TO LIGHT A FIRE

ON

THE EARTH

TO LIGHT A FIRE
ON
THE EARTH

Proclaiming the Gospel in a
Secular Age

BISHOP ROBERT BARRON

With John L. Allen Jr.

IMAGE BOOKS

NEW YORK

*To my entire Word on Fire team and to
all those around the country and around the world
who have supported them*

Contents

TO LIGHT A FIRE

ON

THE EARTH

Introduction

By John L. Allen Jr.

In the history of American Catholicism, 2018 marks an important, if somewhat underappreciated, milestone. It's been fifty years since Archbishop Fulton Sheen, arguably one of the best natural preachers the Church in America ever produced, delivered his last live broadcast on U.S. commercial television. Anyone today south of, say, sixty years of age, probably doesn't have personal memories of watching Sheen in his prime, but for those who do, it's almost impossible to overstate what he meant.

I grew up in rural Western Kansas in the 1970s and '80s, a child of the post–Vatican II era in the American Church. I never saw a Sheen show until much later in life, but I remember my grandparents telling me about getting together with neighbors in front of the one small black-and-white TV they had in the early 1950s, on Tuesday nights, to watch Sheen's *Life Is Worth Living* on the DuMont Network. Expected to be a flop, it was mostly just the New York–based Sheen standing in front of a blackboard with no notes and no cue cards, talking about the faith. Instead of tanking, it became a massive, runaway hit, even challenging Milton Berle at one point for TV's most popular show. (Berle once quipped, "If I'm going to be eased off the top by anyone, it's better that I lose to the One for whom Bishop Sheen is speaking.")

I remember asking Grandpa and Grandma what they remembered from those broadcasts, and they couldn't summon many specifics, except to say that "we learned a lot." What came through with crystal clarity, however, was the pride they felt about Sheen's success. It's important to remember that this was all happening at a time when anti-Catholicism was still very much part of the fabric of rural American life—just a decade before, my grandpa had to join a few other Catholic men of the small town where they lived in standing guard as their parish was being built, for fear somebody might try to burn it down. In that context, to see a Catholic bishop holding his own with the country's most popular stars, even winning an Emmy over Lucille Ball, Arthur Godfrey, Edward R. Murrow, and Jimmy Durante, did more for their Catholic self-esteem than anything else they could ever recall. It told them, "We've arrived!"

In a different way, we too live in an era of widespread hostility to belief—if not always to Catholicism specifically, although there's certainly some of that, then to religious faith in general. American Catholics today generally don't have to worry about Protestant bigots swooping down with pitchforks and torches to destroy their parishes, but they do have to cope with an elite snobbery that says religion is backward, benighted, superstitious, and dangerous because of the primitive hatreds and prejudices it unleashes. They have to live in a culture that tries to force them, in a thousand ways, to separate their minds from their hearts—telling them that if they insist, for sentimental or psychological reasons, on clinging to a religious faith, it can't have anything to do with the way they see the world, or with their lives as professionals and as citizens.

That, by a short route, brings us to Auxiliary Bishop Robert Barron of Los Angeles, born and bred in Chicago, who is to American Catholicism in the early twenty-first century what Sheen was in the mid-twentieth. Barron is the Catholic personality in the English-speaking world today who can stand toe-to-toe with the best and brightest of the secular world, either in person or online, and swell Catholic hearts everywhere by making the faith appear not only plausible but more convincing, more humane, and ultimately more loving than its cultured despisers are. Here's one clear sign of his success: In the English language, after Pope Francis, Barron is the most-followed Catholic figure on social media.

(For those unfamiliar with the argot, an "auxiliary" bishop is one who is not the head of a diocese but rather assists the bishop in charge. Because Los Angeles's Catholic population is so sprawling, the Archdiocese of Los Angeles has several bishops, five of whom are responsible for different regions. Barron is the Episcopal Vicar for the Santa Barbara Pastoral Region. His status as an auxiliary, however, doesn't mean he's any less a bishop, a point we'll explore in a later chapter.)

Such is Barron's reputation that when he met Pope Francis for the first time, in 2015, wondering if the pontiff would have any idea who he is, Francis exclaimed: "Ah, the great preacher, who makes the airwaves tremble!" Presumably the pope meant tremble with excitement, not fear, since Barron is nobody's idea of a fire-and-brimstone televangelist.

To be clear from the outset about the nature of this book, I'm a journalist with a reputation for interviewing senior churchmen on whatever the news of the day may be, from the latest chapter in the Church's clerical sexual abuse scandals to debate over papal proclamations. While I touch on such matters with Barron, this is a different sort of work, because Robert Barron is a different sort of churchman. He understands that scandals, controversies, and divisions sometimes drive people from the faith, and so he knows he must address them. At the same time, Barron is fundamentally a missionary, driven to change the conversation about the faith—to start not with secondary aspects of Catholicism but with its beating heart, meaning expressions of Catholic art and culture that capture the heart, and a rich Catholic intellectual tradition that fires the mind.

It's on those fundamentals, therefore, that this book concentrates.

To come back to the comparison between Sheen and Barron, the common term isn't exactly that both are big-time media personalities, although that's certainly true. Barron's ten-part documentary series *CATHOLICISM,* a tour de force showcase of Catholic belief, art, thought, and culture, aired on virtually every public television station in America beginning in 2011, and has made Barron the most recognizable Catholic priest in the country. That series has had two follow-ups so far, 2013's *CATHOLICISM: The New Evangelization* and 2016's *CATHOLICISM: The Pivotal Players.*

Nor is it that both Sheen and Barron succeeded in a commercial broadcast arena that's normally tough terrain for religion, especially clergy talking seriously about the faith. Barron's *Word on Fire* program on WGN America is a powerhouse, and like *Life Is Worth Living,* it has an appeal well beyond the boundaries of the Catholic Church.

In truth, however, Barron's media profile is quite different from Sheen's, largely because he lives in a different time. Yes, he's succeeded in the conventional broadcast and print arenas, but Barron is also nearly ubiquitous in the world of social media— YouTube broadcasts, blogs, podcasts, tweets, Facebook posts, online chats, and on and on.

Moreover, on a personal level, Sheen and Barron represent contrasting personality types. Where Sheen held himself with an almost theatrical degree of pomp, Barron comes off as relaxed, self-deprecating, a sort of intellectual everyman. (Case in point: Despite having studied for years in France, he's not a foodie, professing to be content with a Whopper.) Where Sheen could be personally thin-skinned, often involved in conflict with ecclesiastical superiors or fellow clergy, Barron is a remarkably nice guy for being so accomplished, and it's virtually impossible to find anyone with a cross word to say about him personally.

One could go on cataloging differences. For example, Sheen was keenly aware of his standing in Rome, at one stage appealing directly to Pope Pius XII in a dispute with his archbishop, Cardinal Francis Spellman of New York. Barron, on the other hand, is the kind of guy who is much more likely to recite lines from the latest intellectual tomes by Charles Taylor or Simon Blackburn than from the most recent Vatican decrees, and he's definitely not the sort of cleric who makes a point of checking the Vatican's news bulletin each day to see who's up and who's down in court politics.

Further, their focus is different. Sheen was keenly political, emerging as one of the most powerful anti-Communist voices of his day. Perhaps his most famous single broadcast came in February 1953, when he paraphrased Shakespeare's funeral speech from *Julius Caesar* to suggest that Soviet leader Joseph Stalin would soon have to "meet his maker." (Stalin died just a week later, adding to Sheen's legend.)

Barron is hardly apolitical, and he would conventionally be seen as mildly "conservative," but his primary focus is not on politics, either in America or in the Church; instead it's on deeper cultural and intellectual currents. Plus, he's got that rare ability of only a handful of massively successful intellectuals, which is to know what he doesn't know—one that even Sheen's best friends will tell you didn't always come naturally to him.

Barron himself is well aware of the contrast.

"I watch him now, and say to myself, you could never pull that off today," Barron says. "The way he does it is impossible, because the 1960s happened. That self-conscious theatricality just wouldn't work."

Yet there is a real analogy between Sheen and Barron, based on four points.

First, both men flourished in the media world by defying conventional wisdom that you have to dumb stuff down in order to sell it. Both were legitimate, accomplished intellectuals—Sheen earned a doctorate at the Catholic University in Leuven, Belgium, becoming the first American ever to win the Cardinal Mercier Prize for best philosophical treatise, while Barron received his doctorate from the Institut Catholique de Paris, learning to speak fluent French and organizing his thesis around an analysis of Thomas Aquinas and Paul Tillich.

What made Sheen, and what makes Barron, so mesmerizing is that both intuitively understood that when faced with the challenge of trying to get across something complicated, the trick isn't to avoid the complexity but to find engaging ways to explain it. Do that, both men were convinced, and people will respond. This way of putting it, however, smacks of strategy, which is probably a cart-before-the-horse mistake. Maybe a better way to say it is that both men were passionately in love with ideas, they were convinced that the Catholic Church has some awfully good ones, and they devoted their lives to helping others discover the same passion.

"I lived through dumbed-down Catholicism, so I don't want that," Barron says. "I want a smart presentation, but one that also emphasizes the beauty of Catholicism. Smart and beautiful are my two priorities."

Both Sheen and Barron, moreover, drew on the life of the mind in eras in which it wasn't taken especially seriously as a mass-market communications enterprise. Sheen was up against Milton Berle and Lucille Ball in prime time. As Barron will explain later in this book, he came of age in the Church in a period when the dominant idea of how to communicate the faith was to start with people's experience, first and always, and only later try to show how the Christian Gospel might speak to that experience. While he's a strong believer in making things relevant, Barron is convinced that too often essential content was sacrificed in the process. First, he says, you have to immerse people in this "strange, exotic world" of the Gospel and Catholic culture, and only then will you be in a position to suggest ways that world might illuminate and elevate theirs.

One vintage Barron maneuver is to respond to the atheist critique that religion is anti-intellectual by saying the problem is that atheists drop their questions just when they get truly interesting. They're great at explaining, say, how human life evolved from lower species, but what about why there's life at all? Why is there anything at all? At that stage, he says, they generally just shrug, or claim that such queries are fruitless—which, as Barron points out, is essentially an abdication of the intellectual journey.

Second, neither Sheen nor Barron ever divorced his own success from that of the Church, never allowed his own celebrity to become bigger or more central to him than the mission of the Church. Sheen famously put in a brief (and troubled) spell as the Bishop of Rochester, New York, and he also gave sixteen years of his life to heading the American branch of the Society for the Propagation of the Faith, an organization supporting Catholic missions overseas.

Likewise, Barron in 2015 happily accepted his appointment as an auxiliary bishop of Los Angeles despite the fact that he knew it would compete for his time with his media ministry. He's thrown himself into the role of a local shepherd with characteristic zeal. He's also determined to see the circles that have formed around his Word on Fire programs become a full-fledged ecclesiastical movement, so that its contributions to the Church will survive him. He enjoys the life of a pastor, devoting great care to his homilies, cherishing his time in the confessional, and relishing the time he's able to spend moving around the Santa Barbara region of the Los Angeles archdiocese getting to know ordinary people and hearing their stories.

Perhaps that's key to the fascination of both men: When Sheen spoke in his day, and when Barron speaks now, we don't simply hear a charismatic orator. We hear the voice of the faith, of the Church, of a two-thousand-year tradition reaching back to Jesus Christ and passing through centuries of accumulated human and divine wisdom. In other words, precisely because Sheen and Barron were communications geniuses, they grasped that what they had to communicate is much bigger than themselves.

Third, both Sheen in his time and Barron in his have been enormous boons to American Catholic pride.

For my grandparents, living in a period of crass and relatively unthoughtful nativist bias against Catholics, seeing Sheen become a popular culture phenomenon was extremely reassuring. It told them—and, perhaps, just as important, it told their neighbors— that Catholics could not only punch their weight by the accepted standards of American culture but could match and even exceed the highest of those standards.

For Catholics today, living in a time of intellectual and cultural prejudice against religion generally and Catholicism in particular, the fact that Barron can take the stage alongside the best and brightest of the secular world and match their logic premise for premise, match their command of history chapter by chapter, match their humor and wit bon mot for bon mot, and make the "splendor of the truth," to use the phrase St. John Paul II employed in a 1993 encyclical, visible even to the most hostile minds, is enormously satisfying. In fact, Barron does much more than that. By the end of his patient exchanges with secular atheists, he usually has unmasked their positions not as the results of precise scientific logic but as simple prejudice—admittedly, prejudice often cloaked under a fabric of argument, but prejudice nonetheless.

I've often suspected that the lone difference between the farmers in the 1940s who wanted to tear down my grandparents' parish with their hands and today's class of atheist pundits who want to tear down the faith with their minds is that the latter went to college. At his best, Barron puts an exclamation point on that suspicion.

The fact that Barron has delivered such a boost to Catholic pride in the aftermath of the Church's clerical sexual abuse scandals, which were (and remain) a cancer in terms of both the Church's moral authority and its public image, is especially remarkable.

"Everywhere I go in the United States, I hear Catholic people say, 'We've got to try to recover a sense of our identity, a sense of our confidence, a sense of our pride in being Catholic,'" said Cardinal Timothy Dolan of New York in a testimonial for Barron's *CATHOLICISM* series.

"This project does that in spades," Dolan said, referring to the video series. "In tying together art and culture, history and literature, beauty and truth, which is what the timeless genius of *CATHOLICISM* is all about, he does it magnificently."

Noted Catholic author and St. John Paul II biographer George Weigel called the series "the most important media project in the history of the Catholic Church in America."

That's not to say, of course, that Barron is without critics. On the left, columnist Michael Sean Winters of the *National Catholic Reporter* has criticized Barron for propagating an overly "heroic" model of the priesthood, arguing that it valorizes machismo and often goes hand in hand with what Winters describes as "intransigency regarding doctrine." On the right, a 2015 interview in which Barron counseled nonviolence in response to the Paris terror attacks led one Catholic blogger to accuse him of promoting "dhimmitude." (The headline of the piece was "The Incredible Shrinking Bishop Barron." The reference is to a concept in Islamic law that consigns non-Muslims, such as Christians, to second-class citizenship.)

More basically, some on the Catholic left find Barron too acquiescent to the status quo in the Church, so eager to extol and evangelize that he ends up "going soft" on the need for criticism and reform. On the Catholic right, it's the potential for another form of "going soft" that sometimes alarms people—that by intentionally leading with beauty in making the pitch for the faith, emphasizing romance over judgment in the first instance, missionaries such as Barron may blur, or take the edge off, the Church's countercultural message.

As one especially ardent Catholic blogger put it in 2013, "I find this idea of evangelizing through beauty as the first principle to be one of the most dangerous ideas ever uttered in modern Catholicism. It has the potential to turn our faith into the religion of Oscar Wilde's aestheticism."

Yet in an acrimonious age, in which snark is often the currency of the media realm, nobody ever plays to universal acclaim. For the record, Barron acknowledges often being perceived as a conservative, but insists he's not "antiliberal" but rather "postliberal" because he sees "something permanently valuable in the liberal move." He also has no patience for today's more militant, hard-core conservative Catholics, for whom one distinguishing trait is often hostility to the reforming Second Vatican Council (1962–1965).

"There's no going back behind Vatican II," Barron says. "To suggest otherwise is just silly, it seems to me. I lived through the implementation of the council, and that was problematic in many ways, and I reacted against it. But there's no going back, as if Vatican II is a moment we should forget about. I have zero interest in that. I have no nostalgia for the period before the council, and anyway, I didn't know it experientially. I reverence the Vatican II documents. They represent the best of twentieth-century Catholic scholarship and spirituality."

Whatever one calls his outlook, Barron's success would suggest that, for a lot of folks, including many Catholics, he's put something fairly attractive on offer.

This brings us to the fourth element of the analogy between Sheen and Barron, because while both clearly knew who the enemies of the faith are, and both were expert debaters who could debunk a sloppy argument or mean-spirited accusation, neither man was fundamentally negative. Though they could tear down when the situation called for it, their core desire was to build up—to help people discover the beauty of the Catholic experience, progressively order their lives around it, and then construct the kind of deeply humanistic culture in which such an aroused Catholic conscience naturally flowers.

One of Barron's maxims is "The sure sign that God is alive in you is joy."

Whether in his *CATHOLICISM* series or his YouTube videos or his speeches or his Word on Fire program, at his best Barron comes across as subtly intoxicating—subtle because he's neither a fire-breather nor a demagogue, and he relies on persuasion rather than intimidation. Intoxicating because he's so relentlessly positive and persuasive, talking about Catholicism the way rock fans might talk about how Bob Dylan changed their lives (and, in fact, Barron is a huge Dylan fan). His point is that if you're a music lover, and you find an artist who totally turns your world upside down, you're naturally going to feel driven to share that with others. That insight is the root of all authentic Christian missionary work, all the more so when you're dealing not with a cool album but with someone's human happiness and eternal destiny.

To put it as simply as possible, Bob Barron is a man passionately in love with Jesus Christ and the Catholic Church, and he wants you to feel it too—not because you'll go to Hell if you don't, but because your life will be richer, more satisfying, and better if you do.

In Catholic parlance, the word for such missionary work is *evangelization*. In that sense, Barron could perhaps be described as the best English-language evangelizer of the early twenty-first century—not, perhaps, in the sense of the raw number of converts for which he's responsible, though that tally is considerable, but for his capacity in his time to do what Sheen and other great evangelizers reaching all the way back to St. Paul did in theirs, which is to understand their culture from the inside out. He's able to convince men and women in all walks of life that Christianity has the answers to the questions they weren't even necessarily conscious of asking.

One proof of the point is that in early 2017 Barron agreed to be interviewed on a highly popular YouTube program called *The Rubin Report*, hosted by Dave Rubin, who's been described as "a thirty-nine-year-old pro-choice, pro-pot, recently gay-married atheist with a strong allergy to organized religion." After the hour-long show, the avalanche of positive comments on social media about Barron from convinced atheists was positively stunning. Here's a sampling:

- "I'm a hardcore atheist, but this guy is amazing."
- "Yeah! I'm only at 7 minutes, and he's definitely not making me a theist, but I love that [Rubin] chose a priest who seems rather smart."
- "Robert Barron is my favorite religious intellectual. I've been subscribed to him on YouTube for over ten years as a stone-cold atheist."
- "I'm not atheist . . . more ummmm, spiritual (though that is a vague term I agree), but I really do enjoy listen-

ing to a damn good interview with a damn intelligent and well-read man who can really articulate his belief and faith."

The bottom line is that Barron walked into the lion's den of the social media world, and if he didn't quite convert the lion, he certainly appeared to have tamed it. (By the way, just to illustrate Barron's penchant for never assuming his audiences can't handle meaty stuff, two minutes into that video he's summarizing Aquinas's third argument for the existence of God, the one from contingency, and wielding phrases such as "a sufficient explanation for the contingent reality of the world.")

One element of Barron's appeal to secular critics, I suspect, is that he's so reasonable, yet so palpably Catholic. The late Pope Paul VI once said that the great rupture of modernity was that between faith and culture, which has been reflected in Catholic intellectual life. The Church has had a host of talented figures fully committed to the life of the mind in the last fifty years, but many found their explorations taking them progressively further away from traditional expressions of the faith. Catholicism has also had many great apologists in the same span, but few who could truly be termed distinguished scholars or thinkers. Barron, by contrast, probably incarnates the classic Catholic synthesis between faith and reason more thoroughly and overtly than virtually any other living figure—or at least one with a Facebook following of 1.5 million, a Twitter following of 100,000, and more than 20 million views on YouTube.

Today Sheen is a candidate for sainthood, having been declared "Venerable" in 2012 after then Pope Benedict XVI approved a decree recognizing that he had lived a life of heroic virtue. His cause seems to be heating up again, after being sidetracked by a nasty public spat involving his family; the Diocese of

Peoria, Illinois, where he was born; and the Archdiocese of New York, where he achieved fame and where his remains had been interred in St. Patrick's Cathedral.

I have no idea if Barron similarly will one day be considered as a possible saint, but it doesn't matter. What more than twenty years of covering the Catholic Church tells me right now is that Bishop Robert Barron is among the most compelling, influential, and captivating figures in Catholicism in our time. His story demonstrates that the Church is not consigned to a permanent future of decline and of intellectual retrenchment, but it can remain true to itself and still withstand the best shots secularism wants to take, coming away stronger and more appealing.

This book is the result of roughly twenty hours of interviews with Barron at his residence in Santa Barbara, California, during August and September 2016 and January 2017, coupled with study of his writings, video presentations, and speeches, as well as conversations about Barron with a cross section of people in the Catholic Church. Although I set things up, this is very much Barron's story, and therefore primarily his book.

Since Barron is also a massive baseball fan, perhaps it's best to introduce the rest of the story this way: Enough with the pregame chatter . . . let's play ball!

Chapter One

<hr>

THE BARRON STORY

One charming aspect of Bishop Robert Barron's personality, though it is frustrating for an interviewer, is that he doesn't really much like talking about himself. I've come to think the reason is not only genuine humility but also impatience to get on to what he thinks is the far more important element of any conversation—namely, the Catholic faith, and why it's the best answer to the questions that well up from every human heart.

Yet it's important to begin with some basics about Barron's life and background, not only because doing so helps us get a read on where he's coming from but also because it provides fodder for one of the towering questions about the ministry of evangelization: Are great evangelizers born, or made? That is to say, can the kind of missionary talent Barron possesses be taught, or do you just have to be gifted with it?

As we'll see, Barron's own answer to that question is the classic Catholic "both/and"—natural talent helps, he concedes, but he also firmly believes that certain techniques can be taught that will make anyone seriously interested in evangelizing better at doing it.

Also as we'll see, the basic "technique" Barron proposes is doing one's homework. He's convinced that one can't defend and extol the nearly two-thousand-year intellectual history of the Catholic Church without mastering it oneself. Understanding how he went about that, and what drove him to do it, may help others find their own path.

Today, an equally important component of Barron's life and self-understanding is his role as a bishop. Precisely because it's so fundamental, we'll cover his thoughts on that front in a separate chapter, Chapter 9).

CHILDHOOD

Robert Emmet Barron was born on November 19, 1959, in Chicago. His father worked for John Sexton & Company, a wholesale grocer and food supplier serving restaurants, hotels, and institutions, which had been founded in Chicago in 1883. Robert has a younger sister and an older brother, and he says he was especially tight with his brother growing up since their ages are only fifteen months apart. (Communications run in the Barron gene pool, since his brother would go on to become the publisher of the *Chicago Sun-Times*. His sister worked in PR for a while, took a break to start a family, and is today a teaching assistant in a Chicago-area high school.)

Barron says his was a "good, solid" Catholic family, if not overly demonstrative about their faith.

"My parents are Catholic to the core," he says. "It would never in a million years occur to them not to go to Mass on Sunday. We weren't superprayerful . . . my parents had respect for the rosary, for example, but we didn't always pray it. When I was a little tiny kid, my mother would come in and pray with us before we went to bed."

Echoes of that deep Catholic faith passed on by his parents have stayed with Barron over the years.

"My mother gave me, and I still have it, a crucifix belonging to my uncle who was a Christian Brother, and who died many years ago. He had this pectoral cross–type of thing that he probably tucked into his habit, and I slept with it under my pillow when I was a kid. My mother told me that was a good thing to do, and I had little prayers I'd pray. Sunday Mass, holy days and all that, were absolutes, plus going to Catholic school and regular Confession."

Barron says his parents were never really part of the debates over the changes in Catholic faith and life introduced by Vatican II, content with the philosophy "If the Church wants it, it's okay with me." Apparently, they passed that spirit on to their son.

"I remember being trained as an altar boy, it would've been about 1969, right when the *novus ordo* Mass came," he recalled. "For us it was like, 'Oh, hey, this is a new Mass, and you guys have been trained to serve, so off we go.' There was no sense of 'Oh, I'm going through a rupture with the old and this is a challenging change,' none of that. It was just like, that was the way it is."

The family moved to Detroit in 1963, when Barron was four, because his father's job took them there, and they would remain in Detroit until 1968. Among other things, it was during that period Barron acquired his lifelong love for baseball.

"Our last year in Detroit was when the Tigers won the World Series with Denny McLain and Mickey Lolich . . . that was the era when I first learned baseball. My first professional baseball game was a Tigers game in 1967, so my earliest memories of pro baseball are the Tigers," Barron recalled. (Like the good Chicagoan he is, however, Barron says he cheers only for the Tigers these days only in the American League—overall, he's a die-hard Cubs fan.) The next year he moved back to Chicago just in time to agonize through the Cubs' legendary collapse to the "Miracle Mets"—an early lesson, he now ruefully concedes, in how life often blends elation with heartbreak.

Barron's period in Detroit occurred in the middle of the drama in Catholicism unleashed by Vatican II, though he says he had little awareness of it at the time, despite attending a Catholic grade school. One experience from that time, however, did leave an impression.

"When I was in third grade, the nuns went to a modified habit. I remember vividly how it caused a near riot when Sister walked into third grade and we saw her in the new habit; we all went berserk," he says. "We loved her. Her name was Sister Jean Marie, and she came in with the shorter veil and the dress that showed her legs, we just freaked out. That's a transitional memory, I suppose you could say, of moving to the postconciliar period."

Later on, Barron attended the Dominican-run Fenwick High School in Oak Park, Illinois, the only high school in the United States directly operated and staffed by the Dominican order. It was during that time, as an intellectually precocious teenager, that he discovered what he calls the "two Thomases"—Merton and Aquinas, who would become touchstones for his entire career.

Here's how Barron tells the story on Merton.

I worked at Kroch's and Brentano's bookstore chain. It's gone now, but it was a big deal at the time. There was a huge store in Chicago and about sixteen satellite stores in the area. I worked at one of the branches, and the policy was if a book got too worn out, the manager could tear the cover off and we could take it home. My brother worked there as well; he was seventeen and I was sixteen. He saw that The Seven Storey Mountain *cover had been taken off, so he threw it at me and said, "I bet you would like this. It was written by a Trappist monk." I said, with completely unconscious irony given Merton's interests later in his career, "Oh, I don't want to read a book by some Buddhist." My brother shot back, "Trappists are Catholics, you idiot!" With that, literally landing in my lap was* The Seven Storey Mountain. *I brought this mangled book home with me, no cover, and I read it with full teenage passion ... Merton filled in the spiritual content for me. It was like, wow, if there really is a God, you can be in relationship with him, and you can explore that friendship in all sorts of interesting ways. I read* The Seven Storey Mountain *like a romance novel. I loved the Beatles, and I have a very vivid memory of reading* The Seven Storey Mountain *with the sound track of the Beatles behind me."*

As for Aquinas, Barron has the Dominicans to thank.

It was at Fenwick High School. I'm a freshman and it's spring-time, so the end of my first year. We were out at the playground horsing around, so we all come in kind of sweating, and it's time for religion class. We had this young Dominican, Father Thomas Paulsen. That day, he laid out for us the Aquinas arguments for the existence of God, beginning, I think, with the motion argument. There I was, a fourteen-year-old Catholic kid just going to Mass, and I still don't know why, but I was captivated. I think it was a movement of grace, and I'm sure no one else in that class was all that interested. For some reason, however, it struck me as, Wow, that's right, that's correct. No one up to that point in my experience really had thought seriously about God, you just went to Mass ... That exposure to Aquinas showed me you could actually think deeply and clearly about God. Not that I didn't believe in God, I did, but there was rational depth and clarity to Aquinas that hit me like a revelation.

From there, the young Barron was off to the races.

I guess it never occurred to me to go to the teacher and say, "Hey, I want to know more," so I started going to the library, where I found this volume of Aquinas's writings in Mortimer

Adler's Great Books series. I took it out in my little fourteen-year-old hands, and I brought it home like a treasure. I didn't really know what I was reading, but I knew it was wonderful. It was similar to the experience I had when I discovered Shakespeare that same year. I read Romeo *and* Juliet *and understood precious little of it, but I thought, There should be such a thing! I just knew that Aquinas, like Shakespeare, was someone I could study for the rest of my life.*

After finishing high school, Barron put in one year under the Golden Dome at the University of Notre Dame, and after discovering a vocation to the priesthood, he finished his undergraduate work at the Catholic University of America in Washington, D.C. Since his early attitudes took shape in the context of Vatican II, sorting through how the young Barron reacted to the tumult generated by the council is key to understanding what he would later become.

VATICAN II AND ITS AFTERMATH

Although some Catholics pine for the period before Vatican II, Barron says he's never shared that instinct, mostly because he's too young to remember the Church before the council. What he does remember with great clarity, however, is the postconciliar period of experimentation and change, and that left a deep impression on him.

"It was the high-water mark of what I call 'banners and balloons' Catholicism," Barron says.

"When I was getting religious instruction as a young man, it was the period right after the council: 1969, '70, '71. We did a lot of very experiential kinds of things," he says. "I remember vividly one of the sisters at my grade school played James Taylor's 'You've Got a Friend,' and told us, 'Now as you hear this song, I want you to just draw what you're feeling.' I didn't think it was anything weird, I just did what they told me, but that was religion class. The formation was a little superficial."

Barron says that tendency to reimagine religion largely in terms of emotion and social relevance may have been especially pronounced in Chicago, given all that was going on during that time.

> *We arrived back in Chicago in August 1968, which is when the riots were going on around the Democratic convention. You had the Martin Luther King, Jr., and the Kennedy assassinations. So, the big thing when I was going to school was social justice, the rights of the marginalized, worrying about the poor. If I were to say what they taught me about the spiritual life, I'd probably say it was a deep commitment to social justice. We got that message for sure as kids. What I reacted against, without knowing it at the time, was the reductionism. If that's all that the spiritual life comes down to, then we have an impoverishment on our hands.*

Though Barron says he wouldn't have been able to formulate his thoughts quite that way at the time, part of the direction his life and career would later take was in reaction to the reductionism he sensed as a youth: "I think most of us do that, most of us kind of react to whatever we were formed in and we begin to see the other side, the shadow side of it," he says.

It was while studying at Catholic University in the early 1980s, under legends such as Monsignor Robert Sokolowski, Monsignor John Wippel, and Thomas Prufer, that Barron says he began to articulate to himself what his instincts told him had gone wrong.

By that time, I had begun to see there's a disconnect, there's something that's not making sense [in some elements of how Vatican II was being implemented]. I saw that there was something relatively superficial about the liturgical dimension, for instance. There was also a tension between the way we were living the faith and the more substantial intellectual grounding we were getting at the university, and the discrepancy began to grate on me. Mind you, I arrived at Catholic U in 1979 and John Paul II had just been elected, so the "John Paul effect" hadn't happened yet. Around that time, though, it became clearer to me what the demarcations [in the Church] were.

Looking back, Barron says his reaction to the post–Vatican II period left him with not so much opposition to the liberal Catholic project as a strong sense that on its own, liberalism is not quite enough.

What I emphasize is that I'm not "antiliberal," I'm "postliberal," and that's on purpose. There's something permanently valuable in the liberal project, there's a critique that's permanently valuable. We don't want to reject that, but we do want to move through it on to something else . . . I'm a [Cardinal John Henry] Newman man. He emphasized the development of unfolding things—a plant doesn't just uproot itself and start over again, it's always coming forth and sending off new branches and shoots. I believe in moments of criticism and moments of new growth, but not of rupture. That's my own experience of learning to be in the Church.

PARIS

Barron was ordained to the priesthood in 1986 by Cardinal Joseph Bernardin of Chicago, who had taken over from the flamboyant Cardinal John Cody in 1982 (once described by Father Andrew Greeley, a novelist and sociologist, as a "madcap tyrant"). Barron met Cody only twice, once as a young man when Cody gave him a John Paul II key chain, and the second time toward the end of Cody's life when he visited Catholic University and Barron and a fellow student picked him up at the airport. As they drove by the Shrine of the Immaculate Conception, he remembers Cody telling him, "I built that place!"

Having completed his studies at Catholic U, Barron was faced with the question of what to do next. He decided he wanted to study in Paris, as a chance to deepen his appreciation of Catholic thought and culture generally, and Aquinas in particular, since the Angelic Doctor taught in Paris at two different points in his career. Bernardin needed some persuading, Barron says, since he initially preferred that Barron study in Rome, but he eventually relented. Barron set off for the City of Lights, living at a Redemptorist house on Montparnasse and studying at the famed Institut Catholique de Paris. The other option, Barron says, would have been going to Germany to study under then Father Walter Kasper, a renowned theologian who would later become a bishop and cardinal, but Bernardin was skeptical, fearing it would take Barron too long to finish a degree in the ponderous German system.

It was in Paris that Barron's intellectual perspective came into sharper focus, because while mastering both French and German, he also discovered the work of Swiss theologian Hans Urs von Balthasar. At the time, meaning the late 1980s and early 1990s, much of Catholic theology could be analyzed in terms of whether its point of reference was the German Jesuit Karl Rahner, widely seen as more liberal and oriented to the reform spirit of Vatican II, or Balthasar, generally perceived as more traditional, rooted in both Scripture and centuries of Catholic teaching. Barron eventually took a both/and approach, but with Balthasar in the "major key."

Under the rubric of "postliberal" not "antiliberal," I began to see how deeply anthropological and anthropocentric the Rahner approach is, beginning as it does with the human experience of absolute mystery. It commences with the longing for God, and I think that's legitimate as far as it goes. Rahner is very much like [Friedrich] Schleiermacher [a late eighteenth- to early nineteenth-century German theologian], who says the sense and taste for the infinite is the beginning of religion. I think there is such a thing, and I agree with that. The feeling of absolute dependency Schleiermacher talks about is real . . . the idea that I depend on you, I depend on particular things, and that there's this ultimate dependency, which is upon God. But what Balthasar taught me was that this might be a great place to start, but you don't want to end there. The danger is that theology gets so ordered by an anthropological approach that it tends to name God from the standpoint of experience, and revelation is underplayed. There's this kind of jungle quality to the world of revelation that's worth exploring.

To explain what he means by the "jungle quality" of revelation, Barron invokes an analogy to the Lord of the Rings.

Tolkien's Lord of the Rings—this rollicking adventure story— begins with a lengthy description of Bilbo Baggins's birthday party. When asked to explain this, Tolkien said, "If you're going to understand the story I'm about to tell, you have to understand the distinctive world in which the characters live and move. I've got to open this strange world to you, and you have to have the patience to take it in." To me, it began to have implications for everything, including preaching. So much of the way we were taught to preach was on the liberal model. Try to correlate people's experience. Make sure they have a way in, a route of access through their experience, but it produced in my judgment a too bland and domesticated version of Christianity.

At the time, Barron says, he wasn't thinking of that option in terms of a "liberal" or a "conservative" approach. Rather, he was determined to begin with the uniqueness of revelation and only then move on to find correlations with personal experience, which struck him as "fresh" relative to the kind of formation he'd experienced up to then. With time, Barron says, he came to see that the theological approach associated with Rahner, which he traces back to the influence of another German theologian, Paul Tillich, has great promise but suffers from a fatal flaw.

What you notice about those theologians is how Christologically and Biblically thin they are. Look at Tillich's great Systematic Theology. I love volume one, which is a classic liberal approach to God with all its virtues. But then the Christology is left to this real tiny middle section. It's hyperthin. He construes Jesus as the breakthrough of a new being under the conditions of estrangement and then from that very abstract description derives a Christology. And you're like, yes, but the particularities of the Gospels of Mark, Matthew, and John, the complexity of the Pauline letters . . . all the density of revelation is overlooked. That to me is the great difference. The liberal approach is right, and I use it a lot if people are just getting started and trying to get interested. It's a good point of departure. I've said, By all means, start with this kind of experience of the mystery and so on, but the point is that things can't stop there. The danger, as I began to see clearly, is that it draws the dogma so fully in that my experience becomes the measure of the dogma, and the doctrine loses a lot of its punch and its trans-formative quality. It produces too tame a religion.

One final experience during Barron's Paris years that would leave a lasting impression was watching Cardinal Jean-Marie Lustiger in action. Lustiger was born in 1926 into a French Jewish family, and his mother would eventually be murdered in Auschwitz. He converted to Catholicism at the age of thirteen and went on to a distinguished ecclesiastical career that culminated in being named the Archbishop of Paris in 1981. Lustiger was sometimes criticized by liberal French clergy for being overly authoritarian and dogmatic, but no one seriously disputes that he brought both a keen mind and a beguiling personal story to the post. For Barron, Lustiger's personal example was inspirational.

He would say Mass at 6:30 p.m. on Sundays, and 90 percent of the time I went to Mass at Notre Dame, so I heard him a lot. Just the fact that you've got this Jewish-Catholic cardinal at Notre Dame, not to mention Notre Dame itself, was deeply inspiring. To go to that enchanted place—with the incense rising and Lustiger getting to the microphone and, in the typically French manner, giving a good half-hour homily—was just intoxicating. To hear him speak in beautiful French with all that passion . . . those were very formative moments. He exuded a wonderful, confident, spiritual Catholicism, the Catholicism of someone who had suffered. You couldn't miss it with him. You knew the story of his mother dying in the Shoah. This was someone who had suffered, someone who had come to the faith. There were no histrionics, no arm waving, but

the experience of intense, Israel-based suffering, which led to a
vibrantly confident form of Catholicism.

GEORGE AND GREELEY

Barron finished his studies in Paris in 1992 and immediately returned to Chicago to teach at the archdiocese's Mundelein Seminary. Early on he asked permission to teach a course on Balthasar,
preparing for it by reading some four thousand pages of the theologian's work in roughly four months. (Today Barron says he can
no longer turn in such marathon reading sessions, because "my
eyes are shot"!) At the time of his reentry into the States, Barron says, two trajectories were just taking shape, both of which
would prove enormously consequential for the Church in America: the rise of a new "John Paul II" generation in the seminary
and the priesthood, and the early tremors of what would later
become the earthquake of the sexual abuse scandals.

Barron would spend the rest of the decade teaching at Mundelein, developing a reputation as a prolific and accomplished
scholar. It was during this period that two titans of the Chicago
Catholic scene—Father Andrew Greeley and Cardinal Francis
George—helped steer his career in unanticipated new directions.

Barron first met Greeley, whose occasionally steamy novels made him famous in some circles and infamous in others, in
1988. At the time, Greeley was, as Barron put it, a "total rock
star" in the Windy City. Learning of Barron's intellectual interests, Greeley arranged a lunch with his good friend David Tracy
of the University of Chicago, a moment in which Barron says he
was in "total awe." From there a friendship with Greeley flourished, with Barron spending a chunk of each summer for the
next decade at Greeley's summer residence. Among other things,

Greeley helped pave the way for Barron's first invitation to speak at the Los Angeles Religious Education Congress, the largest annual gathering of Catholics in North America, where Barron has become a perennial crowd favorite.

"If Andy loved you, he loved you all the way, and if he hated you, he hated you all the way." Barron laughs, looking back. "I was happily on the love side, and he showered a lot of love on me."

Greeley also encouraged Barron with his early forays into the media world. Barron says the boost originated with a conversation he had with another priest friend.

I'm grousing about how Catholics are behind the curve, we're not doing what we should be doing and the Protestants are so much better than we are at communication. Fulton Sheen was great, but then we dropped the ball, et cetera, et cetera. He's listening, and he said, "Well, what are you doing about it?" I said, "What can I do? I'm a full-time teacher and writer." He said, "Well, then, stop complaining!" And that's what prompted me to act. I went to WGN in Chicago—I thought, I'll start big—and I asked what would it take for me to have some kind of sermon show? They said, "We have a slot at 5:15 a.m. on Sunday, and for fifty thousand dollars we can let you do that." I went to the parish and told them the story. I said, "If you give me fifty thousand dollars I can get on the radio." They gave me the money for the next three years, so I was on WGN, and that's how it started.

That was in 1999 or 2000, as Barron recalls, and it began as a weekly fifteen-minute program, basically a brief Sunday homily recorded in the seminary basement. Not long afterward, he says, a friend suggested that he really ought to have a website, prompting the then technologically illiterate Barron to ask: "What's that?"

His reaction notwithstanding, a website was soon launched collecting Barron's homilies and other materials.

The decision to create the website raised the question of what it would be called. Barron recalls sitting around with two close friends—Dominican Father Paul Murray, a poet, and Father Steve Grunow, who would go on to become the backbone of many of his ministries. (When Barron moved to Los Angeles, Grunow followed him there.) Barron says he was evoking the Biblical idea of trying to light a fire on the earth to explain his vision, and Grunow suggested "Word on Fire" as a name. As Barron remembers it, Murray, the poet, said, "You're not going to do any better than that."

At that stage, Barron still regarded his growing media presence essentially as a hobby, with his "day job" being academic theology and seminary instruction. That was when Cardinal Francis George, who clearly saw in Barron the potential for a different, and arguably more unique, contribution to the Church, entered the picture.

Barron and George had met shortly after George arrived in Chicago in 1997, bonding over a shared passion for the intellectual life, including their affection for Balthasar. The two men in many ways formed a natural pair, since George was always seen as the deepest thinker among his crop of senior American prelates—in some ways closer to the European model of the intellectual-bishop, as opposed to the vintage American category of "bricks and mortar men."

Barron recalls George then as coming off as "kind of gruff and direct," but nevertheless an impressive figure, all the more so for the quiet way in which he refused to call attention to his disability. (As a result of contracting polio at the age of thirteen, George had lifelong problems with walking.) The two men remained in touch, generally by catching up when George would visit Mundelein, until around 2005, at which point Barron says George decided to "draw me more closely into his orbit."

At roughly the same point, Barron was producing what he calls his "big book," meaning the major intellectual tome upon which academics build their careers. *The Priority of Christ: Toward a Postliberal Catholicism* appeared in 2007, reflecting a solid decade of thought and research. Barron seemed poised for a big-time academic career, fielding offers of teaching positions from both Catholic University and Notre Dame. George, however, discouraged Barron from pursuing the positions.

I think he saw something else in me. What he said to me was "You'd be a fine professor. You'd have your briefcase and walk around the campus and give your lectures and direct doctoral papers, and you'd influence another generation." But then he said, "I think you have a wider and bigger task to accomplish." That's the way he put it to me. They created a chair for me at Mundelein: the Cardinal Francis George Professorship of Faith and Culture. I think he knew I was disappointed [with not taking the academic posts he'd been offered], so the idea was Let's give him a certain status here. By that time, I actually was living part-time with Cardinal George. This happened because of a conversation I had with the cardinal upon returning to the seminary from a speaking trip. I went over to the cafeteria for a reception, and there, to my surprise, was Cardinal George, who said, "I want to talk to you." He said, "I want you to jump-start evangelization." Just like that. And I said, "What do you mean?" He replied, "I don't know, but I want you to do it!" He told me that it was bugging him that I was roaming around the country evangelizing when there was a pressing need in Chicago. He said, "I'd like you to take time away from the seminary, live downtown with me, and I want you to think this through and we'll do it."

Barron says one practical application of George's prompting was a series of talks he began to host at Chicago's downtown University Club and Union League Club.

> *The idea was Let's go to people on their terms. Don't come to church, we'll come to you. We'll serve lunch; I'll give a brief talk; and we'll get you back to work. So I got the money rustled up somehow and we started. It was a good experience: we filled those rooms with three hundred or four hundred people, and I addressed questions such as "Does it make sense to believe in God?" "Who is Jesus Christ?" "Why does the Church matter?" "Why do we need the sacraments?" "What about social teaching?" "What does it mean to be a Catholic in the world?" We called them The Church in the City or something like that. I just gave these quick, punchy half-hour talks, and that's where a lot of our key supporters [for Word on Fire] surfaced.*

For the time being, however, Barron continued to keep a foot in both worlds, teaching at Mundelein and pursuing his academic career while also building a growing media profile. Another key moment came in 2005 with the launch of YouTube, which became an overnight Internet sensation. By 2006, *Time* featured a YouTube screen with a large mirror as its "Person of the Year," extolling the explosion of user-created media. Barron quickly recognized that the plates were shifting in the media world, and he told George that he wanted to enter the fray.

"I said, 'I've got to reach young people, and the Internet is where it's happening,'" Barron recalls. "He totally got it. He never used the Internet—in some ways, he was a total Luddite—but he got it. He said, 'That makes sense.'"

With that seal of approval, Barron plunged into the brave new world of YouTube. Originally he was looking for a hook that would capture the interest of young audiences, and he seized on offering commentaries on popular movies seen through the eyes of faith. For the record, the first film Barron tackled in the new format was the 2006 Martin Scorsese release, *The Departed*. The Word on Fire team shot his comments in a movie theater to give a sort of Siskel and Ebert feel. Barron says he was thrilled when that first video drew 300 views. Now, more than ten years later, his YouTube offerings have generated more than 20 million views cumulatively, with each one drawing around 25,000 to 30,000.

Part of the intent from the beginning, Barron says, was to reach people distant from the faith, who wouldn't be open to talk about God or the Church under ordinary circumstances. One discovery along those lines, Barron says, was that YouTube allows viewers to post comments about what they're seeing, which at first was jarring in terms of the negativity he'd occasionally encounter.

"What I did in the beginning is the 'kill them with kindness' thing," he recalls. "I'd say, 'Good to hear from you. Can you specify what you're upset about?' And then they'd come back. And I thought, Now I've got a little traction, and I can respond." From there, carrying on dialogues prompted by his YouTube videos became an important feature of Barron's evangelical outreach— offering him a window, he says, into what drives young people these days, especially those heavily influenced by a secular cultural perspective on religion and the Catholic Church.

"In some cases, long, long exchanges emerged, and I began to love the dynamism of it," he says. "That got the views up, so it just grew and grew."

Barron says he's been impressed with the creative uses to which people put his videos, such as groups gathering to watch and talk about the movies he discusses. He's also been struck by the global reach of YouTube, saying he regularly gets e-mails and letters from Papua New Guinea, Japan, and points beyond. His capacity to engage people who post comments, he says, has diminished somewhat as his other responsibilities have grown, but he credits the experience with teaching him a great deal about what effective evangelization means in the twenty-first century.

"I love that the videos get out into the wider world very easily," he says. "Fulton Sheen needed people to watch at a particular time, but I'm 24/7 all over the world. It's a whole different game."

Throughout this period of his life, Barron continued to form the next generation of seminarians from his perch at Chicago's Mundelein Seminary, eventually serving as the seminary's rector from 2012 to 2015.

CATHOLICISM

In most remarkable careers, there's that one watershed accomplishment that transforms someone from another face in the crowd to a star, a "somebody." In the case of Bishop Robert Barron, that breakthrough came with his ten-part film series *CATHOLICISM*, which took Barron and his crew to more than fifty locations in fifteen countries, from Israel to Uganda, with stops in settings such as Italy, France, Spain, Mexico, Kolkata, and New York City. The executive producer for the project was Mike Leonard, a veteran NBC *Today* show correspondent and acclaimed filmmaker. Although the series did touch on various scandals and controversies that have marred the Church over the centuries, the accent was on lifting up the marvels of Catholic thought, architecture, art, literature, and culture, as well as Catholicism's great saints.

"I hope this is a shot in the arm that reinvigorates Catholics' sense of faith," Barron said when the first episode debuted. "I want the beauty of the Church to come through."

Originally intended, at least in Barron's mind, largely for small-scale Catholic settings such as parish catechism programs, the series became a runaway hit. It eventually aired on roughly one hundred PBS stations (about 70 percent of the stations in the network) beginning in 2011 and since has been viewed by millions of people. That success has spawned two follow-up series: *CATHOLICISM: The New Evangelization* in 2013 and *CATHOLICISM: The Pivotal Players* in 2016.

That kind of appeal for an explicitly religious program in what's ordinarily a highly secular media environment would be remarkable under any circumstances, but it's especially striking given that it came in the wake of the child sexual abuse scandals, which badly eroded the Church's public standing and seemed to make any TV series extolling its virtues even more of a long shot. Barron, however, says it was no coincidence—he and his team were convinced that the Church needed something to help it recover a sense of pride after the carnage of the scandals, giving them a sense of urgency about bringing *CATHOLICISM* to completion.

Barron remembers discussing with his crew while filming in Jerusalem the impact of the scandals, and the possible role of the series in helping the Church turn a corner.

"We went to a pizza place in East Jerusalem," he says. "The pizza comes, and as we're talking, Mike [Leonard] says to me, 'This could be a tipping point.' I asked what he meant. He said, 'I go to Starbucks and all I hear are people ragging on the Catholic Church, making fun of it. You see a priest and everyone laughs. They ask, "Hey, Mike, why are you still going to these child molesters?" That's what I hear from my peers at Starbucks.' This was at the very beginning, we're barely filming one episode, but he saw that it could be a tipping point."

In order to pull that off, Barron says, he was convinced that if the aim of the series was to reintroduce people to the beauty and romance of the Catholic tradition, its feel and look must itself be beautiful, reflecting the best production values available.

The idea for the series was hatched at a board meeting of Word on Fire. By this time I had really good people and some high-powered people in Chicago. One of them said to me, "Well, what's your dream project? Dream big. The biggest thing you want to do." I said, "Okay, something like Kenneth Clark's Civilization. *I go all over the world and produce a ten-part, beautifully filmed series to show the beauty and truth of Catholicism. That's my project." They all said, "Well, why don't you do it?"*

Two obstacles, he says, loomed immediately. The first was securing permission from George to be away, but that turned out to be easy. A group of his collaborators went to see the cardinal, intentionally leaving Barron out of it, to make the request. Later, Barron says, "they told me he walked into the room and said, 'Whatever I need to do to make this happen, I'll do.'"

The other headache was money. The production company behind the series estimated that a "shoestring" budget for what Barron had in mind would be $4 million, and so, as he puts it, he launched into the process of "running around begging." Eventually, a benefactor agreed to fund the first installment, and the adventure was under way.

We ran off to the Holy Land and we didn't quite know what we were doing. We were kind of making it up as we went along, but somehow we got this episode patched together. Then I started going around to major cities in the United States and we began showing it to Catholic groups, begging for money. When money would come in, we'd go off and do more. Then the economy collapsed in 2008, and a lot of our donors said, "Sorry, can't do it." It was this wild process of begging for money, piecing it together, going all over the world, filming what we could, and then, through God's grace, eventually it came together.

Looking back, Barron is conscious of how both his YouTube presence and the *CATHOLICISM* series, through their unexpected success, changed his profile.

At the beginning, I wasn't a household name by any means. A few people in the Catholic world kind of knew about me, but that was it, and then it just exploded. I remember one commentator saying, "Word on Fire with its massive publicity machine," and I'm thinking, Hey, we're two people, two bozos in the office, just doing their best. But it took off . . . It's funny, because for all these years I was getting on airplanes, going to conferences, going to priest groups, and I would give my talks to polite applause and quietly go home. I did that for years and years—bad hotels, bad lunches, giving talks, so I was used to the idea that nobody knows who I am. The first time I noticed something had changed was World Youth Day in 2011. I arrived with utter innocence and went to our little booth in Madrid, the Word on Fire booth, just to help out . . . well, it was like the Beatles in A Hard Day's Night*! These people were flocking up to me, saying, "Father Barron, can I have your autograph? Can I have a picture?" They were literally chasing me around the arena. I was honestly thinking, What's going on here? It was the popularity of the YouTube videos, and then the series came out and it got launched into the stratosphere. That's how it unfolded.*

In the end, the series's acclaim can probably best be explained by the vision with which Barron and his Word on Fire team went into it, which, looking back, he explains this way:

I grew up in a Church that was fighting with itself. My memory of those early years was of the Church fighting about sex and authority, both liberals and conservatives. What I didn't get was a proud, confident, truthful, and beautiful presentation of Catholicism. The beauty, the density, the texture, the truth of it . . . that was not presented. In making this series, a lot of people said, You have to have an episode on morality, or the theology of the body, or you have to talk about sexual ethics. I said no, I don't want to do it. I didn't want another bickering Catholic position paper, I wanted this to be lyrical.

Although when it comes to rock and roll Barron's deepest passion is Bob Dylan, he's also keenly fond of Bruce Springsteen, who once called his acclaimed 1975 album *Born to Run* his "shot at the title," meaning his stab at the greatest rock album ever made. Asked if he ever felt like that about *CATHOLICISM*, that it was the one work above all else for which he'll eventually be remembered, Barron says simply, "I think I did.

"Our team was all around the same age, in our late forties and early fifties, so we weren't kids but we weren't exactly old yet. We had a lot of experience, but we were still lively enough and energetic enough. I would say things like 'Everyone, savor this!'

"I'd be very happy if, when I die, they'd say, 'This is the man who did the *CATHOLICISM* series,'" Barron says. "I'd be fine with that."

By July 2015, Father Robert Barron had become America's best-known Catholic evangelist, presiding over a mini–media empire that produced weekly YouTube videos and a variety of other social media offerings, and which at that point had already generated two celebrated video series that aired widely, even in non-Catholic settings. He was also in intense demand on the lecture circuit, routinely packing in big audiences to hear his "lyrical" presentation of the Catholic faith. What he couldn't have antici-pated was the next turn his life would take—appointment as a new auxiliary bishop in far-off Los Angeles in July 2015, which meant uprooting his life and ministry and taking on an enormous set of new pastoral responsibilities.

Through it all, and with the support of his superiors in the Church, Barron has remained determined to keep Word on Fire and his evangelizing work going, because he believes it's got something to say to today's secular culture, including fallen-away Catholics, people who've never encountered the faith, and even Catholicism's most determined secular critics. Barron would be the first to insist that the focus should be not on him but rather on the message—which, he'll add, isn't his; it's that of the Church and, ultimately, of a loving God.

It's to the content of that message we now turn.

Chapter Two

BEAUTY

Imagine you're back in grade school, your best friend lives about a mile away, and for some reason the phones are down. Now imagine that somehow you learn, maybe from your older brother or sister, that some big kids are planning to beat your best friend up if he takes a certain path to school that morning. Do you drop whatever you're doing and run over to your friend's house to warn him? If you're any kind of friend, the answer is probably yes.

In very simplistic fashion, that was often the sort of motivation underlying much Catholic missionary work over the centuries. Famously, generations of Catholics grew up being urged to pray for the "pagan babies," premised on the belief that if those babies didn't grow up to come to faith in Jesus Christ and baptism in the Catholic Church, their eternal salvation was at risk. What drove many missionaries, in other words, was the firm conviction that they needed to save people from such a fate.

Now, imagine you're back in grade school again, and this morning instead of your older brother telling you that your best friend is in danger, he shares with you a new rock-and-roll album he just picked up. You're blown away, it opens up a whole new world for you, and you're absolutely convinced your best friend should hear it too, because it might have the same effect on him. Once again, do you go running to your friend's house to catch him before school, in order to share this amazing new discovery? Once again, most real best friends probably would.

That, in a nutshell, is the Bishop Robert Barron approach to missionary work. He wants to draw you into Catholic faith and practice, not because he thinks you'll be punished if you don't become a part of the Church but because he thinks it's so amazing, so rich, so powerful—in three key words—so beautiful, good, and true—that your life will be infinitely better because of it.

Consider where Barron decided to film his landmark *CATHOLICISM* series:

- The Holy Land of Israel, including Nazareth
- Rome, including the Sistine Chapel
- Poland
- Germany
- Spain
- Kolkata (formerly Calcutta), India
- New York City
- Ephesus, Greece
- Lourdes, France
- Guadalupe, Mexico
- São Paulo, Brazil
- Manila, Philippines
- Uganda
- Orvieto, Italy
- Florence, Italy
- Ireland

Barron didn't select those locations just because they help illustrate core principles of the faith, though they do. He picked them because of the drama, the pageantry, and the iconic power each setting wields. In other words, he went to those locales not only because they capture truth and goodness but because they're beautiful.

In Christian tradition, beauty, goodness, and truth are known as "transcendentals," linked to the three core human abilities to feel, to wish, and to think. Jesus refers to them in the Great Commandment when he talks about the mind, the soul, and the heart, and inducements to take the wrong path with each of the transcendentals formed the core of his temptation scene in the Gospels. While Barron is convinced that Catholic Christianity represents the fullness of all three, he's equally convinced that the right way to open up the Catholic world to someone is with its beauty.

In a 2015 essay for a book on St. Patrick's Cathedral in New York, subtitled *The Legacy of America's Parish Church,* Barron unpacks the idea, after noting that many people today find talk about "truth" off-putting, seeing it as a way of imposing one's values or opinions on others.

> *There's something more winsome and less threatening about the beautiful. "Just look," the evangelist might say, "at Chartres Cathedral or the Sainte Chapelle, or the Sistine Chapel ceiling, or the mosaics at Ravenna." "Just read," he might urge, "Dante's* Divine Comedy *or one of Gerard Manley Hopkins's poems, or Chesterton's* Orthodoxy." *"Just watch," he might suggest, "Mother Teresa's Missionaries of Charity at work among the poorest of the poor." The wager is that the encounter with the beautiful will naturally lead someone to ask, "What made such a thing possible?" At that point, the canny evangelizer will begin to speak of the moral behaviors and intellectual convictions that find expression in the beautiful. If I might suggest a simple metaphor, when teaching a young person the game of baseball, a good coach begins, not with the rules or with tiresome drills, but rather with the beauty of the game, with its sounds and smells and the graceful movements of its star players.*

We'll come back to that baseball analogy in a moment. For now, however, we might express the essence of the point this way: Barron is wholeheartedly convinced that Catholicism is true and good, but he's equally convinced that, at its best, it's also gorgeous, fun, fulfilling, life-affirming—and that if you can break through the cultural noise to get people to see all that, they'll respond.

BASEBALL AND BOB DYLAN

Several of the defining passions of Barron's life came together early. As we've seen, he was a teenager when he discovered his "two Thomases," Thomas Aquinas and Thomas Merton, who remain lodestars of his faith today. His childhood was also when two other powerful forces captured his heart and mind—the game of baseball, and rock and roll, perhaps especially the music and poetry of Bob Dylan. It's instructive to see how Barron speaks about both, because it's clear there's a nexus uniting all three that has something to do with the attractive power of beauty.

In baseball, as we've mentioned, Barron is a die-hard Cubs fan, despite his recent relocation to Los Angeles. (He did actually throw out the first pitch at a Dodgers game on "Catholic Night," however, so he's not quite fanatical in his loyalties.) He played the game himself from Little League through high school, generally at the shortstop position, and he wasn't bad, several times making all-star teams. He was playing other sports too, including basketball and football, but it was clear that America's Game had a special pride of place in his heart.

Barron always emphasizes that it was the love of the game that came first, well before he mastered its fine points. It was the smell of the grass, the "crack" that a cleanly hit ball makes when it leaves the bat, the "smack" of a well-fielded ball entering the glove, the infield ballet required to produce a ground ball out, the combination of speed and cunning and power good teams have—just the poetry in motion of it all. The passion he felt for the game, and his drive to share it, he says, was in some ways his first taste of what it means to evangelize.

"I'm an evangelist for baseball. You love something, and you want to share it. Something beautiful has seized you, and you think baseball is terrific, and you want to let people know why. If someone says to you, 'I hate baseball; it's boring,' you want to grab them by the lapels and say, 'Let me tell you why it's not boring. Let me explain it to you.' And you can do that in a way that's not browbeating."

Only when you've had that experience of falling in love with something, Barron believes, will learning the rules that support it make sense. Otherwise, "rule-talk" is always going to seem like someone trying to control another, like an exercise in power rather than liberation to play the game well.

"My analogy is the infield fly rule," Barron says. "It's a good rule, and I love it. I remember distinctly when I learned it in Little League, but there's no way I would have been drawn into the splendor of the game through that rule. To compare it to the life of faith, if you've got someone who wants to know what Catholicism is and who Jesus Christ is, you'd never start with the Pauline privilege!"

(Note: The infield fly rule states that a fair fly ball in the infield, which in the judgment of the umpire could be caught with ordinary effort, is an automatic out, in order to prevent dropping the ball on purpose and catching runners off base. The Pauline privilege is an aspect of Catholic marriage law which states that when two nonbaptized persons are married, the marriage can be dissolved if one partner converts to Christianity and the other leaves the marriage.)

Barron recalls his early baseball coaches as in the sense he's describing, natural-born evangelists.

When I was learning baseball, I had these good coaches. They were young, probably in their twenties, but seemed ancient to us. One of them says, "I want you to get down on your knees, and I want you to feel the infield." What he was doing, I understand now. When you're trying to field the ball, you get kind of skittish. If you're really uncomfortable with the grass and the dirt and all, you've got to get over it, because you have to be comfortable moving in to get the ball. He was literally having us feel the infield. Then they had us watch filmstrips of baseball players to notice the various positions of the bat, where your hips should be in relation to the swing, how high your elbow should be, et cetera. Then, of course, they got us playing. And we played terribly, we were throwing wildly and striking out, but having a blast. It would never have occurred to them to say at this stage, "Let me clarify first the infield fly rule." I think what happened in my experience growing up is something like that. In the Church, we started with the infield fly rule. People looking at it would have said, "Catholicism . . . I guess it's all about rules, especially sexual ethics. It's about getting your sexual life in order." I became convinced, and am still convinced, that a huge swath of Catholics do not know the fundamentals of Christianity. They don't know the beauty of the game. They don't know what the infield feels like. They don't know the texture of it. I want them to feel Catholicism, to know the essential stuff. Furthermore, we won't get the sexual teaching right until we get the essentials right. It will just seem like arbitrary rules being imposed on you, which is how it feels to a lot of people.

In many ways, filling that gap, and in so doing, restoring the proper sequence between falling in love and then learning the rules, has become the idée fixe of Barron's life and career. Today, he says, his favorite sports parallel comes not from baseball, which he can't play anymore, but from golf.

"Golf is a baseball swing on the ground," he says with a laugh. "Notice how golf people are obsessed with rules. We love them. Once you get a few rules and know how this thing works, we love it, reading *Golf Digest* and so on. There's solace in the rules. We understand what the Psalmist was talking about: 'Lord, how I love your law! I meditate on it day and night!'

"Rules are not the enemy of golf," Barron says. "Rules are what make it possible, and what free you to be a good golfer. That's the right way to approach the rules of Catholicism too, but the trouble is we have this rule book and people bicker about prohibitions all the time, especially in regard to sex. Many wonder, Who needs it? I think that's the reaction of a lot of people my generation and younger. Who needs all that?"

Around the same time Barron was developing his appreciation for the proper place of rules in evangelizing through baseball, another equally strong passion began to flourish. He discovered the music of Bob Dylan, and to hear Barron tell it, nothing would ever be quite the same again. (To this day, he's got a picture of Dylan he once drew in his residence, along with Merton, Aquinas, and a beloved fellow Chicago priest.)

I discovered Bob Dylan right around the same time I discovered Thomas Aquinas and Thomas Merton. Remember the Concert for Bangladesh *album that came out in the early seventies? I'm twelve years old, and I was just discovering rock and roll. That's when I was listening to the Beatles, and that was the connection. My brother gets* Concert for Bangladesh. *I was listening to it on the record player, the vinyl. I'm listening to George Harrison's music, and then my brother turned over the record and I hear Harrison say, "I want to bring on a friend of us all, Mr. Bob Dylan." I'd never heard of him, but the crowd went berserk. Here's this really peculiar voice, but I was just old enough and had enough experience in school to get poetry and language, and so I'm listening, and he sings the first song I ever heard by him, "A Hard Rain's A-Gonna Fall." He does "Blowin' in the Wind," "Mr. Tambourine Man," "Just Like a Woman," his biggest songs. I was particularly blown away by "A Hard Rain's A-Gonna Fall." The language, the voice, and the people responding to it . . . that was it. I'm kind of an obsessive guy, so with Aquinas and Merton I went all the way, and with Dylan I started going all the way.*

According to Barron, it's not just the poetry of the lyrics or the quirkiness of the voice that drew him to Dylan but also the strong religious sensibility the singer exudes.

Do you remember at the Rock and Roll Hall of Fame, when Springsteen inducts Bob Dylan and says the snare drum that opens up "Like a Rolling Stone" is like kicking open the door to your mind, and this whole world opens up? This is cliché to say, but the Old Testament prophet is the right rubric for Bob Dylan. He's Biblical. He's a lot of things, of course, but above all, from beginning to end, he's Biblical. He's the one, perhaps more than anyone else in pop music, who brings the Biblical worldview into our time. Buddy Holly, Woody Guthrie, Elvis, and others influenced him, but it's the Biblical take which drives his interest in sin, judgment, eternal life, and God. One of his later songs, called "I'm Trying to Get to Heaven Before They Close the Door," has stayed with me. Often when I'm in prayer in my chapel I'll look up at the tabernacle and say, "I'm just trying to get to Heaven before they close the door." When it gets down to it, that's all I want. I'm just trying to get to Heaven before they close the door.

Once again, Barron says he was seized with such a strong passion for Dylan that he felt compelled to share it, instinctively leading him down a path that he would today recognize as a kind of evangelization.

It's sharing something that I find so compelling and life-giving. I became a Bob Dylan evangelist immediately. I remember saying as a little kid, "Have you ever heard of Bob Dylan? He has a crazy voice, but it's actually great once you get it. You've got to listen to this song." I've had people all my life ask me, "Bob Dylan? Why? He's terrible!" But from the time I was fifteen, I've been a Dylan evangelist, and I don't think I've ever been offensive about it. I think people see a guy who really loves Bob Dylan, and is articulate about him, and can tell you why he likes him. He can introduce him to you. Balthasar says anything beautiful first arrests you—you're stopped in your tracks by it. Then, Balthasar says, the beautiful elects you. You've been chosen. Not everyone who hears Dylan becomes a fan, but I got elected. Finally, he says, the beautiful always sends you. You're sent on a mission.

Another point Barron absorbed from his love for Dylan, he says, is not to be bashful about asserting the superiority of your passion over other possible choices. Today, he thinks, there's sometimes too much skittishness about missionary activity for fear that it may seem to treat Catholicism as better, truer, than other faiths—but he insists, if you're truly convinced of that, why wouldn't you want to share it?

"Do I think Bob Dylan is superior to the vast majority of singers and songwriters? Yes! Absolutely! And I can demonstrate it if you want. I'll sit down and show you," he says. "I'm convinced of it, and frankly, I want you to be convinced of it too. I think it'd be great if you listened to him too, because he's wonderful, and I think he is better than the other ones. But I don't think that's offensive to people. It's the enthusiasm of the missionary.

"So, do I think Catholicism is the fullest way to live the way of Jesus Christ? Yes. Do I think Jesus Christ is the Son of the living God, and the Way and the Truth and the Life? Yes, I do. I'm not apologizing for it, and I'm so on fire about it I want you to know it too."

From baseball and Bob Dylan, therefore, Barron took a strong core belief that the right way to expose people to a new idea, a new way of life, is to start with what makes it beautiful, relentlessly help them see and feel that beauty, and only then introduce them to the structures and rules that make such a way of life possible.

Beauty, in other words, is the key to it all.

THE THEORY OF BEAUTY

Naturally, a mind as voracious and given to reflection as Barron's isn't content to rest its case for beauty simply on the examples of baseball and Bob Dylan, even if those early tastes of enchantment helped launch him down this path. He also grounds the argument in early Church Fathers, such as Origen, and in several leading Catholic thinkers of other eras.

An obvious point of reference is the twentieth-century Swiss theologian Hans Urs von Balthasar, who as we learned in Chapter 1, has long been a touchstone for Barron's own thought. Balthasar's famed multivolume work on theological aesthetics, which rolled out over two decades, from the 1960s to the 1980s, features this line, which resonates deeply with Barron's approach: "Before the beautiful—no, not really *before* but *within* the beautiful—the whole person quivers. He not only 'finds' the beautiful moving; rather, he experiences himself as being moved and possessed by it."

"The beautiful leads to the good and the true," Barron says. "But I think strategically, and I got it from Balthasar, it's better to start with the beautiful in our postmodern society. That's not cowardice. It's a strategic thing."

Another passage from Balthasar's theological aesthetics, intended to drive home what he saw as the inseparable bond uniting beauty, truth, and goodness, captures much of both Barron's thinking and his operational style.

> *Beauty is the word that shall be our first. Beauty is the last thing which the thinking intellect dares to approach, since only it dances as an uncontained splendor around the double constellation of the true and the good and their inseparable relation to one another. Beauty is the disinterested one, without which the ancient world refused to understand itself, a word which both imperceptibly and yet unmistakably has bid farewell to our new world, a world of interests, leaving it to its own avarice and sadness. No longer loved or fostered by religion, beauty is lifted from its face as a mask, and its absence exposes features on that face which threaten to become incomprehensible to man. We no longer dare to believe in beauty and we make of it a mere appearance in order the more easily to dispose of it. Our situation today shows that beauty demands for itself at least as much courage and decision as do truth and goodness, and she will not allow herself to be separated and banned from her two sisters without taking them along with herself in an act of mysterious vengeance. We can be sure that whoever sneers at her name as if she were the ornament of a bourgeois past—whether he admits it or not—can no longer pray and soon will no longer be able to love.*

Barron also cites Cardinal John Henry Newman, the great nineteenth-century English convert to Catholicism, and his famed *Essay in Aid of a Grammar of Assent*, in which he referred to something called the illative sense. "It is a grand word for a common thing," Newman conceded. In essence, it means the natural capacity of all people to sense when they're in the presence of something remarkable, inspiring, ennobling—in a word, something beautiful.

Here's how Andrew M. Greenwell describes the idea:

> *The illative sense is what allows us to take our concrete human experiences—whether they be of nature's beauty, of the demands of conscience (the feeling of guilt, the pangs of remorse, the search for forgiveness), of the sense of the contingency of life, of the peaceful joy elicited by the shallow breathing of your sleeping child beside you in bed, of the honor given to a soldier who sacrificed his life for his fellows, of the haunting beauty of the second movement of Schubert's "Piano Sonata in A major," of the pathos of G. M. Hopkins' poem "Spring and Fall," of indeed any created good or beautiful thing—and come to the conclusion that there must be a transcendent reality behind it all, ultimately, He whom we call or know as God.*

In other words, the illative sense isn't about *ars gratia artis*, the celebrated MGM motto that means "art for the sake of art." It's rather a recognition that the encounter with something beautiful, something so obviously transcendent and powerful, often leads people to wonder how such a thing is possible, what might have fostered it or inspired it, and from there an openness to the divine and to religious thought is often born.

"Leading with beauty has always been important for me," Barron says. "I'll bring Newman into this. He would ask, 'Why does a person assent to something?' Argument, he felt, was only a small part of it, what he called formal inference. The illative sense is what assesses a variety of experiences, hunches, intuitions, and thoughts together. I always loved that in Newman."

Predictably, for someone who spends a lot of his time on You-Tube trying to reach unchurched youth, Barron appeals to a contemporary movie to make the point.

Take the abortion debate. Both sides are talking like mad, arguing endlessly. But the movie Juno *offers an instructive approach. The main character goes to a clinic for an abortion. She meets a protester, who happens to be one of her high school classmates, and the young woman says, "Your baby has fingernails!" The next scene shows people in the waiting room of the clinic drumming their fingernails, examining their fingernails, cleaning their fingernails—and then Juno decides not to have the abortion and she abruptly leaves. That's the Newman thing, yes, there are arguments you could make, but it was this kid saying "Your baby has fingernails" that led her to assent to the proposition not to have an abortion. There's something similar in Catholicism. We have this Grandma's attic, this grab bag of liturgy, song, saints, prayers, processions, public displays, arguments, and so on, and we've got to be flexible and creative enough to use all of it.*

Barron says that during the course of his own life, it's often been those moments of preconscious appreciation of something beautiful that have left the deepest spiritual and personal impression on him.

"It's [Paris Cardinal Jean-Marie] Lustiger walking into Notre Dame Cathedral, or it's Paul Claudel, in the same spot where I stood in 1989, looking up at the north rose windows [of the cathedral] and saying, 'That's it, that's it. I believe.' I get that, I totally do."

At a theological level, and in keeping with his penchant for both/and thinking, Barron insists that the Church must always hold two teachings about itself in tension. On the one hand, the Church is the spotless Bride of Christ, a thing of great beauty and purity. On the other hand, it is also an earthen vessel, composed of flawed and fragile human beings. "As a Catholic, I hyperinsist upon the idea of the Church as the Mystical Body," he says, "which means the body is essential. It's not like a vague purse that carries [the faith] around. But then the other side of the Pauline image is that there is a distinction between the treasure and the fragile vessel that carries it, so that's the theological point you have to insist upon. The Church in its beauty and integrity, in its sacraments and its teaching, remains the spotless Bride of Christ, yet it's also this fractured, fragile vessel. That's the kind of theological clarification I'm trying to get across with people."

In other words, Barron's emphasis on beauty does not mean, as he understands, ignoring or refusing to confront the ugliness, the sin, corruption, and hypocrisy, that can also be part of the Catholic life.

"In the *CATHOLICISM* series, there is this intense little scene where I'm in a darkened church and I talk about the Crusades, the Inquisition, and the witch hunts and everything else. 'Was this a terrible moment?' I ask, and I keep saying, 'Yes, yes, yes.' Then I say, 'Even today there's the sex abuse scandal. Were some priests and bishops horrifically derelict in their responsibilities?' I say, 'Yes,' and we kind of let it echo in the church."

Barron's conviction, however, is that in today's cultural vortex, the ugliness is often easier to see, and so the task of the evangelist is to lift up the beauty so that it's clear why intelligent, well-meaning people would put up with the ugliness, even give their lives to trying to eliminate it, in service of something much greater and more compelling.

CASES OF CATHOLIC BEAUTY

One striking thing about Barron is that he has a fairly expansive notion of what "beauty" encompasses. When pressed for examples of beauty in Catholic life, he'll refer to stock cases in point, such as the soaring architecture of Gothic cathedrals, the haunting melodies of religiously inspired music, great works of art by masters such as Caravaggio, and gripping works of literature such as Dante's *Divine Comedy*. Yet in the same breath, he'll also invoke, say, the grace of Rory McIlroy's golf swing. He even points to the selfless service to the poor offered by Mother Teresa and her Missionaries of Charity sisters—despite the fact that those missions routinely bring the sisters face-to-face with the most appalling, most repugnant, ugliest situations in which human beings can live and die.

Here, then, are four examples of what Barron has in mind when he talks about the beauty of Catholicism; they are all part of his basic evangelical strategy for where one should begin in presenting the faith to the world: "First the beautiful, then the good, then the true."

Great Literature

First published in 1945, the classic novel *Brideshead Revisited* by English writer Evelyn Waugh charts the life and romances of the book's protagonist, Charles Ryder, who's introduced as a sort of breezy agnostic, through the England of the 1920s, '30s, and '40s. *Brideshead* refers to a large manor house and estate owned by an English Catholic family, and it functions in the novel as a sort of metaphor for the Catholic Church writ large.

To Barron's way of thinking, *Brideshead Revisited* is a compelling example of the power of great Catholic literature to capture the deep movements of the soul that lead to faith.

Brideshead *begins with the beautiful. We have the narrator, Charles Ryder, who's like many people today. He's a secularist, an agnostic. He's first intrigued by the beauty of his friend Sebastian, who then brings him to this gloriously beautiful place, Brideshead. He's a painter, so his artist eyes are engaged and he goes through the house and it's the beauty of it that draws him in. Then, the book unfolds as the story of how the beautiful leads him to the good and to the true. The moral demand of the house eventually becomes clear to him. At the very end, the truth claim of the house becomes clear, and he becomes fully engaged. Christ is the head of his bride the Church, and thus Brideshead is an icon of the Catholic Church. Often, what draws you is the beauty of it all.*

Here's how Barron explained the same point in a 2013 column on the novel:

In the course of his many visits, Charles came, of course, to know the inhabitants of the house, Sebastian's strange and beguiling family. Especially through Sebastian's mother, the aristocratic and devoutly Catholic Lady Marchmain, he became familiar with the moral demands of the Catholic Church, especially as they pertained to Sebastian's increasing problem with alcohol. For many years, Charles joined Sebastian in his friend's rebellion against these strictures, but in time, he came to appreciate their importance, indeed their indispensability. Finally, at the very close of the story, we learn that Charles, the erstwhile agnostic, had come to embrace the coherent philosophical system of Catholicism and to worship the Eucharistic Lord, who was enshrined in the beautiful chapel at Brideshead. Many years after entering that chapel as a mere aesthete, he knelt down in it as a believer.

As a footnote, Barron's zeal for *Brideshead Revisited* led to the only indirect contact he ever had with Christopher Hitchens, whose aggressive "evangelization" on behalf of atheism and against religious faith made him an obvious point of reference throughout Barron's career. In 2002, Barron says, he published a book called *The Strangest Way: Walking the Christian Path*, which included a section on Waugh and the novel. Hitchens, he says, apparently read the book and talked about it in an article, agreeing with some things and disagreeing with others, but obviously feeling that Barron's treatment of *Brideshead* was important enough that he needed to engage it. (We'll deal with Barron's thinking on Hitchens, and what Christian evangelists might be able to learn from him, in Chapter 5.)

Rounding out Barron's personal list of all-time great Catholic books, by the way, are *The Diary of a Country Priest* by George Bernanos; *Divine Comedy*, by Dante; and *The Idiot* and *The Brothers Karamazov* by Fyodor Dostoyevsky. (Of course, Dostoyevsky came from the Orthodox tradition, not Catholicism, but Barron says there's enough shared sensibility to make the Russian writer's great works imminently "Catholic.")

Great Cathedrals

When Barron was living and studying in Paris, in the late 1980s and early 1990s, his residence was just a fifteen-minute walk from the historic Cathedral of Notre Dame, and he eventually found himself giving tours to visiting pilgrims every Wednesday. The experience, he says, led him to a lifelong love affair with the great cathedrals of the world, which have often been dubbed a sort of "*Summa Theologica* in stone," meaning an artistic and architectural expression of the whole Catholic faith.

"That turned out to be really influential in my life," Barron says. "It started me on this whole medieval passion, with the cathedrals and the rose windows and all these things that I've used extensively in my theological and evangelical work." Barron says he's always been moved by the stories of people who came to their faith through being swept up in the beauty and majesty of the cathedrals—people such as the great French Catholic poet Paul Claudel and Cardinal Lustiger of Paris.

Notre Dame and Chartres are meant to disorient you. In fact, when you come in you're always in the darkest part of the building on purpose, so you come out of the bright light into the dark so you're disoriented, kind of lost, and then your eyes gradually adjust and it gets brighter as you go to the front. That's on purpose, it's an initiation process. When you pass through a portal in a different dimension of experience—and I know I'm sounding like Rod Serling from The Twilight Zone *here—it's meant to awaken a higher consciousness.*

Barron calls Chartres—formally, the Cathedral of Our Lady of Chartres, widely seen as the apex of French Gothic design and mostly constructed between 1194 and 1220—"my favorite place in the world." He elaborates:

I used to go there whenever I could. I went one weekend, Friday through Sunday, and I stayed at a little hotel, and my purpose was to look at everything in the cathedral. What happened to me, and this is very von Balthasar too, is that my Old Testament imagination was awakened. You walk around Chartres outside, and it's dominated by the Old Testament. It's the prophets, the patriarchs, the stories of the Old Testament. Then you realize the Patristic world that all this came out of. You don't get Jesus apart from Israel, and Chartres brings that home in a compelling, beautiful way.

Barron believes places such as Chartres pack such a spiritual punch precisely because they lift us out of the ordinary, out of our usual expectations of physical space, and put us in a place where we're "uncomfortable."

"Chartres always has that impact on me, like a ship," he says. "It's like you're riding a battleship or a starship or something, when you climb up on one of the towers. But the boat image, of course, is on purpose. It's a Noah's Ark, it's a place of haven; you've stepped out of something into something else. It's the sense of the word *ecclesia*—you've been called out to a new place.

"I don't want to feel comfortable in church; a church should not be a domestic space," Barron says. "I want to feel transfigured in a church, and the great ecclesiastical architects knew how to produce that feeling. There's a lot there in terms of evangelical power."

Asked if he could take a potential convert to one place on earth to demonstrate the power and magic of Catholicism, where it would be, Barron doesn't hesitate: "It would be Chartres," he says. "I've always said Chartres is the most beautiful covered space in the world. Now, I haven't seen all the world, but I've seen a fair amount of it, certainly a lot in the Catholic world, and I'd bring him to Chartres, I think, if I were trying to convert him."

On the Catholic landscape in the United States, Barron says his favorite example of beauty in stone is the Cathedral of St. Paul in St. Paul, Minnesota. "Not only where it's situated, the way it hovers over the city, but the exquisite beauty of that building; it has an obvious transcendent quality to it," he says. "The way it's designed, it's very clever, because it has an intimacy to it when you're inside, even though it's a massive building. I've both preached and lectured in that space, and it's always left an impression."

Great Music

Barron's aesthetic tastes can be remarkably eclectic. He veers back and forth between the classics, such as Gregorian chant and Beethoven's Ninth Symphony, and modern pop songs, such as Dylan's "Every Grain of Sand," Springsteen's "Hungry Heart," and pretty much anything U2 ever recorded.

"To me, rock and roll has always been religious," Barron says. "It's weird to say, but there's something about the primal quality of rock and the way it opened up, for me and my generation, the soul, in a way. 'I Still Haven't Found What I'm Looking For,' the U2 song, has that same kind of religious power." He's serious about his interest, playing a little guitar himself, and spends a lot of time listening to all sorts of music.

Barron's fondness for Gregorian chant, for instance, is clear from the score for *CATHOLICISM*. It's a fifteen-track musical score composed almost entirely by Steve Mullen, a veteran musician and composer who, among other things, has produced scores for programs such as *Wild Kingdom* and *The First 48: Missing Persons*. Drawing on melodies from traditional Gregorian chant, titles of pieces in the sound track include "The Mystery of God," "Mary, Handmaid and Mother," "Veritable Despair," and "Amazed and Afraid."

Developed mainly in western and central Europe during the ninth and tenth centuries, Gregorian chant in many ways is the most distinctive musical genre in the Latin Catholic Church, and in many ways it's music at its most elemental: monophonic, unaccompanied, and when done right, hauntingly beautiful. Yet Barron is no enemy of ornamentation, referring to instances of soaring polyphony such as the works of Palestrina and Mozart's *Requiem* as other great entries in the Catholic musical library. (In that sense, Barron would probably stand with emeritus Pope

Benedict XVI, who once said of Mozart, "His music is by no means just entertainment; it contains the whole tragedy of human existence.")

Ever the attentive evangelist, Barron sees an analogy between coming to appreciate difficult portions of a piece of music and accepting the moral demands that are part and parcel of what it means to be a believing, practicing Catholic.

> *There are certain realities that are so basic in their goodness, beauty, and importance that they are not so much chosen as given. Beethoven's Ninth Symphony, the Swiss Alps, Dante's* Divine Comedy, *the French language, moral absolutes, and the saints are goods that give themselves to us in all of their complexity and compelling power. We don't choose them; they choose us. We don't make demands of them; they impose a demand upon us. We wouldn't presume to excise those sections of Beethoven that are "unpleasant," or those features of French that are too difficult, or those dimensions of morality that are hard to live up to. The Word of God, preserved in the Church, is a supreme value of this type. We shouldn't therefore speak of choosing sections of it that we like and leaving behind those that bother us. Rather, we should let it, in all of its multivalence and complexity, claim us.*

Great Movies

As we've already seen, Barron considers movies to be terrific evangelizing tools, especially for young seekers, who may be drawn in by a conversation about a popular film and then led to a deeper exploration of matters of faith. That's not to say, however, that his view of cinema is purely instrumental. At their best, he believes, movies can be powerful religious works in their own right—and his test for what counts as a "religious" film, it turns out, is anything but conventional.

Asked for a sampling of his favorite "Catholic" films, Barron serves up an idiosyncratic mix of usual suspects and fairly outside-the-box entries.

A Man for All Seasons

On any list of slam-dunk Christian classics, *A Man for All Seasons* would have something close to top billing. It's the story of St. Thomas More, the great English lawyer and politician who refused to sacrifice his conscience in order to approve the divorce and remarriage of the king he served, Henry VIII. Barron has credited More's life, and the 1966 film that captured it, with getting across three basic insights: We're all responsible for upholding the rights of others; accepting one's duties often leads to discomfort; and despite the second point, you don't have to be gloomy about it.

Barron says, "My favorite line is from an early scene with More and Richard Rich, a young, ambitious Cambridge graduate who wants a position at court. More tells him that he can find him a job as a teacher in a local school. Crestfallen, Rich complains, 'If I were a teacher, who would know it?' More replies, 'You, your friends, your pupils, God . . . not a bad public, that.' That statement sums up the whole Christian spiritual life, in many ways. You're playing to one audience. To use Balthasar's language, it's not the ego-drama but the theo-drama that matters."

Ben-Hur

This choice comes with a caveat: Barron is referring to the 1959 version of *Ben-Hur*, with Charlton Heston, although he also liked the 2016 update with Jack Huston. The film is an adaptation of the 1880 Lew Wallace novel, *Ben-Hur: A Tale of the Christ*, and focuses on a once-wealthy Jewish prince whose life is ruined by a Roman commander, and who goes about seeking his revenge. In the end, witnessing the crucifixion of Jesus changes him. "Even though he is on film for only a few brief scenes, Jesus is the key to the entire drama," Barron says. Heston's character, he says, came to understand "God's forgiveness of the sins of all of humanity, and thereby found the grace to become a vehicle of forgiveness to someone who had harmed him so awfully."

Gran Torino

Here's where Barron begins to think a bit outside the box. *Gran Torino* is a 2008 film starring Clint Eastwood that tells the story of an aging curmudgeon and widower in Detroit, alienated from his own children, who improbably befriends the children of a Hmong immigrant family next door. When the brother and sister are menaced and then attacked by members of a gang, Eastwood's character goes to the gang's house, standing outside and berating them loudly, drawing the attention of the neighbors. He then gives the impression of drawing a gun, even though it's only his cigarette lighter, causing the gang to shoot him to death—but because the killing was done in public with so many witnesses, this time the gang is swept up by police, and the brother and sister are free. Barron says that it's "one of the most Christological movies ever made," and that Eastwood's character, Walt Kowalski, "joins a list of a handful of really great cinematic Christ figures." (He also puts Paul Newman's Cool Hand Luke, Jack Nicholson's character in *One Flew Over the Cuckoo's Nest*, and E.T. on that list.)

Fargo

Fargo, a dark comedy crime thriller produced and directed by Joel and Ethan Coen, tells the story of a desperate car salesman who hatches a fake kidnapping plot, which predictably unravels and leads to a series of murders. The bad guys are pursued by a massively pregnant police chief, Marge, played by Frances McDormand. Barron believes the Coen brothers are Jewish versions of the great Catholic novelist Flannery O'Connor, in that her stories too were usually very funny, shockingly violent, and ultimately deeply spiritual. Barron sees Marge as an element of grace running through the story, "an agent of transformation willing to go to the margins and bring back those who have been alienated." In that sense, he says, she calls to mind "the Church at its best."

Chapter Three

GOODNESS

At first glance, there's a seeming paradox in Bishop Robert Barron's attitude toward "the good," roughly meaning personal morality and what constitutes a well-lived life, as an evangelical strategy. On the one hand, he's keenly aware, from long experience, that for today's lapsed Catholics and "nones," meaning secularized folks with no religious affiliation, opening the pitch for belief with "the rules," a catalog of moral prohibitions and restrictions, is generally an exercise in futility. Almost invariably the response is "Who are you to tell me what I can and can't do?" Moreover, Barron believes that Catholicism's rules make sense only to someone who's already been enchanted by the faith and the Church, and being hit over the head with rules at the beginning isn't a very reliable pathway to enchantment.

On the other hand, Barron recognizes that throughout the course of Church history, the most powerful missionary calling cards Catholicism has ever been able to play are the lives of its great saints—people, in other words, who embodied "the good" in an especially compelling or remarkable way. As he puts it, "The concrete living out of the Christian way, especially when done in a heroic manner, can move even the most hardened unbeliever to faith, and the truth of this principle has been proven again and again over the centuries."

As he notes, that lure of the good life has been part of Christianity's appeal from the very beginning.

In the earliest days of the Christian movement, when both Jews and Greeks looked upon the nascent faith as either scandalous or irrational, it was the moral goodness of the followers of Jesus that brought many to belief. The Church father Tertullian conveyed the wondering pagan reaction to the early Church in his famous adage, "How these Christians love one another!" At a time when the exposure of malformed infants was commonplace, when the poor and the sick were often left to their own devices, and when murderous revenge was a matter of course, the early Christians cared for unwanted babies, gave succor to the sick and the dying, and endeavored to forgive the persecutors of the faith. And this goodness extended not simply to their own brothers and sisters but astonishingly, to outsiders and to enemies. This peculiarly excessive form of moral decency convinced many people that something strange was afoot among these disciples of Jesus, something splendid and rare. It compelled them to take a deeper look.

What was true for the early Church has remained the case across time, Barron notes, from the revival of Catholicism in the twelfth and thirteenth centuries led by St. Dominic and St. Francis, the great "beggar saints" who brought Christianity back to its roots and "produced a revolution in the Church and effectively re-evangelized armies of Christians who had grown slack and indifferent in their faith," to the towering Catholic moral and spiritual heroes of the modern age, such as St. John Paul II and Mother Teresa. Barron explains,

There's a wonderful story told of a young man named Gregory, who came to the great Origen of Alexandria in order to learn the fundamentals of Christian doctrine. Origen said to him, "First come and share the life of our community and then you

will understand our dogma." The youthful Gregory took that advice, came in time to embrace the Christian faith in its fullness, and is now known to history as St. Gregory the Wonderworker. Something of the same impulse lay behind Gerard Manley Hopkins's word to a confrere who was struggling to accept the truths of Christianity. The Jesuit poet did not instruct his colleague to read a book or consult an argument but rather said, "Give alms." The living of the Christian thing has persuasive power.

So, what gives? Is Barron saying that "the good" is the right way to capture hearts and minds in the early twenty-first century, or is he saying that it's a concept one should begin to unfold only somewhere down the line, once someone has already begun moving toward the faith? Perhaps the way to resolve the paradox is with that well-worn bit of wisdom about good writing, which Barron would say is equally applicable to evangelization: "Show, don't tell."

Barron is convinced that the moral teachings of Catholicism are true, and that people who strive to practice them will live healthier, happier, more fulfilled lives. At the same time, he knows that in a postmodern, secular world, "rule-talk" often comes off as an attempt to limit people's freedom, not to free them to become the persons God intends them to be. Therefore, the right way to deploy "the good" as a missionary tool is to start by showing people what a genuinely Christian life at its best looks like—and then, gradually, to lead people to appreciate the principles and norms which make that kind of heroic life possible.

The best place to begin to understand how Barron thinks about "the good," therefore, is with those legendary role models of holiness and goodness who, over the centuries, have so fired the imagination, and so often led to bursts of creativity and renewal in both the Church and the wider world. As he puts it, "I'm convinced that, at this moment, we need good arguments, but I'm even more convinced that we need saints."

THE SAINTS

In 1985 then Cardinal Joseph Ratzinger, who would become Pope Benedict XVI, gave a series of extended interviews to Italian Catholic journalist Vittorio Messori, resulting in a book that, in English, was titled *The Ratzinger Report*. It was the book that made Ratzinger a Catholic superstar, not to mention a lightning rod. Messori led his subject, who was then the Vatican's doctrinal chief under Pope John Paul II, through all the controversies of the day, from women priests to the limits of legitimate Catholic dissent.

Ratzinger answered all those questions patiently and clearly, but then insisted that none of that was really the heart of the matter when it came to persuading people of the Christian faith.

"The only really effective apologia for Christianity comes down to two arguments," Ratzinger said, "namely, the saints the Church has produced, and the art which has grown in her womb."

It's a sentiment that resonates with Barron, who sees the saints as among the most powerful examples of the Catholic genius.

"Looking at concrete lives is a very good way to get into the Catholic world, maybe better than ideas," Barron says. "That was John Paul II's instinct in making so many saints, and I think [focusing on the saints] grabs people's imaginations more fully."

(For the record, John Paul II canonized 482 saints during his almost twenty-seven-year papacy and proclaimed 1,338 people "blessed," the final step before sainthood. That was not only more than any previous pope but more than all previous popes combined.)

For his 2016 follow-up to the *CATHOLICISM* series, titled *The Pivotal Players*, Barron chose twelve thinkers, artists, mystics, and saints who, in his estimation, not only shaped the Church in their day but also changed the course of civilization.

- St. Francis of Assisi, the great medieval apostle of poverty, peace, and creation.
- St. Thomas Aquinas, the thirteenth-century Dominican theologian who, in many ways, is Barron's intellectual hero.
- St. Catherine of Siena, the fourteenth-century mystic who was also bold enough to rebuke the popes of her time.
- Blessed John Henry Newman, the famed English convert and nineteenth-century theologian. (*Blessed* means Newman has been beatified but not yet canonized, the formal act of declaring someone a saint.)
- G. K. Chesterton, the twentieth-century English journalist best known for his paradoxical wit and whimsical novels; he surprised the world by converting to Catholicism in midlife.
- Michelangelo, who lived in the Renaissance and was perhaps the greatest artist in the history of Western civilization.
- St. Augustine, the fourth-century bishop and theologian whose works *The Confessions* and *City of God* remain among the all-time classics of Christian literature.
- St. Benedict, the great developer of Western monasticism, who in the sixth century helped keep the Church alive as the ancient Roman world crumbled around it.
- St. Ignatius of Loyola, sixteenth-century founder of the Jesuit order, whose relentless missionary spirit bred a

society of missionaries determined to carry the faith to
the edge of the world.

- Bartolomé de las Casas, a sixteenth-century Spanish missionary who served in Chiapas, Mexico, and is
widely considered a progenitor of human rights.
- Flannery O'Connor, a twentieth-century Catholic writer
who radically changed our idea of what religious fiction
could be.
- Fulton Sheen, the pioneer in Catholic evangelization
through the media, and a patron of Word on Fire.

All twelve, Barron believes, embody the Catholic penchant
for beauty and goodness in their fullest sense, meaning living a
life in which holiness, passion, and love shine through in an ar-
resting way. Anyone who becomes familiar with their stories, he
believes, will wonder what it was about Catholicism that inspired
lives like that, and from there, the door is wide open to leading
someone progressively deeper into the faith.

"I wanted this series to reflect the variety of Catholicism, so
we have Thomas Aquinas and John Henry Newman, who are
pretty academic," he says. "But we also have an episode on Catherine of Siena, which is very lyrical and poetic. We have an episode
on Francis, which basically tells his life story and doesn't delve
so much into theological ideas. And then we have Bartolomé
de las Casas, who defended indigenous people against colonial
authorities.

"I wanted to show the full range—men, women, the ancient
church, the medieval church, the contemporary church, plus the
wide spectrum of issues their lives touch on," he says.

One especially powerful example of a saintly life Barron likes
to cite is Mother Teresa of Calcutta (now called Kolkata), who
was herself canonized by Pope Francis on September 4, 2016, as
one of the high points of his special jubilee Holy Year of Mercy.

Here's how Barron once talked about the legendary "Saint of the Gutters":

John Paul II was the second most powerful evangelist of the twentieth century, but unquestionably the first was a woman who never wrote a major work of theology or apologetics, who never engaged skeptics in public debate, and who never produced a beautiful work of religious art. I'm speaking, of course, of St. Teresa of Kolkata. No one in the last one hundred years propagated the Christian faith more effectively than this simple nun who lived in utter poverty, and who dedicated herself to the service of the most neglected people in our society.

In the end, Barron says, if he could teleport someone contemplating the Catholic faith to see anyone, or any group, in action, in order to persuade them of the appeal of Catholicism, he'd send them to India.

"I would take them to Calcutta, and show them Mother Teresa's nuns working," he says. "I'd bring them there and say, 'Look, I'm not going to tell you what to think or how to behave. Just look at them. Just watch them for a while.' In itself, that would probably be enough."

Barron is convinced that the stories of the saints represent an especially effective way to respond to the Church's most ferocious critics.

"We have to out-narrate them," Barron says. "Pope Francis says we have to out-love them, but the out-narrate part means that we have a more compelling story to tell. That has an extraordinary evangelical power, and I've always had the intuition to lead with the saints."

Moreover, Barron believes that familiarity with the lives of the saints can help disabuse some popular misconceptions about Catholicism. High on that list, he says, is the impression that the

Catholic Church is a patriarchal institution, basically a "boys' club," in which women have no opportunities to lead or to exercise power.

I usually deal with that by talking about the great female saints. Who is truly powerful? What is real power? We tend to identify power with office, but genuine power comes from sanctity, power comes from holiness. In the nineteenth century, I've argued, the most powerful Catholics were the "Little Flower," St. Thérèse of Lisieux, and St. Bernadette of Lourdes. The most powerful Catholic of the twentieth century was Mother Teresa, no question about it. Or, think about a Mother Angelica. Talk about power! I think that's the key to it. Real power comes from holiness, and there's absolutely nothing preventing a woman from becoming holy. Thomas Aquinas was asked, "What must I do to be a saint?" and he said, "Will it." Be a saint, and you'll unleash the power of grace and holiness.

(St. Thérèse of Lisieux, known as the "Little Flower," was a French nun who died at twenty-four and whose writings, including *The Story of a Soul,* have shaped the spirituality of countless Catholics around the world. St. Bernadette of Lourdes was a young French peasant girl to whom Mary is believed to have appeared in 1858, and who inspired the construction of the Lourdes shrine, where miraculous healings are believed to occur and which has become Catholicism's most beloved pilgrimage center for the sick and disabled. Mother Angelica was an American Franciscan nun who founded the EWTN media network, succeeding where bishops and Catholic officialdom had failed, and was widely considered one of the most influential Catholic personalities of her time.)

Finally, Barron believes that a focus on the saints illustrates another point about Catholicism, which is that its moral teaching ultimately isn't intended to hem people in but to allow them to excel, to flourish, and to be great.

The Church is interested in making saints. It's not interested in making spiritual mediocrities. It wants saints. Who's a saint? A saint is someone who's radically conformed to love, because love's what God is. That's the whole point of the moral life, of the spiritual life: to help you conform to love. Is that extreme? Yes, because we want saints, we want people to go all the way with offering the gift of themselves. We're not interested in lowering the bar, or making adjustments, or saying it's okay to settle for mediocrity—our idea is, take it all the way!

If you want to understand the Catholic concept of goodness, in other words, you can certainly read tracts on moral theology, or look up Church teaching on various points in official collections. But if you want to grasp what all that doctrine is intended to foster, by far the best place to see "the good" in flesh and blood, in life-changing action, is by coming to know the saints.

THE MARTYRS

Perhaps the most powerful model of the "radical conformity to love" Barron describes among the saints is found in the martyrs, meaning Christians who laid down their lives for the faith. Martyrdom has always been an important chapter of the Christian story, from believers in the early Church who were killed for refusing to sacrifice to the pagan gods of imperial Rome to great saints of the Middle Ages, such as Thomas Becket and Thomas More, who refused to compromise their beliefs for the sake of the state, to modern martyrs killed in what Pope John Paul II used to call *odium caritatis*, "hatred of charity," such as Archbishop Oscar Romero of El Salvador, who was assassinated while saying Mass in 1980 because of his strong stands in favor of the poor and against human rights abuses.

In the early twenty-first century, martyrdom remains a stunningly common fact of Christian life. One high-end estimate for the number of Christians killed each year for reasons linked to the faith is 100,000, while the low end is usually around 7,000 or 8,000—which works out to a range of between one new martyr every five minutes and one every hour. As Pope Francis repeatedly has observed, there are more new martyrs today than in the early Church, and they come from every Christian denomination, creating what Francis calls a vast "ecumenism of blood."

Centuries of Christian experience show that the example of the martyrs is a highly effective missionary force, drawing people to wonder what it is about the faith that would induce so many to make the ultimate sacrifice. The early Church Father Tertullian once said that "the blood of the martyrs is the seed of the Church," and this is a rare case of a theological maxim for which there's actually empirical confirmation. It's a statistical fact that today the greatest danger zones for Christians often are also the places where the Church is growing most rapidly.

That's not to say, of course, that most Christians aspire to martyrdom. The late Protestant scholar David Barrett, who pioneered the statistical study of global Christianity, liked to tell the story of once addressing a group of Evangelical businessmen committed to using their wealth to spread the Gospel, when someone asked: "Professor Barrett, can you tell us what's the most effective missionary tool the Church has?"

"Based on all our research, I'd have to say the answer is martyrdom," Barrett replied.

As he described the scene, there was a long silence in the room, and then someone raised his hand to ask: "Professor Barrett, can you tell us what the second most effective missionary tool would be?"

Yet the plain fact of the matter is that the stories of the martyrs pack a uniquely powerful punch. Consider, for instance, the story of the Italian Consolata Sister Leonella Sgorbati, who was shot to death in Mogadishu, Somalia.

Sgorbati had studied nursing and then, after becoming a missionary sister, served in a series of hospitals in Kenya before heading to Mogadishu in 2001 to open a training center for nurses. She would move back and forth between Kenya and Somalia for the next few years, and had returned to Mogadishu on September 13, 2006. At the time, Sgorbati was one of only two Westerners left in the Somalian capital because the city was in the grip of Islamic militants. Mahamud Mohammed Osman, a father of four children and a devout Muslim, was Sgorbati's driver, bodyguard, and friend, and he was standing next to her when gunmen staged their ambush. The two were shot as they walked thirty feet from the hospital to the sister's home. Osman tried to shield Sgorbati's body with his own, and he took the first bullet. They died together, their blood mingling on the hospital floor. Sgorbati's last words reportedly were *"Perdono, perdono,"* meaning "I forgive."

It's an undeniably haunting tale, and many might say that Sgorbati's life and death represented Christianity at its very best. Today, the cross that she wore during her life is on display in Rome's Basilica of St. Batholomew, which is entrusted to the Catholic Community of Sant'Egidio and dedicated to modern-day martyrs.

One could go on listing examples, such as Father Jacques Hamel, an eighty-five-year-old French priest whose throat was slit on July 26, 2016, by assassins professing loyalty to ISIS, in

Normandy, while he was saying morning Mass. He is now a candidate for sainthood. The point, however, is that in terms of getting across what the Catholic Church understands by "the good," introducing people to even one martyr often is more effective than untold hours of moral exhortation.

Barron believes the stories of the martyrs are so compelling for a simple reason.

"If you want to see what Christ looks like, look at those who participate in him in the most dramatic way," he says. "It's the Cross, participation in the Cross. It's conforming to Christ, it's Christ appearing vividly in our midst."

When Barron spoke at World Youth Day in Krakow, Poland, in July 2016, shortly after Hamel was killed, he says he set aside his prepared text and talked instead about the French priest and the role of the martyrs in Catholic life. (World Youth Day, launched by St. John Paul II, is a global gathering of Catholic youth held every two or three years, which has become one of the largest regular events in the world, routinely generating crowds in the millions. Despite its name, it actually runs for a week.)

I thought, the only way Europe's going to be reevangelized is through the martyrs. In some ways, it's a terrible thing to say, but it's true. Argument will be part of it, but it's the martyrs. Martyrs will reevangelize Europe, and maybe it's missionary martyrs as in the early centuries of the Church's life. Missionaries from Africa, Latin America, and Asia, coming to Europe and dying for the faith . . . The martyrs are participating in who Jesus is. In some ways, we've so domesticated the Cross that we've forgotten not just that Jesus died, not just that he was put to death, but that he was humiliated. It was the most humiliating, the most dejecting, the most dehumanized way for a person to die. That's why Paul says, "I'm not ashamed of the Gospel." Why should he have been ashamed of his message?

Well, because he was talking about this horrific pain, torture, nudity, humiliation—all of it. That's what the martyrs do; they're embodying Christ on the Cross. The Cross is the great display of divine love, and that's what the martyrs do; they show it.

In terms of understanding the depth of God's love, Barron says, "There's no more intense expression of it than martyrdom. It's showing forth the heart of God, showing forth the Cross, which is where that heart is most clearly on display."

THINKING MORALLY

Part of the reason Barron may be so sold on the saints, and especially the martyrs, as the right way to introduce the Catholic concept of goodness is that in the technical language of moral philosophy, he upholds a "teleological" view, from the Greek word *telos,* meaning "aim" or "goal." The idea is that the morality of an act depends upon whether it's oriented to its proper end, and it's the understanding of morality that great thinkers in the Church such as Augustine and Aquinas inherited from Greek philosophers such as Plato and, especially, Aristotle.

Here's how Barron lays it out: "Classical moral thinkers considered the ethical act in terms of its purpose or finality. What makes an act good is its orientation toward its proper end. Thus, since the end of the speech act is the enunciation of the truth, speaking a lie is morally problematic; and since the end of a political act is the enactment of justice, unjust legislating is unethical, et cetera."

In that sense, Barron believes, the saints and the martyrs illustrate what morality is all about. It's not a matter of checking boxes to make sure you're following the rules but rather one of becoming the kind of person whose own life is fully ordered to the good, and thus has the power to change the world. In other words, it's by looking at the saints that one understands why morality matters, and what it's intended to produce.

To expand on that point, he turns anew to *Brideshead Revisited*: "You're beguiled by the beauty, great, come on in and look around. But then the house will make a moral demand on you, and you have to change your life." His point is that once hooked by the beauty of the faith, people will be more receptive to the idea that such beauty is inextricably connected to a way of life.

Part of what's gone wrong in the modern age, Barron believes, is that the concept of morality being measured by its proper end has been widely abandoned.

> *With final causality relegated to the margins, morality became a matter of self-expression and self-creation. The extreme instance of this attitude can be found in the writings of Friedrich Nietzsche and Jean-Paul Sartre. The nineteenth-century German opined that the supreme morality—beyond good and evil—was the ecstatic self-assertion of the Superman, and the twentieth-century Frenchman held that the "authentic" person is the one who acts in accord with her own deepest instincts. Sartre famously argued that existence (unfettered freedom) precedes essence (who or what a person becomes). That's the polar opposite of [morality] ordered to objective finality.*

Conceding that all this may come across as "hopelessly abstruse and irrelevant to the contemporary situation," Barron insists it's anything but, because he believes that idea has corroded our moral instincts and bred a basically "do-it-yourself" way of thinking about what goodness and the good life really mean. It's also, he says, made Catholic moral teaching almost impenetrable for lots of people raised in this cultural milieu.

"The modern person instinctually says, 'Who are you to tell me what to do?' or 'Who are you to set limits to my freedom?' And the Catholic instinctually says, 'Order your freedom to an objective truth that makes you the person you are meant to be,'" he says.

Interestingly, Barron says the basic problem with postmodern thought on morality is that it's "boring." If there's no objective good to which to aspire, no heroic ideal to push people beyond their natural instincts and to call out the best version of themselves, then there's no moral adventure to be sought, no drama to be played out, nothing really beyond a bleak and bland landscape of "I'm okay, you're okay."

How to resist that slide into moral ennui? Barron thinks one effective way is to shift the focus for a moment away from morality and into other walks of life, where people seem far more willing to embrace the idea that there is an objectively desirable purpose to things, and they're often willing to make the effort to adjust their behavior accordingly.

One way I try to do it is to observe that in any other area of life that people take seriously, they naturally assume there's legitimacy to objective values. Take a golf swing. Nobody would seriously say, "Just go swing it any way you want to, because who am I to tell you what to do?" Well, how would that work out? Horrifically. We know that in something like golf, you start to internalize objective ideals, and in that process, you become freer and freer. You become a freer player of golf, and you can actually do what you want to do. That's true of anything—language, music, politics, anything. You begin to internalize objective values in such a way that they now become the ground for your freedom, and not the enemy of your freedom. The binary option we have to get past is "my freedom versus your oppression." What we need to say is, No, no, the

*objectivity of the moral good enables your freedom, opens free-
dom up. Once you get that, you see the Church is not the enemy
of your flourishing, but the condition for it.*

Finally, Barron is utterly convinced that when Catholic moral
teaching is criticized as harsh, unrealistic, or overly demanding,
the best response is not to water it down. It's to explain that the
Church may be extreme in its demands but it's also exorbitantly,
almost wildly extreme in its mercy too, a point he believes Pope
Francis has brought home with special clarity.

*The Catholic Church's job is to call people to sanctity and to
equip them for living saintly lives. Its mission is not to produce nice people, or people with hearts of gold, or people with
good intentions; its mission is to produce saints, people of heroic
virtue . . . To dial down the demands because they are hard,
and most people have a hard time realizing them, is to compromise the very meaning and purpose of the Church. However,
here's the flip side. The Catholic Church couples its extraordinary moral demand with an extraordinarily lenient peniten-
tial system. The Church mediates the infinite mercy of God to
those who fail to live up to that ideal (which means practi-
cally everyone). This is why its forgiveness is so generous and
so absolute. To grasp both of these extremes is to understand the
Catholic approach to morality.*

Barron explains this duality between high expectations and
deep mercy with a concept he borrows from the English Catholic
writer G. K. Chesterton: "bipolar extremism." For him, this is not
the name of a psychological disorder but rather the best way of
grasping the Catholic moral instinct.

"Chesterton didn't like this rather than that, nor did he like a
compromise between the two," Barron says. "He always said the

Church likes red and it likes white, but it has a healthy hatred of pink. Further, it doesn't want red alone and it doesn't want white alone; it wants them both at full intensity. His ground for that was the incarnation: Jesus is not a little bit human and a little divine; he's fully human and fully divine. He believed that this peculiar logic imbues all of Catholicism, and he was dead right."

Importantly, Barron worries that an inadequate grasp of this balance between ideals and mercy can produce distortions not merely among secularists who reject the very idea of objective aims in the first place, and lapse into a sort of moral complacency, but also among fervent believers who're striving to live up to those ideals and are ill equipped for what happens when they fall short. He says he sees that tendency, for instance, among some of today's young seminarians, meaning men studying for the Catholic priesthood.

"It's the shadow side of the John Paul II generation. I know this generation well from my many years of teaching at Mundelein, and I admire this coterie of young people immensely. But I've noticed that they have a hard time dealing with moral and spiritual failure, with not living up, at every moment, to the heroic ideal."

In that sense, he believes, Pope Francis's emphasis on mercy is especially important.

As I look at Francis, I see a good trainer. You don't just name the pain or the problem; you say, "I'm going to work with you every day. I'm going to tell you how to do it; I'm going to stay with you. I'll do it with you." Watch those training programs on TV—there's always a moment when the person kind of breaks down and swears at the trainer, and the trainer has to yell back, and then there's the moment of tearful embrace and "God bless you, you're doing great." There's the Church in its pastoral outreach, and that's how I read him. It's wrong to see

him as indifferent to the struggles of the human race, or think-
ing everything's fine. He barks at us, but he also walks with us
and will embrace us depending on the circumstances.

SEXUAL MORALITY

All this, by an intentionally long path, brings us to Barron's take on what is usually the most contested zone of the Church's understanding of the good life in the postmodern era—its teaching on sexual morality. Ask Barron what are the most common objections he hears about the Church's approach to sex, and it's a depressingly long list.

"That it's oppressive, it's puritanical, it's anti-joy, it's anti-body, it's the Church imposing itself illegitimately on people," he says. "It's unrealistic, it's hopelessly idealistic, it's out of touch with the way people actually live. I mean I hear all of that; I could go on. We're anti-human, we're anti-body, we're anti-pleasure. We're dualistic and platonic and it's just an impossibly high ideal."

In the teeth of it all, when one listens to Barron talk about sexual morality, three broad principles seem to emerge:

- Don't put the cart before the horse, meaning don't become so focused on the fine points that the true fundamentals of the Catholic faith never come into view.
- Don't water down or avoid the teaching but rather try to help people see why ultimately it expresses a yes rather than a no.
- Get past the notion that the Church is "sex-obsessed" by making sure people grasp that this area of morality is hardly all Catholicism cares about.

On the first point, Barron uses the example of a seminarian interviewed by *The New York Times* roughly a decade ago, who was asked what he wanted to preach about once be became a priest and had the chance to speak to his flock every Sunday from the pulpit.

> *The fellow said, "I really want to tell people that they have to stop masturbating." Now I'm not in favor of masturbation, so don't misconstrue me, but you'd never finish the Gospel of Matthew and say, "Okay, what the evangelist really wants me to know is that I shouldn't masturbate!" You wouldn't finish the Book of Revelation, or read Paul's Letter to the Romans and say that's what it's primarily about: getting my sexual life in order. That's important, obviously, but it's a question of where this teaching fits in a much bigger picture. I became convinced, and am still convinced, and as I've mentioned before, that a huge swath of Catholics do not know the fundamentals of Christianity. They don't know the beauty of the game. They don't know what the infield feels like. They don't know the texture of it.*

For precisely that reason, Barron says, he deliberately avoids extended discussions of sexual morality in his *CATHOLICISM* series.

"I didn't want to do that," he says. "I want people to feel the infield again; I want them to smell the ballpark. I want them to feel Catholicism, to know the essential stuff. Furthermore, we won't get the sexual stuff right until we get that right."

That said, Barron is unabashed in insisting that once you understand the ends it's intended to promote, and the kind of life it's intended to foster, Catholic teaching on sexuality is right on the money, and he's uncomfortable with any attempt to back away from it. Here, for instance, is how Barron responds when asked if he believes the fight against abortion deserves pride of place among the Church's other social concerns.

> *Yes, I do. It's the right to life; it's the protection of innocent life. If anything is the linchpin of a moral program, it's the protection of innocent life. That's why abortion does have a certain pride of place in the hierarchy [of moral concerns]. They're all in the picture, but there is a proper ordering. Whatever threatens innocent life takes priority, morally speaking. Yes, I get the fact that people are especially preoccupied with abortion, but [the Church's position] doesn't mean we're shills for the Republican Party. It means we're trying to bring all of life under the aegis of radical love, but there's a prioritization.*

When asked if he believes it's realistic to think that the 1973 *Roe v. Wade* decision of the U.S. Supreme Court legalizing abortion could be overturned in his lifetime, Barron is cautiously optimistic.

> *Probably not in our lifetime, but I wouldn't rule it out. I'd make a comparison with slavery. At a certain point in American history, nobody would have imagined the possibility of slavery being overturned. Very smart people, very morally plugged-in people, were defenders of slavery in 1830, 1840, including Christians at a very high level. Politicians at the highest level didn't think slavery could be overturned in 1820 or 1840, and yet now slavery is unthinkable. It's the same with civil rights. In the 1930s and '40s, a lot of very high-placed people, including religious people, wouldn't have imagined the overturning of Jim Crow, but now it's a fact. I find that, by the way, from a theoretical standpoint, fascinating, how that happens in a society. How at one point something is commonly accepted, and fifty years later it's unthinkable. I*

don't rule out that, at some point, the same could happen with abortion. I hope, in God's providence, it will become unthinkable that we're murdering children at the rate of millions per year. I don't know if it will happen in our lifetimes, because you and I don't have that much longer to go! But I also don't rule it out.

Finally, Barron says he often finds that one good way to help people appreciate how the Catholic Church approaches sex is to shift the focus for a moment to some other topic of moral concern more congenial to a postmodern sensibility.

One thing I find helpful is to move out of the sexual arena for just a second. For instance, go back to the Church's teaching on what constitutes a "just war." It's every bit as demanding as sexual teaching. If you follow it, and all of its rigorous details, one could argue there's possibly never been a just war. World War II, maybe, in terms of the motives for the war, but the way it was fought? Forget it—Nagasaki, Hiroshima, Dresden, Tokyo, none of it would correspond to the requirements of a just war. Now, would you say we better dial it down, that we're being unrealistic? In 1945, if you had polled Catholics in America on whether we should drop the atomic bomb, I'd say 95 percent would have said, "Yes, of course. End the damn war, save lives!" So, should we have lowered the bar; should we have said, "Bring it down, it's unrealistic?" Today, I think most people would say no, the Church should stay very high in its moral demand.

As a corollary, Barron believes that taking the discussion out of the arena of sexual ethics also can help people better appreciate the link between high expectations and deep mercy in Catholic morality.

"Consider the man who dropped the bomb from the *Enola Gay*, who was Catholic," he says. "I don't know anything about his inner life, but let's suppose he came to confession and said, 'I want to confess that I dropped this bomb and killed 75,000 people, and I feel this great regret before God the Father and I want to confess my sin.' He'd receive total absolution of his sin, right? So, the Church is extreme in its demand but it's also extreme in its mercy."

In the end, Barron concedes that no amount of rhetorical repackaging and pastoral accompaniment will make Catholic teaching on sex anything but a tough sell for a broad swath of the contemporary culture, but as he sees it, that's no excuse for bowing out of the conversation.

"Do we need shepherds who are willing to walk and accompany people? Yes, I'll say it as passionately as Pope Francis," he says. "Now, is this all going to work out really well in the confines of a fallen world? The answer is no. Will this be a source, for some people, of permanent frustration? Yes, it will. I get that, but I don't think we have another choice."

Chapter Four

TRUTH

O ddly enough for someone convinced that beauty rather than truth is the best way to begin presenting the Catholic story to the world, Bishop Robert Barron himself is a counterexample. We learned in Chapter 1 that a foundational experience for Barron was his chance encounter with St. Thomas Aquinas at the age of fourteen, which put him on a journey to penetrating the depths of Catholic thought which he's never abandoned and which, for a long time, he envisioned as the core of his career. In a sense, Barron was convinced that Catholicism is true before he fully appreciated the beauty and goodness he believes it also incarnates, reversing his usual dictum about the proper evangelical sequence.

"My way in was the truth," he says. "It happened when I was a little kid hearing Thomas Aquinas, so my natural propensity was to lead with the mind. I love the life of the mind, and I've spent my whole life studying and reading. Yet because of where we are now, the 'true' and the 'good' are offensive in a culture that is so radically subjective and relativist, and the minute you say, 'Hey, I've got the truth for you,' every defense goes up, and even more if you say, 'I've got what's good for you.'"

Perhaps that disjunction between his personal experience, in which being persuaded of the truth of Catholicism was all-important, and his professional experience, which has taught him that truth claims often backfire until several other pieces of the puzzle have fallen into place, accounts for the rather unique style Barron brings to talking about Catholic doctrine, especially when dealing with people who either have fallen away from the faith or never had it in the first place.

On the one hand, when the situation calls for it, Barron can expound and defend Catholic teaching with the best of them. He can take up the Trinity, the claim that God is three persons in one being—which is, let's face it, a fairly counterintuitive idea—and make it seem utterly plausible. He can present the Catholic understanding of revelation as a blend of Scripture and tradition, and leave you completely convinced this is indeed the way a loving God would gradually guide humanity to a deeper understanding of his will. Along the way, Barron won't just present his own answers but will cite from memory the best and brightest of the Catholic tradition, invariably leaving listeners with the impression that this is obviously someone who knows his stuff. He's nobody's idea of a theological dissenter, and he says the more he reads and studies Church teaching, generally the more convinced he becomes.

At the same time, Barron is not the sort of preacher or missionary who believes the primary aim of every encounter regarding the Church has to be absolute clarity on doctrine—as if the primary obstacle to faith in a postmodern, secular culture is that Catholicism has been insufficiently clear. To be sure, he's no fan of fudging what the Church teaches, as we'll see in a moment, but he's also able to keep his eyes on the evangelical prize. Winning a debate doesn't do much good, he understands, if you haven't first won hearts and minds, and he knows that all his erudition, however precious it may be, often can't accomplish that latter goal by itself.

Barron's approach to what he deeply believes to be the truth of Catholicism perhaps can be understood as a both/and synthesis of two extremes, which can be illustrated by possibly apocryphal stories about two legendary men of the Church.

On the one hand is a story told about St. John XXIII, "Good Pope John," who called the Second Vatican Council. In 1962 Pope John received a group of Protestants from the ecumenical monastery of Taizé in France, which had been founded in 1940. Legend has it that the pontiff asked the group why Catholics and Protestants couldn't put the past behind and get together.

"We have different ideas," one of them is supposed to have said.

"Ideas, ideas!" Pope John was said to have replied. "What are ideas among friends?"

Whether or not John XXIII actually said that, the story was widely repeated in Rome during the opening period of Vatican II—predictably, eliciting delight in some quarters and horror in others.

The other story is about Cardinal Henry Edward Manning, who served as Archbishop of Westminster in England from 1865 until his death in 1892, and who took part in the First Vatican Council under Pope Pius IX, which produced the dogma of papal infallibility.

It was well known that another famous English Catholic personality of the time, John Henry Newman, had his doubts about declaring the pope to be infallible when he speaks on faith and morals. Such reservations irked Manning, who had a highly exalted notion of papal authority, especially when the pope was propounding Catholic teaching to the world.

Manning was so enthusiastic about clarity on doctrine that his friend William Ward quipped, "Manning would like nothing so much as to find a papal encyclical on his breakfast table every morning alongside *The Times*."

Barron probably wouldn't be fully comfortable with either of the instincts those anecdotes capture. On the one hand, he's anything but casual about ideas. He's devoted much of his life to intellectual research and writing, and he's also convinced that some extremely dangerous ideas got unleashed at the beginning of the modern period, ideas that have had disastrous consequences. As a result, he's firmly persuaded that the Catholic Church must always speak its truths to the surrounding culture, without adjusting those teachings to make them more palatable.

Yet neither is Barron an "encyclical a day" sort of Catholic, who believes the Church is always at its best when it's insisting that it has the truth and others don't. Instead, he believes restraint is sometimes the better part of valor—and further, exhortations full of truths, however convincing they may be, generally preach only to the choir. The real trick is leading people into a space where they may be ready to hear and embrace those truths, which is an entirely different challenge.

That, then, is the distinctive Barron touch: being utterly, completely convinced of the truths of Catholicism, ever eager to plumb those truths more deeply, and prepared to defend them against all comers; yet at the same time, never fussy or rancorous in the way he presents, never polemical or pugnacious with people who don't share those truths, and also fully aware that the Church itself may share some measure of the blame for creating a cultural context, at least in the West, in which many people find the truth claims of Catholicism hard to swallow. All of that is generally blended with a deep calm, a lack of any agitation and angst.

"I'm at war with dumbed-down Catholicism, and so I always try to make sure my presentations are smart, crisply organized, and draw on the tradition," he says. "But I also try to project a certain friendliness, a certain invitational quality. I'm inviting you to get in the conversation with me, rather than I'm here to pound something into your head. I try not to be histrionic."

In the end, Barron believes that anyone who's attracted by the beauty of Catholicism, or by the extraordinary goodness of the lives the Church fosters in the saints, will naturally be impelled to begin discovering the truths that underlie those marvels. Truth, for him, is indeed the heart of the matter, but it does not stand alone either strategically or theologically.

BEIGE CATHOLICISM

Probably the right place to begin unpacking Barron's vision of the importance of truth in Catholicism is his well-known antipathy for what he calls "beige Catholicism," meaning a sort of watered-down version of the faith. (He says he drew the inspiration for the term from his own parish church in the Chicago suburbs, "because it was built in the 1970s in the classic style of that time, brick empty walls, wooden ceiling, open space, asymmetrical, nothing resolved"—meaning, not quite a monument to the great Catholic tradition.)

Here's a fuller version of how Barron defines *beige Catholicism*, from a 2016 podcast.

> *It's a Catholicism that's become bland, apologetic, unsure of itself, hand-wringing, overly accommodating, that's allowed its distinctive color to blend into beige, so that it's hard to distinguish it from other religions and the wider culture. That's what I was worrying about, and it was the Catholicism of the postconciliar period and the poor reception of the council. It was the church I grew up in, the church of the 1970s and '80s. It was mirrored and expressed in the literally beige structures we built, that looked like they belonged in a shopping mall and were hardly distinguishable from the suburban environment. That became symbolic for me of a deeper problem, of a Catholicism that's lost its purpose, energy, confidence, color,*

distinctiveness . . . its sharp edges had been dulled, and its dis-
tinctive colors muted.

Barron started referring to "beige Catholicism" early on, and
the expression was picked up by a number of other Catholic writers and commentators, including his fellow Chicagoan Father
Andrew Greeley, who helped popularize the term. Barron is self-
aware enough to realize that many such adult convictions are, in
part, a reaction against things people experienced in their child-
hoods. For him, growing up in the immediate post–Vatican II era
in Chicago and later as a young theologian, beige Catholicism
was the order of the day, and it left him cold.

"I lived through dumbed-down Catholicism, so I stand
athwart that," he says. "I want a smart presentation of the faith.
The dumbed-down Catholicism that I received has served us
very, very poorly. I'd go so far as to say it's been a pastoral disas-
ter. We've lost two generations because of it." His point is that
because young Catholics were never given any reason to believe
there's something intellectually and rationally compelling about
the faith, they could be easily persuaded of the secular view that
religion is no more than superstition and prejudice.

In his view, it's simply laughable to contend that young people
can't be expected to understand and reflect on complicated religious ideas, or even systems of ideas, in the same way they do in
virtually every other area of their lives.

There was a young lady who worked at Word on Fire five or
six years ago, and she had two kids. Her daughter was nine at
the time. In she comes one day, and her mom says, "Hey, tell
Father Bob all about Star Wars." *So off she goes, recounting in*
infinite detail the whole Star Wars *saga—every minor player*
and every complicated name. I'm smiling as she told me all

about it, and when she finished, I said to her mother, "Now, don't tell me little kids can't understand the Bible." Excuse me, but this kid knows the Star Wars *story from start to finish, but she can't tell me the story of salvation? Yet time and again, I have heard teachers and catechists say, "Oh no, Father, kids can't read the Bible; it's just too complicated—and all of those long names." Give me a break! I frankly don't see how Habbakuk and Nebuchadnezzar are necessarily harder to memorize than Obi-Wan Kenobi and Lando Calrissian.*

(As a footnote, Barron hardly has a salty tongue, but such is his passion on this subject that he actually used a couple of minor off-color terms to punctuate that story—they've been excised in the interest of decorum!)

To hear Barron tell it, based in part on the experience of his own family, things haven't improved much, at least in many places, in the years since he was moving through the system.

When my niece was a senior in high school, attending a very good Catholic academy outside Chicago, I came to my brother's house toward the end of the summer, and he said, "Look at Neala's books for the coming school year." There they were, and there's Hamlet *on the top, the full text, and Virgil's* Aeneid *in Latin, and under that was some bristlingly complex mathematics book, and underneath all that, in paperback with big print and pictures, was a religion book. Well, I went out and I bought her volume one of the* Summa Contra Gentiles *[by Aquinas],* The Confessions *of Saint Augustine, Bonaventure's* The Mind's Road to God, *maybe Chesterton and Dante too, the* Divine Comedy. *I brought these to her and I said, "These are the Catholic versions of the other books you're reading."*

Barron has told some version of that story many times, but he still grows visibly irritated every time he recounts it.

I remember in Los Angeles many years ago, I was speaking at the Religious Education Congress. I'm the keynoter in that giant room, and at the end I said, "Hey, can I just tell everybody how I hate dumbed-down Catholicism?" I told a version of that story [about his niece], and I'm banging the podium like a madman saying I hate dumbed-down Catholicism. The whole arena burst into raucous applause, and so I said, "Don't applaud; do something about it." The room was filled with publishers, teachers, catechists, and I told them to do something, because we have no one else to blame. We've met the enemy, and it's us. We did this to ourselves. High school kids can handle a lot of serious stuff, so why aren't they reading C. S. Lewis? Why aren't they reading Orthodoxy *by Chesterton? Why aren't they reading Aquinas, for that matter? My nephew, he's a smart kid, he's a junior in high school, and he's a math guy, which I'm not. Man alive, the complexity of the math books he's dealing with . . . why couldn't we give him Augustine or Thomas Aquinas? I have very strong feelings about that. We dumbed it down out of this attempt to be relevant.*

That reference to "relevance" is key to Barron's thought, because he believes that it was the search for relevance, characteristic of classic Christian liberalism, where things began to head off the rails toward beige Catholicism. The roots of that move in Christian thought and theology, he believes, run deep.

You have to go way back to the beginning of the modern period philosophically, and the option for a very subjective and experiential reading of religion . . . go back to people like Des-

cartes and Kant, Schleiermacher and Hegel, and many others.
Then you come into our century with people like Paul Tillich
and Karl Rahner. What you get is an approach to Christian-
ity that emphasizes what it has in common with all the great
religions and spiritualities. There's nothing really wrong with
that in itself, but when it becomes consistently the point of de-
parture, or the point of orientation, what you hear is "Catholi-
cism is a spiritual path among many others. There are many
ways up the mountain. Catholicism is kind of like Buddhism,
et cetera." That was born of the typically modern approach
that emphasized the universality of all religions. They were
worried that religions were warring with each other, battling
over their distinctive theologies. One way around that, they
thought, was to emphasize the universal dimension. Taken to
an extreme, however, what it produces is a bland, watered-
down Catholicism.

As part of that picture, Barron believes, Catholics influenced
by these theological currents began assigning an undue weight to
personal experience in communicating the faith, believing that
the Gospel always must be made "relevant," in ways that ended up
domesticating the Christian message.

My formation in the 1970s and '80s would have been expe-
rience, experience, experience. Good preaching, for example,
meant you begin with your own experience. Begin with a joke
or story, then draw it into your experience, and only then cor-
relate it to the Bible. But the trouble with this way of going
about it is that experience runs the show, experience asks the
questions, experience sets the agenda, experience sets the con-
text. The Bible is drawn into experience, but that's getting it
backwards.

In general, Barron argues, the post–Vatican II push in Catholicism for engaging the surrounding culture in dialogue oftentimes took a wrong turn, shifting from "dialogue" into one-way communication, and from there into a form of accommodation.

> *Dialogue between religion and culture dominated the conversation when I was a young man, and when I was coming of age as a student of theology. Yet it seemed to me it was always the Church reaching out to the culture, and not vice versa. The call for dialogue was coming almost exclusively from the Church. I didn't see a lot of the avatars of culture interested in making themselves understandable to us, on our terms, and making contact with religion. A slogan I heard a lot as a young man was "The world sets the agenda for the Church." That's simply not the case. Vatican II called us to "read the signs of the times," and let me tell you, that phrase was used to produce a lot of beige Catholicism. It was taken to mean, "See what's going on around you, and become like that." No, the point wasn't to accommodate those signs, but to read them in light of the Gospel. Now, when you read culture through the Gospel, you'll find good things, but also lots of bad things. The point is, the culture is not the interpretive lens for the Church. It's Christ, and everything must be read through him. The problem that produces beige Catholicism is attempting to read Christ from a standpoint higher than himself.*

All that helps explain why for Barron, "the truth" is a foundational pillar of the entire Catholic edifice. He has no patience for blurring or fudging Catholic doctrine, or for tweaking it to suit the shifting tides of a given era's fashion. That certainly doesn't make him a "traditionalist" or a hawk in doctrinal disputes—and in reality, few people familiar with the dynamics of Catholic debate these days would see him in those terms—but it does prove that his strategic option for not beginning the conversation about the Church with its claims to truth doesn't mean he isn't firmly convinced it has to get there eventually.

THE PRIORITY OF CHRIST

One question that often gets asked about people who become prominent in the media, thereby garnering some degree of celebrity and fame (however minor compared to others—think Kardashian and Bieber, for instance), is whether the experience has changed them. It's a common tale, that people who become celebrated in some walk of life can become so addicted to that acclaim that they begin tailoring their personalities or ideas to try to cling to it.

That clearly isn't the case with Barron, and one proof of the point is that one of his core ideas, in a sense the pillar upon which everything else is based, is what he calls "the priority of Christ" in all aspects of Christian life, teaching, and evangelization. As we've seen, his "big book" as an academic carried that title—2007's *The Priority of Christ: Toward a Postliberal Catholicism*. In effect it was a work of Christology, meaning doctrine about Jesus Christ, but it was much more than that. It was also a diagnosis of what had gone wrong in Catholicism in the post–Vatican II period, meaning the rise of "beige Catholicism," and how to set things right. It was the product of years of reflection and study, including a sabbatical period at the University of Notre Dame in 2002 to do much of the writing.

Among the core ideas of the book, Barron argues that for its overt rejection of religion and the supernatural, contemporary secular culture nevertheless remains "Christ-haunted," longing for the answers to questions that the culture has lost the ability to even ask, and that can be found only in Christ. So important is that idea to Barron that later on, when his Word on Fire ministry took its early steps toward thinking of itself as a movement, outlining eight core principles, the very first was "Christocentrism," which is another way of saying that Christ is the priority.

"The idea is that everything we talk about and try to introduce people to—all of it revolves around and returns to Christ, in the manner of the medallions in a rose window," Barron says. "Relationships, theology, politics, art, philosophy, all find their center in Christ."

Although the book appeared early in the papacy of Benedict XVI, it was seen in many quarters as a classic expression of the St. John Paul II spirit in the Church. John Paul was, in a sense, very much a "postliberal" pope—not rejecting the positive aspects of the liberal reforms unleashed in the postconciliar era but leavening them with stronger doses of Catholic identity, doctrinal clarity, and, well, verve. That was the distinctive John Paul II touch, a desire for a bolder, less skittish and self-absorbed Church, one with the self-confidence to get back into the game by being clear on what it stands for.

Barron's book very much breathed that air. In the foreword, Chicago's Cardinal Francis George called *The Priority of Christ* "a hopeful work, designed to help the Church today work through many sterile debates and express the truths of the apostolic faith clearly and persuasively."

"A lot of that book is an argument with people like Kant, Schleiermacher, and, in the twentieth century, with Rahner and Tillich and many others who had followed the liberal line," Barron says. "It's a reversal of the epistemic momentum of the last two hundred years, which formed the basic instinct of most liberal theologians, and so I'm proposing a postliberal Catholicism. That means that a densely textured, detailed picture of Jesus becomes the permanent point of reference."

At the time, *The Priority of Christ* was Barron's seventh published work, and in academic circles it was a reputation-making watershed. It would have set Barron up for a distinguished career as a theologian and university professor, and it was around that time that job offers came in from both the Catholic University of America and Notre Dame. A colleague of Barron's at Mundelein Seminary called the book "a robust short *summa*," and for someone as in love with Aquinas as Barron, that had to be high praise indeed.

Barron says that when it appeared, he felt the book might be the high point of his career. "I thought that if I had an obituary which said I was the author of *The Priority of Christ* and a few other books that influenced the academic world of Catholicism, that would be enough," he says.

Life, of course, had other plans for Barron. Yet today, in a different key, he is as convinced of the importance of the priority of Christ as an evangelist and a bishop as he was as a theologian. Here's how he talked about the priority of Christ is our interviews for this book.

It runs counter to so much of the theological momentum of the last two hundred years, which was to position Christ by something exterior to himself. One of the basic moves of liberalism, and why I identify as a postliberal, is a tendency to read Christ from the standpoint of human experience. It positioned him, it didn't ignore him, but it positioned him from a point of view external to himself. My argument is that you've got to reverse the momentum, because liberalism in the sense I'm describing it is repugnant to the structure and logic of the New Testament, which holds Jesus to be the Logos [meaning "the Word of God," the principle around which the universe is structured]. If he is the Logos, or as the Letter to the Colossians would say, he's that through whom all things subsist, then he can't be positioned by a Logos higher than himself or external to himself. He's the Logos by which all other Logoi are read and positioned. It doesn't mean you eliminate experience, you eliminate symbolism, you eliminate history, rather that you read all those things from the standpoint of Jesus.

Barron insists that his self-description as a "postliberal" doesn't imply a rejection of liberalism but rather a course adjustment.

"I get liberalism," he says, "which is why I'm not antiliberal, I'm postliberal. I get it, because it's very effective apologetically. It's a great way to reach out to a skeptical audience, but the price that we paid for a wholesale and uncritical embrace of liberalism was too high, because it flattened out Jesus. It made him like many other founders and other religious teachers. It gave priority to experience, in a way that rendered Christ less than he should be."

In the end, Barron believes that placing the priority on Christ—the raw, undomesticated, almost spiritually feral Christ—is a more effective evangelical move than trying to sand off the rough edges to make him palatable, or easily comprehensible, to a secular sensibility.

My wager is, and here I'm with Balthasar and others, that it's actually more evangelically effective when you begin with Jesus and bring his dense texture forward, drawing experience into him, not the other way around. It's all those moves, that reversal of momentum, that I think are decisively important for the way we do theology, the way we preach, the way we evangelize. I'm speaking abstractly here, but if you want to look at it this way, everything I'm involved in—Word on Fire, the CATHOLICISM series, my books, my preaching, all of it—is an expression of this transition.

Part of what placing priority on Christ means, as Barron sees it, is grasping what the New Testament message about Christ really is. Too often, he believes—and this perhaps is another symptom of the tendency to begin talking about the Bible in terms of contemporary experience, rather than letting Christ himself set the agenda—that second-order matters such as sexual ethics get top billing, instead of what the Biblical text is actually trying to say.

I've argued for years that when you read the Gospel of Matthew or the Book of Revelation, you're not going to finish and say the number one concern of these people is to get my sexual life in proper order. It's part of the picture, but the New Testament is really about a lot of people who want to grab the whole world by the shoulders and shake them, saying, "Do you realize that Jesus Christ has risen from the dead? Therefore, he's the Lord, and therefore, your whole life has to be situated around him." The primary message is "Jesus Kyrios—Jesus is Lord." That means your country isn't Lord, the Roman empire isn't Lord, no other figure is Lord. He's the Lord. That, to me, makes the New Testament crackle with excitement in a way that other spiritual texts don't. They can be true and good and right, but they're not crackling with the excitement of this message.

Barron says he detects a hunger among many Catholics to recover this sort of Christocentric approach to talking about, and living, the faith, which to some extent had gone into eclipse for a long stretch of time. He drives the point home with an anecdote about an evangelization conference where he spoke several years ago.

I spoke on the third day of the conference. My opening line was "Evangelization is about the resurrection of Jesus from

the dead," at which point the whole audience broke into ap-
plause. I joked, "On behalf of the risen Jesus, I want to thank
you all!" But I was honestly puzzled, so afterward I talked to
people and asked what the ovation was all about. They said
it was because they'd been here for three days, and heard all
about sociology and statistics and this and that, but not a word
about Jesus or the resurrection. I thought, Thereupon hangs a
tale. If the Catholic Church, in a conference on evangelization,
hasn't gotten around to the resurrection until day three, there's
something fundamentally wrong. It's one of the practical im-
plications of a hyperliberalism that would so stress experience
that we miss the heart of the matter.

As part of this Christocentric emphasis, Barron is deeply fond
of the traditional description of Christ as "priest, prophet, and
king," which is rooted in the Old Testament and was developed
by the early Fathers of the Church.

"It means a lot to me, and it's a category Newman used," Barron says. "Newman got it from Calvin. That's actually a significant way that Protestant thinking came into the Catholic world,
because it moved from Calvin to Newman, and then Newman influenced Balthasar and [Henri] de Lubac and others, and then it
got into Vatican II. In the council's documents on the laity, on the
priesthood, the idea of priest, prophet, and king is everywhere.

"I found in my own work these archetypes are incomparably
rich; they keep generating meaning," Barron says. "It's a way of
naming who we are, and who Jesus is."

Here's how Barron briefly explains what he regards as the
timeless truths expressed in the concept of "priest, prophet, and
king."

Priest

"The priest is the one who gives right praise. That's the Biblical way of naming who we are. What goes wrong is that we praise the wrong things. Augustine said that too, that we end up worshipping creatures rather than the Creator. We become priests of the wrong god. From bad worship flows everything else, meaning the disintegration of the self, sin, violence, and so on.

"Getting us back on track means we're like Adam before the Fall," he says. "He's a priest, because he's in the attitude of right worship. I was playing with this idea in the episode on Michelangelo in *The Pivotal Players* because on the ceiling of the Sistine Chapel, where Eve comes forth from the side of Adam, she's facing God and she has her hands folded in an attitude of prayer. That's humanity before the Fall; it knew how to worship right."

Prophet

"Before the Fall, Adam names the animals, that is to say, he catalogs them. He names them according to the Logos (*kata logon*) that God has placed in them. He's not making up their meaning, he's recognizing (*re-cognizing*, to use the term of Joseph Ratzinger). He's thinking again what's already been thought into them, so he's a prophet. From that prophecy, correct speech flows, the whole range of literature and science, philosophy, everything."

King

"The idea of king is that Adam, and the rabbis talked about this, is made to expand out. Now that Eden's okay, let's move out and turn the whole world into a place of right praise. What it gives you is the whole vocation of Israel. It is a priestly people, a prophetic people that knows the divine truth, and then, finally, a kingly people that will go on the march."

Barron stresses that all this comes into clear focus only through the lens of Christ.

"That vocation wasn't fully achieved until Christ, who is very richly described as a priest, prophet, and king," he says.

"He, in his own person, is the place of right praise," Barron says. "It's humanity turned to divinity. He's not just the speaker of truth, he is the Logos incarnate, so he's prophet in the full sense. Then he's king, because he's going on the march to 'Edenize' the world, to 'Christify' the world.

"What goes wrong with us," he added, "is that we get all three of those things wrong. We worship the wrong things, we start making up our own meaning, and then we also privatize the faith." A restored focus on Christ, Barron believes, is the only exit strategy from those temptations.

In the end, Robert Barron is a man who believes that while Catholicism propounds a galaxy of truths to the world, its core truth, the claim that must never fade from view, is that Jesus Christ is the center of history and the answer to the meaning of human life. Because of that conviction, he's palpably impatient with any presentation that, in his view, plays down the centrality of Christ.

To make the point, he cites the example of a Catholic Biblical scholar who once said he wanted to produce a book on the New Testament's presentation of Jesus with which a Jew, a Muslim, or an atheist could also agree.

"What you end up with often is this very desiccated Jesus, just a few little nuggets of truth," he says. "I get the method, and I appreciate it, but it's not evangelically compelling. You can undertake that exercise, and do it very well, but what do you end up with? It's a Jesus no one really cares about, a Jesus whom you can't really preach."

BEYOND SCIENTISM

Both as a theologian and as an evangelist, Barron puts forward the key belief that modernity has a truncated view of "truth," reducing it to what can be established through the empirical sciences. "Truth," for such a worldview, boils down to scientific truth, brushing aside other truths from philosophy, the arts, and so on.

> *The trouble is, we're so conditioned by the sciences, we've come to think the only way to know truth is through scientifically verifiable evidence. But there are so many important nonscientific ways to know the truth. Many people ask me, "Is there evidence for God?" I always say, "No, if by that you mean physical traces and data you can do experiments on." But if the question is, "Are there rational warrants for believing in God?" I say absolutely, and then I bring them into the philosophical discussion.*

Barron believes that a breakdown in the humanities in Western culture is partly to blame for this myopic view of what counts as "truth."

"It's a giant problem," he says, "because all we've got now is the binary option of science and nonsense. Those are the only two things many people recognize. Well, how about all these literary forms? What about philosophy, and poetry, and all these different ways of conveying the truth? I've had a lot of young people say they don't get that. They get science, and that's truth and then there's all this unverifiable nonsense.

"Many young people believe that philosophy, for instance, is just a bunch of people irresponsibly mouthing off opinions about things," he says. "A young person will lay out a version of logical positivism, and I'll say, 'So, Plato, Aquinas, Heidegger, Kant, and so on, are just spouting nonsense, because they're not speaking in the scientific manner?' That's a deep problem, which goes by the technical name of scientism."

For clarity's sake, it's important to state that Barron has no issue with the sciences. His complaint is rather with "scientism," meaning the conviction (which for the record, is philosophical rather than scientific) that the hard sciences are the only way to arrive at truth.

"Science can't demonstrate the secular worldview," Barron argues. "The secular worldview is a philosophical conviction born of certain assumptions, all of which can be questioned. In reality, scientism is self-refuting. That's the problem, and in a certain way, secularism too is self-refuting, and that's what we're up against.

"Where did you empirically verify the principle that only empirically verifiable things are true?" Barron asked. "That's the problem with logical positivism in all its forms, and it's as old as the hills. Augustine made the same argument against the academics."

Barron has called scientism "comically arrogant," a position held by sloppy thinkers "who have simply closed themselves off to what a thousand generations of human beings have taken for granted . . . How, precisely, did the advocate of scientism see, measure, or empirically verify through experimentation the truth of the claim that only empirically measurable things are true?"

Given that landscape, Barron believes, it's the responsibility of Catholicism to help the surrounding culture recover a deeper and richer sense of truth, which was actually at the origins of Western culture—including, he points out, the rise of the empirical sciences.

Just tell the wider story. Think about the number of Jesuits around the time of Galileo who were deeply involved in the sciences. Think about the founders of modern science—

Descartes, Copernicus, Pascal, Galileo himself—who were devoutly religious, not just accidentally but devoutly so, with Newton maybe being the most famous. I always cap it off with Georges Lemaître, the formulator of the Big Bang theory, which is now pretty much accepted by all serious cosmologists. Lemaître had to convince Einstein of it. Well, Lemaître was a Catholic priest. That's massively unknown, especially among young people, because all they know is the Galileo myth that the Church is a great persecutor of scientists.

In that regard, Barron believes the Church must do a much better job of demonstrating convincingly that its understanding of truth is not antiscientific. He made that point, he says, in a recent address to California Catholic high school teachers.

I was in Santa Barbara, speaking to around three hundred Catholic high school teachers. I told them what I really believe, which is that they are massively important and influential people. Then I asked a simple question: "Could I have all the science teachers stand up, and could I have all the religion teachers stand up?" Then I said, "Okay, you two groups seriously need to talk to each other!" I did this, because the number one reason young people tell us they're leaving the Church is that science refutes religion. It's nonsense, of course, but we haven't gotten through to our kids on this score and we have to get our act together.

THE DANGER OF PRIVATIZATION

To this day, Barron keeps up his commentary on popular movies through his YouTube channel, seeing it as an especially effective way to raise issues of faith in a secular milieu. In December 2016 he offered a take on the Martin Scorsese movie *Silence*, which to a great extent swam against the tide of much commentary from faith-based reviewers. In essence, the movie tells the story of a group of Jesuit missionaries in Japan who face horrific struggles, including excruciating torture, and eventually renounce Christianity to become wards of the Japanese state, embracing Buddhism. Yet at the end, there are haunting indications that their Christian faith isn't entirely vanquished.

Most Christian commentators praised the film for its complex and respectful treatment of spiritual themes, and Barron didn't disagree. He did, however, weigh in with a somewhat dissenting perspective, which raised some hackles. Here's what he wrote:

> *I would like to propose a comparison, altogether warranted by the instincts of a one-time soldier named Ignatius of Loyola, who founded the Jesuit order, to which all the* Silence *missionaries belonged. Suppose a small team of highly trained American special ops was smuggled behind enemy lines for a dangerous mission. Suppose furthermore that they were aided by loyal civilians on the ground, who were eventually captured and proved willing to die rather than betray the mission. Suppose finally that the troops themselves were eventually detained and, under torture, renounced their loyalty to the United States, joined their opponents, and lived comfortable lives under the aegis of their former enemies. Would anyone be eager to celebrate the layered complexity and rich ambiguity of their patriotism? Wouldn't we see them rather straightforwardly as cowards and traitors?*

Ultimately, the point Barron wanted to make wasn't so much to condemn the choices made by the Jesuit missionaries but rather to suggest that *Silence* expresses the strong prejudice in secular culture against religion—which is that it's fine if you want to harbor religious beliefs, as long as you keep quiet about them and don't disturb the social order.

"The secular establishment always prefers Christians who are vacillating, unsure, divided, and altogether eager to privatize their religion," Barron wrote. "That's the kind of Christianity the regnant culture likes: utterly privatized, hidden away, harmless."

Recovering a full-throated and bold understanding of the priority of Christ, Barron believes, is the best antidote to this tendency toward privatization.

> *That's my point about priest, prophet, king. Paul, who understood the fullness of his Jewish tradition, was running around the whole world, frantically, to say, "You have a new king, Jesus Kyrios [Lord]. Caesar isn't Kyrios." That's called evangelization, and these are evangelical categories. They're also Vatican II categories . . . Cardinal George always said that Vatican II was a missionary council, and I think that's dead right. It's not the Church fussing with itself about authority; it's the Church going out. It's* Lumen Gentium, *you know? [*Lumen Gentium, *"Light of the Nations," was the Dogmatic Constitution on the Church issued by Vatican II.] Let the Cross be the light of the nations.*

The privatization of faith in a secular world, Barron believes, has toxic consequences—including for secularism itself, which is premised on the two great values of equality and liberty yet has a hard time explaining where those values come from apart from the Biblical frame of reference in which they originally arose. Barron says,

> *I taught political philosophy for a long time at the seminary level. I had my students read everyone from Plato to Aristotle to Cicero, all the ancient political writers. All the classic*

philosophers took it as axiomatic that human beings are not equal. This was a fundamental assumption for their political philosophy. A tiny handful of people had the right to enter public life, but most people don't. Women and slaves and the ignorant and children must all remain in the private realm, and recognizing that fundamental inequality was seen as basic to political flourishing. Then something happened with Biblical religion, which gave us a sense that even though we are unequal in beauty and courage and power and everything else, we are, nevertheless, equal as children of God. I would argue that that's what haunts the West to the present day. If you take away the Biblical ground, you have a very hard time, it seems to me, arguing for equality and liberty. I use the image of the flowers and the water, because if you take the flowers out of the water, they'll look okay for a while, but pretty quickly they're going to wither. That's the fear, that when you take these values, such as freedom and equality, out of the water of their deep spiritual source, then they will be compromised.

To be clear, that outlook by no means leads Barron into anything like explicit political activism. In truth, from an interviewer's point of view, it's far easier to get him to express an opinion on Georg Hegel or Immanuel Kant than on, say, Donald Trump, and he'll respond with considerably more passion about the former. Barron insists that he has no interest in theocracy, saying, "That's been a dangerous road."

However, Barron is certain that when Catholicism retreats from a clear proclamation of Christ as the lone Savior of the world, when it tailors its truth about Christ to become more easily digestible, it's not only the Church's self-understanding that suffers. It's also the cultures to which faith in Christ once gave rise, and which today seem increasingly fractured and disoriented, as well as all those other cultures in the world for which the message of Christ could act as a leaven.

The bottom line for Barron is expressed in a famous expression from Pope Benedict XVI, in his 2005 document *Deus Caritas Est*: "Being Christian is not the result of an ethical choice or a lofty idea, but the encounter with an event, a person, which gives life a new horizon and a decisive direction." Keep that clear, Barron believes, and all will be well; lose sight of it, and nothing else in the long run will really matter.

TRUTH AND THE EVANGELIST

As a final observation about Barron's understanding of the third of the great transcendentals, truth, he may not believe that in a postmodern age that's generally where *evangelization* should begin, but he is absolutely convinced it's where *the evangelist* must start. Without understanding the doctrinal content of Catholicism, he believes, an evangelist won't be able to explain it well when pressed; and without being convinced that it's the truth, he says, the evangelist won't be credible.

> *I always go back to what John Paul said about the New Evangelization, which is that it's really the old evangelization, meaning it declares that Jesus Christ is Lord. What's new about it, he said, is that it's new in ardor, it's new in method, it's new in expression. He too was worried about beige Catholicism, that we'd lost our edge, lost our fire. We had fallen into a sort of relativism, thinking that if all religions are the same, what's the point in drawing people to Jesus? Aren't we all walking up the holy mountain on different paths, and so on? I think that led to a loss of ardor, and I think that's what*

Ratzinger feared when he spoke of a "dictatorship of relativism." I've got my truth, you've got your truth, and so we're all on this big lake and we're all floating along with our private opinions. I'm not going to get in your way, and you won't get in mine. You're not going to become an evangelist under those circumstances.

We'll expand on this point in the next chapter, but Barron's unwavering belief in the importance of truth is why his standard response to anyone who asks his advice about how to get started as an evangelist is "read, read, read." He insists that before delving into the brave new world of social media, for instance, would-be evangelists need to master the "old technology," meaning the printed word, the classics of Catholic thought. Only by grasping those classics, and by being persuaded of the truths they contain, he thinks, can an evangelist be effective.

Chapter Five

EVANGELIZATION

My day job as a journalist is covering the Vatican and the papacy, and if there's one ironclad conclusion I've come to after twenty years on this beat, it's this: The papacy, as we've come to understand it in the modern era, is an impossible gig. I'm talking not about the official descriptions of the papacy in sources such as the *Catechism of the Catholic Church* or the Code of Canon Law, but rather about the popular understanding of what it means to be pope.

Think about all the things people now expect popes to be. They want popes to be world-class statesmen, able to wave a magic wand and make wars, or poverty, or other social ills disappear. They want popes to be Fortune 500 CEOs, responsible for everything that happens in the Catholic Church around the world. If my parish doesn't have enough paper clips this month, by God, then the pope should do something about it. We also expect popes to be intellectual giants, with something incisive to say about whatever's bubbling in the culture. If a scientist somewhere develops a new cloning technique, for instance, and the pope doesn't address it, many people would take that as an abdication of responsibility. We want popes to be media rock stars, dominating the airwaves, and if they're not, we begin talking about their papacies as failures. (Just ask Benedict XVI about that one.) Finally, of course, people also expect popes to be living saints, embodying a path of holiness and virtue for the entire world, and if there's even a hint of irascibility, or ego, or any of the other classic forms in which real human beings sometimes fall short of the ideal, people go nuts.

The truth, which anyone would recognize upon a moment's reflection, is that doing any one of these things even moderately well is a life's work. Rolling them all up into one job description, therefore, is a prescription for perpetual frustration and heartburn. The net result is that popes always have to choose where to invest their time and resources, prioritizing one thing over another, which is a choice generally driven by their reading of what their life experience has prepared them to do especially well, and by what God's providence expects of them at a given moment in time.

At a lower level, Bishop Robert Barron faces something of the same dilemma. By this stage in his career, he's distinguished himself in multiple fields. He's an academic and a theologian, very much interested in the life of the mind. He's been a pastor and still understands himself as a pastor, someone devoted to the care of souls. For a long time he was a molder of future priests, culminating in his role as rector of Mundelein Seminary in Chicago. He's a media personality, forever in demand to comment on the issues of the day vis-à-vis the Catholic Church. Now he's a bishop, responsible for his own pastoral region of Santa Barbara in the Archdiocese of Los Angeles, and also a member of the U.S. Conference of Catholic Bishops, which means he also faces obligations on the national scene.

While Barron takes all of those demands seriously, it's clear that when he gets out of bed in the morning, he doesn't fundamentally think of himself as an intellectual, or a celebrity, or an administrator. Instead, if Barron had to choose one word to describe how he sees himself and his role in the Church in our time, it would probably be this: *evangelist*.

When asked if he sees himself primarily as an evangelist, Barron doesn't hesitate.

"I'd be happy to take that title," he says. "I was trained as a theologian, so I was trained to do technical theology, to write, to teach, which I did for a long time and still do. But I'm happy to claim that title, because I think there's something global about that term. Aquinas was an evangelist. I reverence Pope Benedict, and he was a great evangelist at the intellectual level. And he was very keen on the engagement of the secular culture at the high academic level. I think the great theologians are evangelists, and I think especially now it's what's needed."

Given that *evangelist* is the way Barron sees himself, it's critical to consider more closely how he views the evangelical enterprise in order to grasp the role he plays in the Catholic Church in the early twenty-first century, both in the United States and on the universal level. We've already established what Barron sees as the right way to evangelize a secular culture, which is to begin with what's beautiful about Catholic life, and then proceed from there to the good and the true. As a result, this chapter focuses more on the background to his understanding of contemporary evangelization, and the techniques necessary to support it, rather than on its content.

TWO CAVEATS

Before diving in, we need to make two preliminary points about how Barron sees evangelization—what it is and, just as important, what it isn't.

First, for Barron evangelization is not an exercise in marketing or salesmanship, though there are certain natural affinities among these activities. His fundamental concern is not about third-quarter sales numbers or market share but about the welfare of the individual people who come into his orbit.

In a certain way, it has something in common with marketing, but I hope the main difference is that the evangelist is not dealing with a product but a person. You're trying to draw people into a friendship. Evangelization isn't about a concept or an idea, but about a friendship with Christ that you have, and that you want someone else to have too. In that sense, it's not like marketing at all, which is always in some way trying to sell a product. But it is like marketing in that it's telling a story as convincingly as you can. In the end, though, it's about sharing a friendship, an intimacy that's enlivened you, and that you feel will benefit other people.

A further distinction from marketing is the way Barron measures the success of his evangelizing activity.

I'm always delighted when someone says, "Because of something you did, I'm coming back to Mass." There's the ultimate goal. You measure success by whether people are coming to Mass, which is the source and summit of the Christian life. Some people say, "Because I heard you, I'm thinking about the faith again," or "You made me see things in a new way." Good, I'm happy with that too, because it means I'm drawing people closer. The ultimate measure, however, would be the Mass. It would be full communion with the Catholic Church and going to Mass on a regular basis, receiving the sacraments, that's the measure of it. You draw people at all kinds of levels in different ways, and I think you measure success relatively at different stages, but getting them to come to Mass and enter more deeply into the life of the Church is the ultimate aim of it all.

The second caveat is that Barron is in complete agreement with recent popes, including Pope Francis, and other Church leaders who have insisted that although the Catholic Church should be bold in its missionary efforts, it must never practice what the Vatican usually calls "proselytism"—which in that context usually refers to overly aggressive or manipulative forms of evangelization that don't really respect people's freedom.

"I'm with John Paul II," Barron says. "Never impose, always propose. We should never be browbeating, aggressive, prideful, and all that. You don't want to impose the faith, and it's counterproductive anyway. It's almost self-parodying: You know, 'Here's the Prince of Peace, and let me knock you over the head to make sure you accept Him.' Or, 'Here's the Lord of nonviolence, let me bomb you into submission.' Of course, that's ridiculous."

Yet Barron doesn't want anyone to take that as a prescription for going soft or slack in terms of the Church's missionary drive.

"By God, we should propose with a lot of energy and enthusiasm," he says, "convinced that we have the best thing on the market. I think that's the right way to do it."

With those stipulations read into the record, we can move to what Barron considers the right way to evangelize with energy.

THE NEW EVANGELIZATION

In contemporary Catholic argot, Bishop Robert Barron would be seen as a prime mover in America of what's called the New Evangelization. To get a handle on how Barron understands his role, therefore, we first need to get a sense of what *New Evangelization* actually means.

The term originated with an Italian priest named Monsignor

Luigi Giussani, who was the founder of a Catholic movement called Comunione e Liberazione (Communion and Liberation). In general, the *ciellini,* as Giussani's followers are known in Italian, have been seen as embodying a more conservative brand of Catholicism, more interested in changing the world based on the teaching of the Church than in changing the Church based on the insights of the world. Comunione e Liberazione, which is based in Milan, was seen as a sort of "parallel church" during the tenure of the Jesuit Cardinal Carlo Maria Martini, who during the 1980s and '90s was the preferred candidate of the liberal wing of the Catholic Church to become the next pope.

Despite all that, Giussani wasn't primarily a political figure but a theologian and intellectual, whose core idea was that the Christian faith in its most primary form isn't a set of doctrines but rather a relationship with Jesus Christ. Morals and doctrines, as Giussani presented things, are important, but they are secondary to the encounter with Christ. As a result, he was critical of any effort to expound Christianity that didn't begin with the person of Christ. From there, he drew the conclusion that what Western culture really needed was a "new evangelization," meaning a new determination to preach Christ to the world.

Giussani initially presented that idea to Pope John Paul II, who was beguiled by it and in many ways could be said to have incarnated it. John Paul began to call for a "new evangelization" frequently, which is how the phrase entered Catholic conversation. Then came Pope Benedict XVI, who was an admirer of Giussani, and one of whose last public acts before being elected pope was to travel to Milan, at his own initiative, to celebrate Giussani's funeral Mass in 2005. Benedict was so convinced of the need for a new evangelization that in 2010 he created a new Vatican department, the Pontifical Council for Promoting the New Evangelization, to carry the project forward—and that came despite Benedict's well-known skepticism about ecclesiastical bureaucracy.

At the time, Pope Benedict said that "the process of secularization has produced a serious crisis of the sense of the Christian faith and role of the Church," so the new pontifical council would "promote a renewed evangelization" in countries where the Church has long existed "but which are living a progressive secularization of society and a sort of 'eclipse of the sense of God.'"

Barron believes that what distinguishes the New Evangelization from the old isn't content—now, as it was then, it's about preaching Christ as the Risen Lord—but rather the fervor one brings to it, and perhaps above all, the modes of expression and media one employs.

In terms of the techniques that drive the New Evangelization, Barron believes it's listening to the culture and figuring out how best to engage it.

> It's a matter of being aware of our times. How do you say it to an early twenty-first-century audience? We live in a time that's racked by secularism, racked by skepticism about religion, that's experienced 9/11. I think that's a huge phenomenon, because the new atheists emerged in the wake of 9/11. It reawakened the old Enlightenment argument that religion is irrational, therefore it's violent. So, what are the new expressions you have to use to get this thing across to people today? It's also a question of new methods, including the new media, social media, and all that business. We've got these tremendous new methods to evangelize.

It's worth saying at this point that Barron believes the rise of social media is the most important communications revolution since the printing press, more decisive even than the telegraph, radio, and television in terms of the way people receive and process information.

Barron grants that quite often, social media platforms such as Twitter and Facebook don't exactly bring out the better angels of people's natures, seeming to give them license to attack and demean those with whom they don't agree, but he insists that his own experience shows that another path can succeed.

> *When we got going with the YouTube commentaries, and that was right at the beginning of YouTube itself, I wanted them not to be mean and polemical. I've tended to avoid polemics. I don't respond to people like that, and I don't provoke. I wanted them to be smart, so my typical YouTube video lasts for nine or ten minutes, which is fairly long for that format. They're basically video versions of my columns. We wanted them to be positive, and encouraging, reaching out to the culture in a more open way. We didn't go the route of quick, nasty, polemical, or provocative . . . I didn't do that. And we've been pretty successful.*

For Barron, it's not really a question of whether social media are a flawed forum, because every new media technology throughout the ages has had its defects.

> *I remember being at a conference years ago at the Vatican on the new media. It was hosted by [Cardinal Gianfranco] Ravasi's office [the Pontifical Council for Culture], and I was invited to give a presentation on what I was doing. Someone was making all the usual critiques of the new media, and legitimately so. Then one of the bishops got up—he was a Polish bishop, I can't remember his name now—but he said, "My grandmother used to complain that the telephone is a very inelegant form of communication." And then, he said, "Of course she was right."*

There was a long pause. Eventually, I think, people realized, would any of us for a moment think we shouldn't use the telephone? I thought his point well taken. Every new mode of communication has a shadow side.

Under the heading of "new ways," Barron also believes it's important to be paying attention to what's bubbling in the culture, including popular culture, to see what one might be able to pick up on or employ as a bridge to talking about faith. To illustrate the point, he cited the example of *House of Cards,* the acclaimed Netflix series about an utterly amoral American politician.

Recently I was binge-watching the show, and Frank [President Francis Underwood], who's this really demonic sort of figure, has ordered a drone attack. It's killed both soldiers and civilians. He's at Arlington Cemetery for a funeral and a bishop is preaching. You can tell it's kind of affecting him. He calls the bishop and asks to meet him, so they go to an Episcopal church, late at night, and the bishop comes in, and they talk a bit about Isaac and Abraham and the Son of God. Frank asks, "May I be alone to pray for a moment?" The bishop leaves, and Frank looks up at the crucifix and says to Jesus, "So, love is what you're selling? Well, I'm not buying." Then he spits at the crucifix. When he takes his handkerchief to wipe off his spit, the corpus [the image of Christ on the Cross] falls off onto him, and then shatters on the ground. I thought that was an interesting little moment. I'm very alive to that sort of thing, how is this Christian instinct still around? I love how it pops up everywhere.

This, then, is Barron's understanding of the New Evangelization: a confident, Christocentric presentation of Catholicism, attentive to the questions being asked today, and deeply conversant with all the new ways those questions are being asked and answered, especially in the digital realm of social media.

EVANGELIZATION AND BUREAUCRACY

Although there's a sense in which Barron is today an ecclesiastical bureaucrat, since he's now a bishop and has administrative responsibilities, he's keenly aware that the most effective forms of evangelization generally don't spring to life as the products of some institutional initiative.

"That's totally my instinct," he says. "I'm with Cardinal Newman, who said that nothing great is ever accomplished by a committee. That doesn't mean they're useless; they accomplish certain things. But nothing great is accomplished by a committee."

For an example of the point, American Catholics might think of Mother Angelica, the founder of the EWTN media network. To be sure, her feisty brand of conservative Catholicism wasn't to everyone's liking. She once publicly excoriated then-Cardinal Roger Mahony of Los Angeles for a pastoral letter he produced on the Eucharist, saying if she lived in Mahony's archdiocese she would offer "zero obedience" to such a heterodox approach. Over the years liberal Catholics have often rued the rise of EWTN, arguing that it presents an overly dogmatic and selective version of what Catholic life is about.

Whatever one makes of EWTN, there's no denying the fact that at the time it began broadcasting, in 1981, the U.S. bishops' conference had been looking at trying to establish a national Catholic presence on cable television, and they would eventually pour millions of dollars into an effort that ultimately proved fruitless. In the meantime, one charismatic Catholic nun, who at the beginning, had nothing but Scotch tape and glue, managed to build the world's most successful Catholic media empire. In effect, it was a lesson in how content is king—you can buy all the hardware and delivery platforms you want, but if you don't have content that people are willing to walk across hot coals to access, none of it will really matter.

Barron says Mother Angelica and EWTN offer a compelling example of how effective evangelization generally works.

"I think certain people emerge through God's grace, and they lead the way, and then eventually committees help to focus it, but it's usually great figures that get the ball rolling," he says. "Whether it's Fulton Sheen, or Billy Graham, or Matteo Ricci, or whoever it may be. At the beginning, it's not driven by bureaucracy. It's not driven by official programs. Programs have to be developed around the charism or person, not vice versa."

In reality, Barron says, the key to the success of the Word on Fire ministry is that it too was born outside any bureaucratic structure, and has continued to develop without being subsumed into officialdom within the Church.

I've been around Church bureaucracy for a long time, and it takes care of itself. I'll go out on a limb here—Word on Fire succeeded largely because it operated outside of the Church bureaucracy, and that was because of Cardinal [Francis] George, God bless him, plus my own instincts. I don't mean to bad-mouth Church bureaucracy, because it's absolutely essential and the people who serve within it are critical, but there's something about bureaucracy that's resistant to real creativity. The bureaucratic element of the Church exists to serve the charismatic, but the trouble, and it happens very often in the Church, is that the charismatic element gets smothered by the bureaucratic. What we did at Word on Fire is to build our own bureaucracy, with people I know and trust who are committed to the mission. In other words, we've created our own bureaucracy that will serve our mission.

That's not to say, however, that Barron believes that the infrastructure and resources of the Church's official structures have no role to play, or that they can't be useful in promoting the work of evangelization. In November 2016 he was elected to head the U.S. bishops' Committee on Evangelization and Catechesis, and he sees several possibilities for it to play a positive role.

"A committee can help the bishops understand things," he says. "If we could explore and propagate best practices in regard to the use of the new media, for example, and help dioceses get geared around this issue, we could produce some positive results. We could help bishops think about the things bugging the nones, and how we could reengage them. If we can assist them with that, it might be very useful."

REACHING THE NONES, NOT THE NUNS

Any salesman will tell you—and salesmanship, in a terribly inexact sense, would be the secular analogue to evangelization—that the key to success is knowing your customers. In the same way, Barron is clear about whom he's trying to evangelize. Although he spends a fair bit of his time addressing already convinced Catholic audiences, that's not really his target demographic. Instead, Barron's bold ambition is nothing short of evangelizing secularism itself.

Barron describes the people he's trying to reach in terms of two basic cohorts. First are lapsed, fallen-away, and alienated Catholics, people who have left the faith, often because they've imbibed and accepted parts of the secular critique of religion and the Church. Second, Barron is angling to engage the "nones," people of no religious faith, many of whom have had no contact with the Catholic Church at all, and who carry around a bushel basket full of prejudices and instinctive biases against it.

"I'm much more interested in those who are drifting toward secularism, so those who are moving away from the Church world completely," Barron says. "I want to get to those people and engage them again. Catholic insider baseball is largely irrelevant to the people I'm interested in. I'm more worried about the nones than I am about the nuns, I guess. Those are the people I'm focused on."

Though Barron is not especially self-promotional, he's self-aware enough to realize that there are certain aspects of his personality and background that dispose him to be effective in reaching out to those groups.

It's hard to reflect on that, because I don't think I ever went into it thinking, Oh, I've got the right personality for this work. In retrospect, though, I think I can identify certain qualities. For instance, I've never used, or rarely used, a directly confrontational approach. I try not to go into warfare immediately. Once in a while, like with the new atheists, I'll do a little of that, and actually get into it and battle away. But it tends to be a more, I think, winsome, more positive approach . . . I think my YouTube videos are the same thing. I think that quality too, a certain calm intelligence, a certain invitational quality, is consistently in play.

Barron believes his personal background, including his family and his early experience of the Church, as well as his enchantment with the entire breadth of the Catholic experience, helped equip him to project that sort of style.

First of all, I just love the Catholic Church's cultural and artistic and spiritual tradition. I find it very beautiful and life-giving, and so that naturally comes out. I'm eager to tell you about it. I've also always been a teacher, so most of my life I've taught in a formal way. I remember even as a kid I always liked teaching, explaining something, or bringing something to the table, so I'm kind of a natural teacher, I think. I'm pretty articulate, so I can usually say what I'm thinking. The verbal thing, which I think I got from my mother . . . my dad was a great man, a beautiful, holy man, but my mother is the talker in the family. My brother and I both got our communication skills from her. Also, we've talked about the postconciliar time in the Church that I've reacted against, but I actually came of age in kind of a relatively calm and happy period, so it's not like I was in this deep confrontational situation. It was a friendlier kind of Catholicism that I came of age in, and maybe that shaped me in some ways too.

Asked if his nonconfrontational, "friendly" tone is a matter of instinct or deliberate choice, Barron says it's a little of both.

"It's born of an awareness of where we are in the cultural moment," he says. "You're not going to get a lot of nones coming back to church if you're ranting and raving. You have to be more inviting, finding positive things in the culture you can identify with, so that's been a conscious strategy."

He went on,

I think you have to read the signs of the times, what's going to be effective? Yes, I could do that [be more pugnacious], but would that be effective? Would I actually bring more people to church with that style? I would say no. So, some of it is personality, but some of it is reading the signs of the times. What do you need to do at this moment? And sometimes I do get tougher. I can show you lots of videos when I take on a more pugnacious tone, with "this is really bad" and "we have really got to be against this" on certain issues. Maybe at a different time in the

Church's life that approach would be called for more often, but now we're trying to attract the nones. That approach is just not going to do it. The question we always have to ask is, "What's going to work now?"

That focus on the positive, however, doesn't mean that Barron wants Catholic evangelists to play down the Church's distinctive identity, or to shrink from being clear about the truth claims discussed in the previous chapter.

Cardinal Newman made a comparison with an animal navigating its way through its environment. An animal that is utterly resistant to the environment will be dead in short order, but an animal completely open to its environment is also dead in short order. To be alive is to be in this subtle space of both resisting and assimilating. There's the Church. It's a living body, which indeed it is. It's got to be holding off, all the time. It's got to be defining itself, but at the same time it has to be assimilating and taking in. If it's not doing both those things, it's dead by definition. That's the trick, and the great figures in the Church have always done that; they've struck this delicate balance. Pope John Paul II was a prime example of it, I think. Talk about someone who knew legitimately how to hunker down, and yet also reach out like mad. It's a delicate operation, and that's what I'm trying to do. Of course, I understand that at the abstract level, almost nobody would disagree that the Church should be doing both these things. The hard part is to figure out when to do what. I come back to the analogy of the animal kingdom: Let's say a porcupine has moved to the countryside and is doing pretty well, assimilating and eating and taking things in, and then suddenly it's being attacked. At that moment, the porcupine will stop and put every single quill up, sit there, and hunker down and defend itself with all its might. Those are the sorts of concrete judgments the Church has to make all the time.

When you are listening to Barron talk about the fine art of evangelization, you notice that certain adjectives keep coming up: *nimble, quick,* and *canny* are obvious favorites. They reflect his view that while personal conviction, knowledge of the tradition, and zeal for the missionary enterprise are all essential, they have to be rounded out by good instincts for where the target audience is at any given moment, and which strategies are likely to reach those folks best.

"I think an evangelist has to be nimble, and smart, and know all that is up there in Grandma's attic so you can respond to the needs of the time," Barron says. ("Grandma's attic" is a favorite Barron image for talking about all the expressions of Catholic culture over the centuries, from literature and art to liturgy and spirituality, including the doctrinal and theological tradition.) "You've got to be nimble and know what you can use."

That's why, as mentioned earlier, Barron's stock advice to aspiring evangelists is to "read, read, read," meaning to immerse oneself in Catholic thought and teaching, and in the great works of Catholic literature. Secular nones sometimes ask a lot of smart questions of believers, Barron says, and without a solid intellectual foundation, evangelists will find themselves flustered, frustrated, and ultimately, ineffective.

Again, however, Barron stresses that being nimble isn't being infinitely elastic.

"I know sometimes part of that nimble presentation is to put up your quills," he says. "Sometimes you have to present what you're against, not just what you're for. You're a little porcupine moving through the environment."

EVANGELIZATION AND CHRISTOPHER HITCHENS

Asked to name some of the great evangelizing role models of the modern age, Barron rolls out many of the usual suspects— Archbishop Fulton Sheen, Billy Graham, Pope John Paul II, even Mother Teresa, who may not always have been evangelical in the explicit sense but whose life and example had powerful evangelical resonance all over the world. Then, however, Barron comes to a more counterintuitive answer, at least from a Catholic point of view: the great atheist intellectual and pundit Christopher Hitchens.

Born in Portsmouth, England, in 1949, Hitchens was among the most extraordinarily prolific writers and commentators of his generation. He authored, coauthored, edited, or coedited thirty books, beyond a staggering output of columns and essays as well as television appearances and speaking engagements all over the world. A self-described socialist, Marxist, and "anti-theist," Hitchens was an acerbic critic of religion, seeing faith in God as a form of totalitarianism that erodes personal liberty. The title of a 2007 bestseller by him pretty much sums it up—*God Is Not Great: How Religion Poisons Everything*. Hitchens often had a special animus for the Catholic Church, among other things penning a blistering critique of Mother Teresa in 1995 called *The Missionary Position*, which accused her of indifference to the causes of poverty and willingness to take money for her missions from dictators, human rights abusers, and other dubious benefactors. He died in December 2011, his last words reportedly having been "Capitalism. Downfall."

We learned earlier that Barron never had any personal interaction with Hitchens, and that there was only one case in which Hitchens ever engaged his work, which came with regard to an essay Barron had written on *Brideshead Revisited*. Nevertheless, Barron was a careful student of Hitchens's work, and he insists that Catholic evangelists could learn a lot from Hitchens—and they need to, he insists, because although Hitchens himself may be gone, his disciples and followers are still going strong.

"The disciples of Hitchens and Dawkins are out there, and man are they feisty and angry," he says, referring to another noted atheist intellectual, Hitchens's fellow Englishman Richard Dawkins.

Barron speaks admiringly of the qualities Hitchens brought to his own brand of evangelization.

> *He was smart and articulate, but unapologetic. It wasn't a namby-pamby, "let me reach out to you and talk about your experience" sort of presentation. He was a smart guy, convinced he was right, and willing to share his ideas in an articulate way. It was done with a consciously media-savvy approach. He knew how to reach a wider audience, and he knew how to use the media. He was a great debater. He knew the arguments and counterarguments very well, and he was nimble and fast on his feet. He was able to respond to objections. It was so disheartening to me, in the early years with the new atheists like Dawkins and especially Hitchens, when Christians went up against them, it was like feeding them to the lions.*

Barron acknowledges that some of those Hitchens victims were well-meaning but ill-equipped Catholics.

"Some of them were bishops and archbishops, and they were completely destroyed by Hitchens," he says.

One exception on that dismal landscape, Barron added, was a Protestant philosopher, theologian, and apologist named William Lane Craig, who's the founder of an online apologetics ministry called ReasonableFaith.org.

"Craig was one fellow who really stood up to Hitchens," Barron says. "He's Evangelical, and deeply grounded in the philosophical tradition and the scientific tradition. He gives the new atheists a run for their money. He's the best Christian [apologist], and they knew it too. One leading skeptic, Sam Harris, said that Craig is 'the one Christian apologist who seems to have put the fear of God into many of my fellow atheists.'"

"The Catholics who went forward [to challenge modern atheists] were terrible, and I'll tell you why," Barron says. "After Vatican II, we threw away all of our apologetic weapons. When I was coming of age, apologetics was a bad thing. It was defensive, it was anti-ecumenical, it was antiquated, and we're not into that anymore. Then along comes September 11, which seemed to confirm the Enlightenment view that says religion is irrational and violent, and we were unprepared."

From there, Barron draws a fundamental conclusion about how the evangelical enterprise has to work in the face of such determined critics.

The banners-and-balloons way was not up to the task. Hitchens was offering hard arguments, and we weren't ready to give answers. That's why I've reacted a bit to the sort of romanticism about simple language, and the aversion to highfalutin concepts. Man, we need highfalutin concepts right now. We need counterarguments. We need smart people who can really delve into our own tradition and meet the opponents, because they're not backing down. They've got science, they think, they believe science and philosophy are on their side, and they use the idea of a link between violence and religion all the time.

The way atheist pundits such as Hitchens and Dawkins deploy language, Barron says, is another area in which Catholics could learn some lessons.

"Dawkins is awful in his intellectual arguments," he says. "I completely disagree with him, but look at the way he uses language in his writing and public speaking. It has massive appeal to young people, because it's imaginative, it's edgy. Watch Hitchens as he skewers his opponents. It's a very creative, theatrical use of language.

"Then you switch to the Vatican's website, and you get these long gray pages of text," he says. "That's not going to do it. That's an example of how we need to be much more creative, theatrical, nimble, and smart in the way we do our work."

In the end, perhaps the greatest backhanded tribute Barron could offer came in response to a question about whether he's the "Catholic Christopher Hitchens."

"I'd say no," he replied, "but in many ways I wouldn't mind being that. I admire Hitchens for many reasons, and I wrote some nice things about him. Man, if I had his facility with language, and his breadth of culture . . . he had a great grasp of the literary tradition, the artistic tradition, and if I had his rhetorical gifts, I'd be happy to claim that."

As a footnote, Barron notes that Hitchens's brother Peter, formerly an atheist himself, is now a "passionately believing" Anglican. "I was on vacation and I had a dream that the two Hitchens brothers were arguing, because I had been reading Peter Hitchens, and it was like two sides of my own brain fighting each other.

("If anyone is the Christian Christopher Hitchens," Barron says, "it's Peter Hitchens.")

EVANGELIZATION AND POPE FRANCIS

Robert Barron, unabashedly and unmistakably, is a St. John Paul II sort of Catholic cleric. He was swept up by the boldness of

John Paul, his swagger and confidence and bravado in presenting the Catholic faith to the world, and he doesn't hesitate to say that John Paul deserves to go down as one of the great Doctors of the Church.

"There's something about Wojtyla's breadth of mind that I think he would qualify," Barron says, using John Paul's given name, Karol Wojtyla.

Yet Barron also very much has a both/and mind, which makes him a big Pope Francis fan as well. In fact, Barron believes that history's first pope from the developing world, perhaps without thinking about it in quite these terms, is a living role model of the kind of evangelization that works in the cultural milieu of the early twenty-first century.

"Pope Francis hasn't changed the faith, but he has changed the conversation," Barron says. "What Francis has done in terms of public conversation about the Church is to make it clearer to people we're not just about sex. That's been extremely helpful in our wider outreach."

By placing such an emphasis on humility and simplicity, on service to the poor, on concern for the environment and social justice, on immigrants and refugees, on opposition to war and the arms trade, and with his ardent outreach to the "peripheries" of the world, Barron believes, Francis has succeeded in lifting up aspects of the Church's thought and life that were always there but that sometimes got lost amid a myopic focus on sex and the culture wars.

"Pope Benedict was a great evangelist at the intellectual level, and he was very keen on the engagement of the secular culture at the high academic level," Barron says. "But I would say our prospects are better under Pope Francis than they were before in terms of the engagement of the wider world. It's a skeptical world, skeptical for reasons both intellectual and moral, and this pope has been extremely effective in reconnecting to it."

Barron is especially enthusiastic about Pope Francis's 2013 document *Evangelii Gaudium*, which he sees as a sort of Magna Carta for effective evangelization in our day.

When I read Evangelii Gaudium, *my first reaction was "Yes!" These are my themes; it's what I've been talking about for years—not that Pope Francis consulted me, because, believe me, he didn't! For example, he strongly stresses the* via pulchritudinis *(way of beauty), and when I read that, I said, That's right out of my playbook. Don't begin with the true or the good, begin with the beautiful, and it leads you to the true and the good. But begin with the* beau geste, *the kind gesture. You know he's a master of the* beau geste. *He's not a theologian and he's not an academic, but he's a genius at the beautiful gesture that draws people to Christianity. Then there's a sense of urgency, how an emergency will concentrate the mind, focus the mind. This is not bland spirituality, but a message of immediate urgency that we have to announce to the world, and I think that comes through strongly in Pope Francis. Then there's his sense of joyfulness, which echoes* Gaudium et Spes. *It's the Beatitudes as the heart of Christian life. We all think of the Church as giving laws, wagging fingers, and clarifying sexual ethics, but in the great tradition, certainly Aquinas, the project begins with* beatitudo, *with happiness, with joy, and that's John Paul II and Vatican II, and I saw it very strongly in* Evangelii Gaudium. *I love all that stuff, you know, and to me, it's the great statement of his papacy.*

Barron believes it's especially striking that Pope Francis has been able to pull all this off in the wake of the Church's clerical sexual abuse scandals. On the other hand, he argues, Francis seems to have intuited the only way for the Church to recover.

"That's the genius of Francis, frankly," he says. "We were at an absolute low ebb of credibility after the scandals, especially on sexual ethics. We kept just harping at sexual ethics? I think we had zero credibility, and we wouldn't get anywhere. It's like Gallipoli," he says, referring to a famous battle during the First World War in which Allied forces, primarily troops from Australia and New Zealand, were forced to withdraw after massive losses.

"It was a good cause, but the wrong strategy," he says. "I think Francis's genius was to change the subject, and it was an astute strategic move."

Barron is no naïf, so he's well aware that some Catholics, including some conservatives who are among his biggest fans, don't always see Pope Francis in such rosy terms. At times, they find the pontiff alarming, confusing on doctrine, and given to appointing more liberal figures to senior positions than either of the previous two popes. Barron says he's aware of those objections but fundamentally doesn't share them.

> *To my mind, if you read Francis honestly and faithfully, there's nothing in him that's opposed to the great tradition, or that undermines either John Paul II or Benedict. I think there's a tremendous continuity. The difference is in style, pastoral outreach, focus, audience . . . those have all changed, I suppose, but I don't see anything substantially different. I wouldn't feel that the pope is turning us in some dramatic new direction. I try to emphasize the hermeneutic of continuity between him and the other popes, partly in order to reassure Catholics who are more on the inside and may have those concerns. And if you doubt me on this score, take a look at Pope Benedict's own words about his successor. He strongly affirms that though there is a difference in style between himself and Francis, there is no difference in substance.*

Moreover, Barron says, whatever objections some commentators or bloggers may have, Francis remains enormously beloved at the grass roots.

"Most Catholics I deal with, when you go into parishes, they just love the pope," he says. "I don't see a great divide over him. I just finished a preface to a book that Orbis Books is bringing out with a title like *Francis Speaks to Priests*. They had sent me all these texts of his sermons, speeches, and exhortations to seminarians and priests, and it was a delight to read. It's bracing, and funny."

That said, Barron worries that sometimes Francis's emphasis on the beautiful, his emphasis on mercy rather than judgment, and his dialogic style, can be misunderstood.

There is a sense among some that Francis is this kind of hippie, an anything goes, everything's fine, sort of figure, but this is completely out of step with his use of the image of the Church as a field hospital. That's an intense, dire image. You go to a field hospital if you're mortally wounded in battle, or severely wounded, and you need immediate care. Field hospital does not imply "Oh, everyone's fine." It's acknowledging that you might not even know it, but you've just been very, very seriously wounded. You need a lot of intensive care. The assumption is, at the objective level, there's a lot wrong with us, especially in a postmodern world. We're very badly wounded, and therefore the Church has to bring to bear lots and lots of pastoral care. That's the combination to get right. My fear is that Francis is read wrongly over and over again. So many people say to me, "I love this new pope," and when I ask why, I often get a response like "Because he's not as tough, and he kind of understands us." Well, yes, but don't take that to mean he thinks anything goes, that everything is just peachy. The field hospital is a super-Augustinian kind of image. Augustine said the Church is like a hospital where we're in intensive care our whole life long. That's Francis, and I think that part of it tends to get overlooked.

For Barron, the bottom line is that Pope Francis has successfully opened new evangelical horizons for Catholicism—the result, he believes, not of watering down doctrine or jettisoning tradition but of making a strategic calculation to back up a bit and then move down a different path.

"As I read Francis, it's a Gallipoli kind of moment," he says. "Yes, we could keep pouring all of our energy into the sexual issues, but let's change it to environment, let's change it to the poor, to immigration, and to other parts of our Church. That has had a very liberating effect, and I don't mean that for a minute cynically.

"I don't think he's a bit soft on abortion, for instance," Barron says. "He's said very strong things about it. He's not soft on transgenderism or same-sex marriage, but he's changed the subject. It's Gallipoli: 'Look we're getting mowed down over here. We're not making any progress, so maybe let's bring some men and material elsewhere in this grand struggle.' That's what I see him doing, and it strikes me as just the right move."

Chapter Six

PRAYER AND THE SUPERNATURAL

I n terms of his temperament, Bishop Robert Barron comes across as a highly rational, calm, thoughtful sort of guy. He's definitely not your stereotypical televangelist, shouting from the rooftops and spotting miracles and wonders under every rock. While Barron is utterly at ease talking about ideas and the Church, he's often reticent to make himself the focus of the conversation, and so he doesn't naturally incline to sharing private details about his prayer life, the touches of divine grace he may have experienced, or his inner spiritual journey.

Barron is also not what one might call a Catholic spiritual enthusiast, meaning someone who gets carried away at the latest report of a Marian apparition, or the latest end-times prophecy. He's not part of the charismatic scene, which stresses the "gifts of the Holy Spirit" expressed in signs and wonders such as healings and speaking in tongues—though, in principle, he has no problem with it, and understands its appeal over a bland Christianity that's basically given up on the supernatural altogether.

"I admire the Pentecostal revival within Catholicism, the charismatic movement," he says. "I think we should benefit from it, we should take in some of that experience, that confidence. To call upon the gifts of the Holy Spirit is good, though not in a mechanical way. It's not really my cup of tea, but there are people in the Church who do some of those things, and I think they're great."

Yet if your cup of tea is the kind of priest willing to perform an exorcism at the drop of a hat, Barron is probably not your best option as a pastor, since his first instinct would be to consult a therapist. (Though he accepts that demonic possession is real and that, properly performed, exorcisms are effective.)

Yet for all his rational reserve, Barron is also a true believer, someone who accepts a priori that God is real, that prayer is genuine communion with God, and that the miraculous, while possibly rare, is nevertheless very much a feature of human experience. He also has a deep appreciation for Catholic liturgy, takes seriously that it's a way of participating in the Heavenly chorus of praise, and firmly believes that in the Mass, believers receive the actual flesh and blood of Christ.

In that sense, Barron stands with the great English Christian writer C. S. Lewis, who noted that Christianity is premised on the most audacious miracle claim of all time—that God himself chose to take on human flesh in the person of Jesus of Nazareth, in order to save the world. If we're willing to accept that idea, Lewis asked, why would we reject, as a matter of principle, the possibility of smaller, and—from the point of view of worldly logic—arguably more plausible interferences in nature by a supernatural power?

"The Christian story is precisely the story of one grand miracle, the Christian assertion being that what is beyond all space and time, what is uncreated, eternal, came into nature, into human nature, descended into His own universe, and rose again, bringing nature up with Him," Lewis wrote in *God in the Dock*. "If you take that away, there is nothing specifically Christian left. There may be many admirable human things which Christianity shares with all other systems in the world, but there would be nothing specifically Christian."

Lewis devoted an entire book, *Miracles*, to the subject, arguing that Christianity is the only one of the world's great religions that depends, for its overall coherence, on the authenticity of miracles. "The mind which asks for a non-miraculous Christianity," he wrote, "is a mind in the process of relapsing from Christianity into mere 'religion.'"

Barron says much the same thing: "Miracles stand at the heart of Christianity the way they don't with other religions," he says. "The Virgin Birth, the Immaculate Conception, the Resurrection, the Incarnation . . . we're a faith based on miracles."

Typically, Barron begins explaining his attitudes toward the supernatural by citing the theological classics.

> *The Augustinian starting point is that we have this hungry heart, hungry for God, and that means we're ordered for something that goes beyond nature, beyond what we can see and organize and categorize. No amount of the merely natural will satisfy the hungry heart. We're ordered to the supernatural, and that's why people are fascinated, interested, drawn to it. We're like homing pigeons. That also explains why, and I'll use this slippery term, "liberal Catholicism" is not going to carry the day. I'm defining it here simply as the reduction of the supernatural to the natural, the tendency to interpret everything in terms of natural categories. That's not going to carry the day, because it's not classical Christianity and it's not religion in most parts of the world. At best, it's one form of religion in the West.*

In a sense, Barron sees the popular zeal for the supernatural as an antidote to what philosopher Charles Taylor calls the "buffered self" created by secularism. (We'll come back to that idea, and its importance to Barron, later.) In a nutshell, it means an individual isolated from any sense of the transcendent, anything beyond this world.

"We have such a buffered sense of who we are, and such a

self-limited world, so [supernatural phenomena] all poke holes in that buffered self and let light in," Barron says. "I think people find that attractive."

In all honesty, Barron concedes, the vista of the supernatural has grown on him over time. First, he says, he had to work through some youthful prejudices.

"Keep in mind I was raised and educated within a very liberal Catholic framework, as everybody was in the 1970s," he says. "It was just taken for granted. It was sort of the general view, and anything other than that was seen as prerevolutionary. It was a weird way to be formed, but that's what happened with my generation.

"For a lot of us, awakening to the authentic Vatican II was wonderful; it brought an opening to the concept of continuity with what came before. So yes, the supernatural grew on me over time. I thought through the prejudice of liberal Catholicism, that form of it anyway, and it opened things up."

As a result, it would be a serious mistake to style Barron as any kind of skeptic with regard to the supernatural, miraculous, and mystical dimensions of Christian life. Sometimes he may be skeptical vis-à-vis certain specific alleged wonders—because, of course, the story of Christianity is also rife with bogus miracle claims, usually the products of either overheated imaginations or outright chicanery.

That said, Barron is also firmly convinced that God can and does act in human affairs, that God doesn't simply leave his creatures to fend for themselves, and that the most routine and efficacious way to put oneself in the presence of God is through prayer.

Prayer, therefore, is the obvious place to begin.

PRAYER

Typically for such a rational mind, Barron's thinking about prayer begins not with a mystical experience but with an empirical fact: "Studies have shown that nearly everybody prays," he says. "Even atheists say they pray. You could almost define the human being as 'the animal that prays.'"

After a lifetime of study and thought about prayer, coupled with his personal experiences of prayer, here's how Barron sums up what it's all about.

"Prayer is a conversation between friends," he says. "It's our friendship with God, expressed in this lively conversation."

Barron absorbed a habit of prayer as a child from his faithful but not "superprayer" Catholic family growing up in Chicago, especially from his mother, who made a point of praying with the Barron kids at night before bed. He says that instinct that prayer is important was reinforced when he was a young man glimpsing the centrality it had for figures he admired, including some of the renowned theologians under whom he studied.

Barron came of age at a time when overt demonstrations of piety, even of one's priestly identity, were usually frowned upon. Giants in the theological guild, such as Father David Tracy at the University of Chicago, or Father Claude Geffré at the Institut Catholique de Paris, where Barron studied, generally wore coats and ties rather than the Roman collar, and struck what Barron called a "very rationalistic" tone.

Yet one day in Paris, Barron says, he was preparing to walk into a seminar led by Jesuit Father Michel Corbin, another celebrity of Catholic theology in his day. Like the good American he was, Barron got to the seminar room early, and burst into the room before any of his fellow students had arrived.

"There's Corbin by himself, and he has a rosary in his right hand," Barron recalled. "I kind of surprised him, and I thought, Wow, here's a French professor of theology praying the rosary. Corbin really helped me to see the liturgical and spiritual and prayerful dimension of what we were doing. I think that opened a door that I went through."

(As a footnote, Barron says that when he first arrived back at Mundelein Seminary in Chicago, he followed the fashion of the time and wore casual clothes while teaching. It was only later, he says, when the "John Paul II" generation began to crest in the 1990s in the seminary, that he rethought that choice. A few faculty members began wearing the collar, largely prompted by the students, and eventually it became mandatory. "The students kind of led in many ways," he says, "and the faculty had to rethink some things.")

Barron says another experience in Paris also left a deep impression: frequenting a church entrusted by Cardinal Jean-Marie Lustiger to the Monastic Fraternities of Jerusalem, founded in 1975 by a French Catholic brother with the aim of fostering the spirituality of the monastic desert.

"I actually knew one of the nuns there," Barron says. "It's a long story, but she was from Park Ridge, Illinois, and was living with the community in Paris. I used to go a lot, with my little backpack, and walk to St. Gervais for the evening prayer. It was gorgeous, and very Byzantine, very Eastern, with the icons and the smoke. That began to sing to me, so I would go there a lot."

Today, Barron takes the importance of daily prayer seriously. He passes a Holy Hour in his chapel in his residence in Santa Barbara every morning, right after he wakes up, including quiet time in front of the tabernacle, which is the container in which consecrated Eucharist hosts are reserved. He says the Divine Office, the daily prayer of the Church. He says a personal favorite, one he says every day, is the Jesus Prayer, which is especially popular in Orthodox Christianity: "Lord Jesus Christ, Son of God, have mercy on me, a sinner."

"You breathe in on the first part, and out on the second," he says. "It becomes part of the rhythm of your own body. It's a very simple, calming, centering prayer."

Barron is aware that for many believers, prayer can be a difficult exercise, in the sense that it can seem empty and hollow, like a one-way conversation that doesn't always seem to produce clear spiritual fruits. He says a friend and colleague of his at Word on Fire recently gave him a helpful high-tech analogy for thinking about prayer.

I was in my office, and I'm in touch with my friend Brandon Vogt, who works at Word on Fire. I was having computer issues, so he said, "Let me get on it," and he did this magic thing where he can take control of my computer remotely from Orlando, where he was. I have no science background and he's an engineer, so I said to him, "Brandon, how are you doing this? Is it by telephone lines, or are we in outer space, or what?" He said, "Well, it does involve outer space," and then explained what's happening with satellites and so forth. I said, This is kind of a cool metaphor for the communion of saints. You pray, you send up a personal prayer or a Hail Mary, and maybe it seems like it doesn't make any sense. You wonder, Is Mary actually hearing this prayer of mine? Does it really make any sense, blathering away to the open sky? Well, here's this satellite, which is a man-made contraption, able to take in enormous amounts of data. The satellite can take it in and do its thing, sending it and connecting Orlando to Santa Barbara just like that. So why not the angelic realm, and the saints, who are connected to the mind of God? I send up a Hail Mary, and yes, Mary hears it and is able to communicate. I thought of

Cardinal George, who's now in the communion of saints and whom I invoke in prayer a lot . . . Why is reaching out to him so weird? If the satellite is up there, linking and communicating, then why not? If you believe in this much higher level of communication and connection that we call the communion of saints, why couldn't this be true? In the end, you finally get the insight that there are souls moving through space the way these impulses move and enable us. All the stuff you can't see is actually more real, more efficacious, than what you can, and I thought, That's it. Somehow, we've got an instinct for that.

Ever the practical pastor, Barron has also offered some tips for the prayer life, consciously intended to be simple and within the reach of pretty much everybody.

"Take the time"

Barron says Thomas Merton, the great twentieth-century Trappist, was once asked what's the one thing people could do to improve their prayer life, and Merton's instant reply was "Take the time." For contemporary Americans, especially those who live in big cities and spend a lot of time in traffic gridlock, Barron suggests praying in the car. "It can become your own little monastic cell," he says.

"Speak with honesty"

Too often, Barron believes, people think prayer is about reciting "a bunch of pious language." Such language certainly is important, he says, but if prayer is a conversation between friends, then it has to be open and honest, including the anger and disappointment all of us feel sometimes. He tells a story to illustrate the point.

"There was this lady who spent a long time in a Catholic

hospital while her husband was dying, going through months and months of agony," he says. "Finally she goes outside and sees a statue of Mary. She starts picking up clots of dirt and throwing them at the statue in a rage. Security sees what's happening and starts to pull her back, but the hospital chaplain comes out and says, 'Don't stop her . . . she's praying.'"

"Listen attentively"

Granted, Barron says, except with the great saints, most of the time God doesn't talk back directly in prayer. However, by striving to listen—perhaps by paying careful attention to a Scripture passage, perhaps by pondering what Jesus's answer might be to whatever question you're asking—a message may nevertheless come through. That's why Barron doesn't like the statement "I'm going to say my prayers," because as he puts it, "This isn't supposed to be a one-way conversation."

"Work on the silent savoring"

"We have a really noisy culture," Barron says, "and we're constantly stimulating ourselves. But do we sit in silence, allowing God to speak in that space?" Citing Thomas Aquinas, he notes that the human will has two instincts with respect to the good. First, the will seeks the good; and then, having acquired it, the will "sits in the good it possesses," what Barron calls a sort of "silent savoring." He says people today are still pretty good at seeking the good, but perhaps we need to work on the silent savoring.

Barron suggests two specific prayer techniques. The first is the habit of a daily Holy Hour—an hour spent in prayer and reflection on Scripture—and the second is prayer before the Blessed Sacrament, a practice, he notes, that went into decline after Vatican II but that today has made a strong comeback. Both, he says, have proven spiritually useful for untold numbers of believers around the world.

LITURGY

In terms of Catholic worship, what the Church calls "liturgy," from the Greek word *leitourgia*, meaning "public service," Barron would be the first to admit that he's not one of those Catholics for whom debate over the precise details is all-consuming. We've already seen that although in his youth he had a fleeting experience of the pre–Vatican II Mass in Latin, he has no nostalgia for the Mass in Latin, and no basic objection to the revised form of worship that's most common in the Church today.

Yet as a man of Catholic tradition, Barron understands the role liturgy has played over the centuries in shaping both Catholic culture and Catholic teaching—as the old saying goes, *Lex orandi, lex credendi*, meaning "The rule of prayer is the rule of belief." Noting that Vatican II defined liturgy as the "source and summit of Christian life," Barron says simply, "in a way, the liturgy is everything."

Given those convictions, Barron has thought deeply about the nature of the liturgy, and he's a careful and committed celebrant of the Mass himself. In keeping with a defining feature of his both/and style of thought, Barron views the key to good Catholic liturgy in terms of striking the right balance among three possible extremes.

He quotes American Catholic liturgical scholar Monsignor Francis Mannion, who at the invitation of Cardinal Francis George, founded the Mundelein Liturgical Institute in 2000.

"According to Mannion," Barron says, "good liturgy is the result of a balanced play between priest, people, and rite. When the first becomes exaggerated, we find the clerical abuse of the liturgy; when the second is overstressed, we encounter the congregationalist abuse; and when the third is exaggerated, we have the ritualistic problem. These three elements are meant to go together in a kind of coherence, a kind of dance or ballet."

Here's how he explained each of those risks, in a 2005 homily for the feast of Corpus Christi.

Clericalism

"Let's say the priest's role becomes exaggerated, then the liturgy begins to suffer because it's under a clericalistic burden. When the priest is imposing his own ideas, his own personality, his own style, over the liturgy, then he comes to dominate it personally. This transcends ideology, by the way—there's a clericalism of the right, and a clericalism of the left. In both cases, it's the priest imposing himself too much: 'Look how clever, look how funny, look how interesting, look how impressive I am.' In a certain way, the priest is meant to efface himself at the liturgy. When I put liturgical vestments on for Mass, the idea, in part, is to cover me up. It's not Robert Barron acting, it's Christ acting."

Congregationalism

On the role of laity in the liturgy, Barron begins by citing a famous line attributed to Cardinal Newman when he was asked to explain his view of the lay role in the Church.

"Well, we'd look awfully silly without them," he replied.

Barron concurs: "We need the people, we need a congregation," he says. Yet, he asks, "What happens if the congregation gets too aggressive?

"That's congregationalism, and the liturgy is also burdened by that weight," he says. "For example, it can be as if the people are demanding to be entertained: 'I find this ritual tedious, I find it boring, entertain me. Do things the way I want them done, I'm tired of hearing those old words, I'm tired of hearing that ritual.' It's the congregation asserting itself, its demands, inordinately. I'm not saying the Mass should be boring, but if we try to entertain through the liturgy, we'll never compete with professional entertainers. I don't care how good our choirs are, I don't care how clever and funny our homilists are, we'll never compete. The liturgy is not meant to entertain the congregation, or to respond to their private desires."

Ritualism

"Yes, we need the ritual, and yes, it's not there for us to play with," says Barron. "But can there be an excessive obsession with the ritual? I think so, and then it begins to look like a form of aestheticism. It's the way an aesthete will appreciate a beautiful work of art. 'There it is, it's the *Mona Lisa,* how beautiful, how pristine, how untouchable! Don't go near it, just admire it from a distance.' There are some people who approach the liturgy that way, as if it's a precious work of art, and I can't in any way fuss with it. That's not an active participation in the Mass; that's distant admiration of it. Some people treat the Mass as an object in a museum, and that's ritualism."

In summation, Barron says, "Allow the elegant and delicate dance among these three elements to take place, each one, as it were, contributing to the others and correcting the excesses of the others, then the liturgy is most itself," Barron says.

MYSTICAL EXPERIENCE

Barron is a passionate devotee of great figures in the Catholic tradition whose lives are believed to have been marked by a rich inner spiritual life, including mystical experiences such as the stigmata (the five wounds of Christ spontaneously appearing in one's own body, as was the case, for instance, with St. Francis) or direct revelations by God (think of St. Teresa of Avila, for instance, or St. John of the Cross).

Yet as he sees it, such phenomena are the spiritual exceptions rather than the norm. He says he's never really had anything that would qualify in the classic sense as a "mystical experience" such as a locution, meaning a direct verbal revelation, or a vision, such as an appearance by Jesus to St. Faustina Kowalska or Mary to St. Bernadette of Lourdes.

Nonetheless, he says, he has had moments of grace in which the divine seemed especially real.

"I've had experiences that were intense, that I'd describe as an experience of God, as a breakthrough of God into my life or into my consciousness," he says. "They were a heightened, intense experience of God."

One came in his early twenties, when Barron was studying at the Catholic University of America, going through what he describes as a "real period of doubt." In his philosophy studies, he says, he'd encountered Marx and was kind of "drifting away from faith." He says he wasn't praying much at the time. One day over the summer, at his parents' house, he found himself—not reading, he says, but just "musing" about some of the ideas he'd been studying. Out of the blue, Barron says, he was seized with an "overwhelming sense of the reality of God.

"It was a sense that the object of these arguments we've talked about, God, is something overwhelmingly real," he says.

Barron concedes that his realization probably was "mediated to a degree by the intellect, by remembering arguments and rational propositions," but he insists the experience went far beyond that.

"The reality of God struck me as unavoidable," he says. "It felt like being seized. Not like discovering something, but like being seized by something." The net result, he says, was that he became newly "totally on fire again with the faith."

Another such moment, he says, came during the filming of his film series *CATHOLICISM*.

We're about halfway through, and we're at Gethsemani Abbey, Thomas Merton's home, which is already a charged place for me. I'd been there before. I'd been to Merton's grave maybe three times before, so now we're back. We've been filming at Merton's hermitage. We're in the church and we're not actively filming, our camera man is taking B-roll footage. I went up to the balcony overlooking the church where Merton was ordained and celebrated his first Mass and sang in choir. I'm praying, not in a structured way, just praying. To call what happened next a locution would not be correct, but to say it was just a passing thought would be way too inadequate. What I had was a sense that, "It's all been for this. It's all been for this." It was sort of like, "If you build it, they will come!" Eventually, what became clear to me was that all of my experience, my religious searching, studies, had been to produce this series. Maybe it was the fact that I was praying in Merton's place, and Merton, along with Thomas Aquinas and Bob Dylan, are these decisive figures at an early point in my life. I don't know exactly why it happened, but somehow I just knew it's all been for this. I'd call that an intense experience of prayer, a sort of mystical experience.

Finally, Barron says he experienced a touch of the divine at Sainte-Chapelle, a thirteenth-century royal chapel built in the Gothic style in the heart of Paris.

"I knew it very well," he says. "I'd been to Sainte-Chapelle a number of times, and once when I was there, there weren't too many people and I sat down on the floor and stayed for a long time. I stayed for a good hour, longer maybe, and just soaked in the spiritual power of that place. I felt so deeply connected to believers across the ages, to the Church, to God. I would describe it as a charged, mystical moment."

Barron's basic advice with regard to such grace-filled moments is to be grateful when, and if, they come but not to depend on them as the life's blood of your ordinary spirituality. On that score, he's with Pope Benedict XVI, another legendarily feet-on-the-ground Catholic thinker, who insisted that while mystical experiences, private revelations, apparitions, and so on can and do happen, they're never "essential," because everything needed for the life of the faith is already contained in Scripture, Church doctrine, the Church's liturgy, and the sacraments.

"In my own life, I think of Robert Sokolowski, one of my professors at Catholic University, who's one of the most religious people I know and a model of Catholicism," Barron says. "He once said very blandly in class, 'I've never had a religious experience.' He was trying to make that point, I think, that faith is not dependent upon the extraordinary."

MARIAN APPARITIONS

When it comes to Catholics and the supernatural, nothing seems to fire the imagination or stir the blood more than reported appearances of the Virgin Mary, sometimes carrying a new revelation, sometimes making a request, such as for a church to be built in her honor, and sometimes even producing miraculous events, such as the sun dancing in the sky. A handful have been officially embraced by the Catholic Church as miraculous, such as those in Fátima in Portugal and Guadalupe in Mexico, while others have been rejected as hoaxes or delusions, such as claims that "Our Lady of Surbiton" was appearing every day under a pine tree in England for more than twenty years during the 1980s and '90s.

Many alleged Marian apparitions occupy a sort of ecclesiastical limbo, neither officially condemned nor confirmed, leaving Catholics basically free to make up their own minds. Some of the faithful incline to skepticism about this sort of private revelation, others to almost immediate credulity, while lots of folks keep an open mind, neither rejecting nor embracing these claims.

For that in-the-middle constituency, Bishop Robert Barron probably could serve as chaplain. He doesn't scoff at such reports, and he firmly accepts, even celebrates, those cases sanctioned by the Church. On the other hand, he's also not inclined to book a plane ticket at every fresh report that the Virgin Mary has turned up with a sensational revelation.

"There's always the danger of the superstitious creeping in," he says. "That's the [Cardinal John Henry] Newman perspective, which is that if the 'priestly' instinct gets separated from the 'prophetic,' which is a properly critical function, trying to understand things at first in terms of natural causalities, then something has gone wrong. Yes, let's see a lively belief in the supernatural expressed, celebrated, let it awaken people's hearts, but also put it in conversation with a properly prophetic and rational faculty, lest it get wildly out of hand."

Barron's attitude toward reports of ongoing appearances by Mary in Medjugorje, in Bosnia and Herzegovina, is illustrative. Beginning in 1981, six Herzegovinian children claimed that Mary began appearing to them, in some cases offering extensive daily revelations. The site has become a popular pilgrimage center, but the veracity of those claims remains a matter of debate, and for years the Vatican has been engaged in a still-inconclusive investigation.

On the one hand, Barron says, he strains to believe that the Virgin has been appearing every day at a regularly appointed hour, "saying fairly banal things over and over." On the other hand, he says, he can't deny the spiritual fruits that have come out of the experience: "I know a lot of people whose lives were utterly changed by Medjugorje," he says, "including priests who were completely secular, uninterested, who are now on fire as ardent disciples of Christ."

As a result, Barron says, he's taken a basically "wait and see" stance, content to await whatever ruling may come down from Rome.

On such cases of private revelation generally, Barron has a similarly balanced view.

I think they happen in rare circumstances. But they have to be received by the family of the Church; they've got to be taken in by the family, which means being judged, weighed, their consequences assessed, and their good points and bad points evaluated. That's the right way to do it. They're there, and they happen. Some are good, some bad, some mixed. The Church, at the end of the day, makes a call on it. If the body can receive it, and it becomes something life-giving, great. If the body determines it's toxic and we have to get rid of it, then it should do so, and does. That's my take.

Among the shrines where appearances of the Virgin have been officially ratified, Barron cites two personal favorites: Lourdes in France, and Guadalupe in Mexico. He says Lourdes especially, which is Catholicism's premier healing shrine, where care of the sick and disabled is the priority—the town's streets have, instead of bicycle lanes, wheelchair lanes—has left a deep impression.

The one that moves me the most is Lourdes. I've been there a number of times, and I find it deeply inspiring. It's a good ex-ample of what I was talking about: how the Church receives, judges, evaluates, and eventually accepts an event as super-natural. In the CATHOLICISM *series, maybe the most memorable moment was the candlelight procession at Lourdes, that long midsummer night. Even people on our crew who were pretty skeptical were moved, watching the sick come in. I think it's also a good example of how private revelation works, because at first everyone thought Bernadette was nuts, and she was tested thoroughly in her own lifetime. But after exhaus-tive investigation, the Church signed off on the Lourdes event, and it has indeed borne marvelous fruit. Here the Gamaliel principle applies [a reference to a passage from the Acts of the Apostles in which a Jewish rabbi stopped a crowd from stoning Peter and the other apostles by saying: "If this endeavor or this activity is of human origin, it will destroy itself. But if it comes from God, you will not be able to destroy them; you may even find yourselves fighting against God"]. I'm with Gamaliel.*

Of Guadalupe, Barron says, "You can't be anywhere near the Hispanic world and not be overwhelmed by Guadalupe. I've got six parishes called Guadalupe in my region alone. Talk about one apparition that's borne fruit . . . there's something about Guada-lupe that's just completely unavoidable.

I asked someone one time to explain to me what's the key to the endurance of the Church in Mexico, given the horrific persecu-tion of Catholics in the 1920s. Today up they come to Califor-nia, you know Mexicans come in great numbers, and by God, they have the faith. I asked someone who's in the know, and plugged in theologically, "What's the key?" And the answer came back without hesitation, "Guadalupe." That's the key to why the Mexican faith is so strong. It's a supernatural thing, and I get that totally.

Barron also says there are moments when invoking the Church's approved Marian apparitions, which are generally those with the clearest witness testimony and empirical backing, can be useful evangelically.

Maybe there's a right moment when the buffered self needs to really be punched through and you say, "How do you explain that?" This thing happened to these people. Take, for example, the miracle of the sun at Fátima, which is truly extraordinary, because you have these accounts from agnostics and atheists, and some seventy thousand people who witnessed the phenomenon. I'll ask, "What do you make of that?" Often people will respond, "Oh, it's a mass hallucination." To that, I'll say, "Do you really find that credible as an explanation? Suddenly seventy thousand people have a mass hallucination? Really?" Wouldn't a mass hallucination on the part of a football stadium of people be more miraculous than the sun spinning around?

EXORCISM

The practice of exorcism, meaning the casting out of demons, in Christianity goes all the way back to Christ himself in the New Testament. It's been a constant in Christian life throughout the centuries, very much up to the present day. In Catholicism, an exorcism is considered a "sacramental," not a sacrament, which means its effectiveness isn't understood to be dependent on a precise formula being observed. There's a sequence laid out for exorcism in the *Rituale Romanum*, the Church's official collection of rites and prayers, but not every exorcist follows it in detail.

In the years following Vatican II, the whole idea of exorcism went into decline among theologians, clergy, and cultured elites in the Church, who tended to see it as anachronistic and embarrassing. That didn't make popular demand for exorcism go away, however, and today in Catholicism there's something of a resurgence under way. There's even an annual summer seminar cosponsored by the Vatican on exorcism, and in 2015 a priest of the diocese of Rome said that one-third of the phone calls Catholic officials receive are requests for exorcism.

To recognize a case of demonic possession that might warrant an exorcism, the Catholic Church has a series of typical tests, though no one, or even several together, is regarded as decisive:

- Loss or lack of appetite
- Cutting, scratching, and biting of skin
- A cold feeling in the room
- Unnatural bodily postures and changes in the person's face and body
- The person losing control of his or her personality and entering into a frenzy or rage, and/or attacking others
- Changes in the person's voice
- Supernatural physical strength, out of keeping with the person's build or age
- Speaking or understanding a language the person has never learned
- Knowledge of things that are obscure or that the person would never have had the chance to discover
- Accurate prediction of future events
- Levitation and nonphysical moving of objects
- The person expelling objects from his or her body
- A violent reaction toward all religious objects or items
- Aversion to entering a church, speaking Jesus's name, or hearing Scripture

Many Catholic priests were trained to boil that list down to four points, known as the "classical criteria": supernatural or superhuman strength, a fierce reaction to holy things, hidden knowledge, and the use of languages that the person normally wouldn't understand. Generally, the understanding has been that all four need to manifest themselves in order for a situation to be attributed to supernatural phenomena.

Barron doesn't blink when asked: Yes, he believes that demonic possession is real.

> *I haven't seen it, but I know people I trust who have been involved in it and talked about it in a way that's persuasive. I'll say 98.9 percent of the time, we're dealing with a physiological or psychological malady, but I do think there is this tiny, rare percentage of cases where you're dealing with a supernatural force. I've known people involved in that world of exorcism, and they'll use the language of "very rare." Not long ago, I dealt with someone who's bringing forward a case, and I applied the four classical criteria. If those four criteria are really in place, okay, but I think that's pretty rare. I like the fact the Church has said I need all four. Don't give me one or two—all four have to be in place before we make a move—and I think that's a good instinct.*

Barron says that if he ever encountered such a case, in which all the necessary tests had been satisfied, he wouldn't feel comfortable performing the exorcism ritual himself, but he would authorize a priest with the necessary preparation to do so.

MIRACULOUS HEALINGS

Like exorcism, healings have always been part of the Christian tradition, once again going back to Christ himself. The New Testament records thirty-one healings performed by Jesus, including the paralyzed servant of a Roman centurion, several people with blindness, and scores of lepers. Jesus's healing power culminated in the ability to raise people from the dead, including the son of the widow of Nain. Through the ages, holy men and women believed to have healing powers have arisen in Christianity, and as we've seen, Marian sanctuaries such as Lourdes have been the sites of untold numbers of reports of miraculous healings.

Here too Barron says that while he takes that aspect of Christian experience seriously, he doesn't believe healing is his own calling.

"I don't think I have that charism at all," he says. "I've known people and priests who have it. Again, I think it's rare, but I think some people have it. I think the Lord, for whatever purpose, deigns to work that way. I have a charism for preaching, and although I don't know if that's substantially different from a charism for healing or exorcism or whatever, they're different expressions of the spirit."

Characteristically, he adds a healthy dose of reserve.

"These things can all be abused," he says. "You know, 'Line up here, give me fifty dollars,' and so on. But I think there are some people who really have this gift."

Barron says he's never actually witnessed a miraculous healing, but he insists there are enough credible accounts from enough different sources that one can't simply dismiss them all as folklore or mass hysteria.

I've never seen it, in the sense of being in the room when it happens. But again, I've heard stories from people I trust and find reliable who have talked about it. Something that impacted me was Craig Keener's book Miracles. *He's an Evangelical Protestant who'd been an atheist, and who had some experience that he won't describe exactly, but it was of the risen Jesus and it turned him around. He's now one of the most prolific and seriously academic writers on religious matters. The book is extraordinary, first of all because it looks at things philosophically, taking on David Hume and company. But then, mostly it's case after case after case, all over the world, of these miraculous, wonderful things happening. In our Catholic context, we know that's possible from the saints, so I think that it's real.*

THREE PATHS OF HOLINESS

As the rector of Mundelein Seminary in Chicago, Barron worked out a threefold path to holiness he would share with the seminarians, and he's used the same framework in a number of his writings and videos. In essence, it's his distilled pastoral wisdom, expressed in typically practical and accessible fashion—though as Barron would no doubt concede, it's easier to lay out these aims than to achieve them.

"I wanted to give the young guys at the seminary a specific path for spiritual formation. And for years I have been using these three stages, which are not really my own invention, but are based on wisdom from the saints," Barron says.

Find the Center

Given Barron's emphasis on the priority of Christ, it's no surprise that what he means by "finding the center" is rooting one's life in a relationship with Christ.

"When a life is centered on Christ, all the energies, aspirations, and powers of the soul fall into a beautiful and satisfying pattern," he says.

> *We see this on display in our medieval Gothic cathedrals. These structures were not only marvels of engineering and artistry; they were also symbols of the well-ordered soul, particularly their rose windows. At the center of every rose window is a depiction of Christ. Wheeling around Christ in lyrical and harmonious patterns are many saints and scenes from the Scriptures. The message is clear: When our lives revolve around Christ we find order and harmony. And by implication, whenever something other than Christ—money, power, pleasure, honor—fills the center, the soul falls into disharmony. The well-ordered soul begins to wobble and go off-kilter. So the rose windows illustrate the first requirement, which is making Christ the center of our lives.*

Barron makes the point that this emphasis on Christ at the center is a keenly Biblical theme.

"It's all over the place," he says. "Perhaps the most powerful example of this centeredness is when Jesus calms the stormy sea. As Christ and his disciples are making their way to the other side of the Sea of Galilee, storms blow up and the apostles panic, fearing for their lives. Yet despite the roaring of the waves and the tumult of the screaming men, Jesus remains asleep. The sleeping Christ suggests that place in us where we are rooted in the divine power, that space in our souls where despite all the worries and dangers that smash against our shores, we still find peace and rest," he says.

"Of course, we see that Christ, once awakened by the disciples, rebukes the winds and calms the waves. This means our greatest source of peace is the inner Christ, the ground of the soul," Barron says.

Know You're a Sinner

Famously, when Pope Francis was asked to define himself in his first interview after his election, in March 2013, his answer was simple: "I am a sinner," he said. That bit of self-awareness reflects a line from G. K. Chesterton, who once said the saint is one who knows he's a sinner.

"When you study the saints, you see this over and over again: the holiest people are paradoxically those who are most conscious of their sinfulness," Barron says. "Look at Teresa of Avila, John of the Cross, Augustine, or Thérèse of Lisieux—all spiritual masters—and you'll find people who were painfully aware of how much they fall short of sanctity.

> I use the metaphor of a windshield. When you're driving a car in the morning, when it's still a little dark out, your windshield looks pretty clean and transparent. But in the middle of the day, when the sun shines on it? You notice all the defects and smudges. That's how the spiritual life works. The closer we move to the luminosity of God, the more intensely our inner life is exposed for what it really is. This is nothing to be afraid of, just the contrary, for once we know and see the truth about ourselves, through the graceful light of God, our sin can be healed and cleansed.

Barron believes that with this knowledge of our own sinfulness comes a healthy degree of realism about our ability to fix our own problems.

"Christianity is a salvation religion, and thus its basic assumption is that there is something wrong with us, indeed something so wrong that we could never in principle fix it ourselves," he says. "We are members of the dysfunctional family of humanity, and egotism, fear, violence, and pride have all crept into our institutions and into our blood and bones.

"Therefore, any attempt to lift ourselves out of the problem, any schema of perfectibility, whether it's political, psychological, or religious, any conviction that we can make it right on our own, is illusory and dangerous. We are saved from the dysfunction of sin only when Jesus's way of nonviolence and love, a path not of the world, appears in our world," he says.

Barron believes that Dante's *Divine Comedy* captures this point in especially vivid fashion.

The Divine Comedy *could be described as a spiritual itinerary, a holy journey of the soul. The poem ends with a vision of angels and saints, surrounding the blinding light of the Trinitarian God, but it begins with this dark but liberating insight that something is wrong: "Midway upon the journey of our life / I found myself within a forest dark / For the straightforward pathway had been lost." Before he can find the right path, Dante has to make a side trip through Hell, witnessing firsthand the suffering of the damned. What he is really seeing, of course, is his own sinfulness, and the vision is very harsh and relentless. In fact, when Dante even swoons from the horror of a particular view, his mystic guide, Virgil, has to kick him to wake him, to force him to be aware. Finally, Dante leaves Hell by the only possible route: climbing down the hairy sides of Satan himself. So what's the message? There's no way up but down, no real holiness without awareness; at least part of being a saint is knowing you're a sinner.*

Your Life Is Not About You

The final stage of spiritual maturity, Barron believes, is to get beyond one's own desires and cravings, and begin living for something bigger—or, more accurately put, Someone bigger.

"When we live wrapped up around our own egos, and our pathetic fears and aspirations, we live in the narrow space of the *pusilla anima* (the little soul)," he says. "But when we forget all that, when we live in a risky freedom, when we leap beyond what we can know and control, we move into the expansive *magna anima* (the great soul)."

To take a non-Christian example, Barron says he's struck by the fact that the title given to Mohandas Gandhi, "Mahatma," is etymologically close to this Latin phrase, and it means the same thing.

"Holy people are those who realize that they participate in something and Someone infinitely greater than themselves, that they are but fragments of Reality," he says. "Far from crushing them, this awareness makes them great, capacious, whole."

In a hundred ways, our spiritual tradition attempts to cultivate the great soul, to lure us into that wonderful conviction that it is not about us. Here's one example: at the very end of John's Gospel, the risen Jesus confronts Peter. After moving him from confession to mission, Jesus tells him a secret: "When you were young you put on your own belt and walked where you liked; but when you grow old you will stretch out your hands and somebody else . . . will take you where you would rather not go." When he was young, Peter thought he could control his life: he walked where he liked, fished where he liked, and he tied his own belt. But in his old age—the time of wisdom—he will realize that, all along, his life has been under the direction of a Power that his ego cannot understand or control. In taking him where he does not want to go, this Power will introduce him to the magna anima.

Barron says that the theologian Hans Urs von Balthasar expressed the same concept using a different vocabulary.

"Balthasar speaks often of the 'Theodrama,'" he says. "This is the drama written and directed by God, and involving every creature in the cosmos, including those sometimes reluctant actors, human beings. On the great stage which is the created universe and according to the prototype which is Christ, we are invited to 'act,' to find and play our role in God's theater."

The problem, Barron says, is that most of us instead live our lives in what Balthasar called the "egodrama."

"We think we are the directors, writers, and above all, stars of our own dramas," Barron says. "The rest of the world just provides the pleasing backdrop, and other people function as either our supporting players or, at worst, the villains."

Of course, our dramas are always uninteresting, even if we are playing the lead role. The key is to find the role that God has designed for us, even if it looks like a bit part. Sometimes, in a lengthy and complex novel, a character who has seemed minor throughout the story emerges, by the end, as the fulcrum around which the entire narrative has been turning. In fact, the "main" characters sometimes even fade into relative insignificance with regard to the great-souled player. That's what I'm talking about in this step; that's what we need to find. When, through faith, we see every moment and every creature as an ingredient in the divine plan, when we know that there is a gracious providence at work in the universe, we live in joyful surrender and with a great sense of wonder. When we decenter the ego, and live in exciting and unpredictable relationship to God, we realize very clearly that our lives are not about us. And that's a liberating discovery.

Chapter Seven

THE BIBLE

For centuries Catholics were considered the laggards in terms of mastery of the Bible. Given that one of the defining fault lines in the Protestant Reformation was over Scripture, with Protestants insisting that revelation is a matter of *sola Scriptura,* meaning "Scripture alone," a certain indifference or ambivalence about the Bible became a characteristic trait of Catholicism. To be honest, that instinct was sometimes fed and encouraged by an overweening clerical caste, which just didn't trust simple laity to be able to read and understand the Bible on their own.

To put the point in the simplest possible terms, in many parts of the Christian world, a Protestant was the one who could recite verses from Scripture by heart; a Catholic, meanwhile, was the one who knew all the prayers for the Mass. I still remember my grandparents in rural western Kansas showing me their cherished family Bible, which they'd inherited from another side of the family. For a long time, they said, they felt they had to take it off the coffee table when fellow Catholics from the town were coming over to visit. In a largely Protestant environment, they worried, people might see it as a sign of a creeping "Protestantization."

All that began to change in the wake of the Second Vatican Council, which stimulated a widespread Catholic recovery of the Bible. Theologians, pastors, catechists, and others learned anew to see Scripture as fundamental, not just as a privileged source of revelation but also as a resource for faith formation and the spiritual life.

Early in his life, Barron says, it was actually something of a discovery for him that a Catholic priest could also be an expert on the Bible.

"When I was a little kid, I remember this was the sixties or seventies, there was a series of paperbacks that were done by Raymond E. Brown," he says. (A member of the Sulpician religious order, Brown, who died in 1998, was considered among the foremost Catholic experts on the Bible in his day. He taught for almost thirty years at the Union Theological Seminary in New York, and several of his books, including his final work, *The Birth of the Messiah*, on the infancy narratives of Jesus in the New Testament, are considered classics.)

"There was this picture of Brown on the back of the book with his glasses on, and his Roman collar, and there he was reading an ancient manuscript. That picture had a big impact on me. There's this priest, this really smart man who knows the Biblical languages, and he's poring over ancient manuscripts. That a priest would know all these high-level things, I thought it was just cool."

The transformation in Catholicism had flowered by the time Barron was maturing as a young theologian and later, a pastor himself, and he found himself thrilled by it. When he was studying at the Institut Catholique in Paris, for instance, he says he picked up a more Biblical way of reading Thomas Aquinas from his Dominican teachers, for whom the focus was on not merely intellectual clarification but the whole narrative world Aquinas was trying to explicate.

Indeed, Barron has come to see neglect of the Bible as one of the cardinal sins, so to speak, in currents in Catholic theology both before and after Vatican II, and today he insists there can be no authentic presentation of Christianity that doesn't begin with immersion in the "density" of the Biblical universe. Earlier, we saw that one of the realizations that began to cause Barron to distance himself from the thinking of the giants of liberal Christian theology, such as Paul Tillich and later, in the Catholic tradition, Karl Rahner—though without ever abandoning those influences—was the dawning understanding that their works are often "Christologically and Biblically thin."

"That's what I began to see when I read Balthasar," Barron says, "because Balthasar is the Catholic Karl Barth." (Barth was a twentieth-century Swiss Reformed theologian who's often regarded as a more conservative alternative to figures such as Tillich.) "With all his limitations, I bought Barth in lots of ways. What I love about him is his willingness to say, 'Okay, we're going to go into the Bible, and we're going to spend hundreds of pages interpreting it on its own terms.' He doesn't feel obliged to say at every turn, 'Now, let's make sure this is linking to my experience.'"

It's fine to find analogies to your experience. I'm not opposed to that. Barth used to talk about the preacher standing with a Bible in one hand, and in the other a newspaper. That's great. However, there's a noncompetitive but asymmetrical relationship between the two things. It's not just Bible and newspaper. What I was trained to do was newspaper first, Bible second. However, it ought to be Bible first, newspaper second. Begin with the Bible, and then move on to experience. Draw the experience into the Biblical world. In other words, don't let the question so dominate that the answer gets compromised. There's a correlation between the Biblical world and our world, but it's asymmetrical and noncompetitive.

We've also seen, of course, that part of Barron's passion for Bob Dylan—though admittedly, this is a take on Dylan that occurred to him later, as opposed to being fully formed in his teenage years—is that he regards Dylan as being the most "Biblical" of pop stars. Moreover, some of Barron's favorite figures in contemporary Catholicism—from Archbishop Mark Coleridge in Brisbane, Australia, to Italian Cardinal Gianfranco Ravasi, President of the Vatican's Pontifical Council for Culture to Brant Pitre, Scott Hahn, and Gary Anderson—are figures whose training and intellectual backgrounds are in Scripture studies.

Barron believes that in the post–Vatican II period in the Church, many Catholic scholars went so far in the direction of an overly technical and historical reading of the Bible that they never really got around to unleashing its spiritual power.

"I still think it's a largely unrealized goal of Vatican II, to awaken the Biblical consciousness. Part of the problem was that the intelligentsia became so dominated by the historical-critical approach, they didn't preach. It's a good tool, and we need it and all that, but it didn't preach. There was a rupture with the spiritual experience of ordinary people, which is an important point because it has crucial evangelical consequences."

Further, Barron argues, a lack of familiarity with the worldview shaped by the Bible means that many well-meaning Christians, including many Catholics, take their points of reference from alternative narratives in the contemporary culture. He cites British scholar N. T. Wright in this regard.

Wright says we're all dressed up for Hamlet, *we know the lines and themes of* Hamlet, *but the trouble is we're supposed to be in* Macbeth! *We're in the wrong play. The play we're in is the play of secular modernity, which reached its climax in, say, 1776 and the great political revolutions whose purpose was to throw off oppressive forms of government. Everyone knows that story, and everyone knows where we are in that story, moving toward ever more freedom and equality. But the Bib-*

lical story does not climax in 1776; it climaxes in A.D. 33. It does not climax in Philadelphia with the Declaration of Independence; it climaxes on that weird instrument of death, the Cross, which positions everything else. That's the story we're supposed to be in. Now, there's room within that story for 1776, but that isn't the story. The Bible is the story, and to get that is to be evangelized.

Among other things, Barron believes that immersion in the Biblical worldview could help American Catholics reflect better on the binary nature of national politics, and how it often skews perceptions of the Church's social teachings and the social and political priorities delineated by the U.S. bishops.

That's the key to this left-right dichotomy that many people don't get. When you say, "I'm not a Republican or a Democrat, I'm a Catholic," what you're invoking is a whole different set of criteria. Because the Democrat-Republican contest breaks along a very modern fault line for understanding politics and economics. But when you say, "No, I'm actually going to move onto a different ground," then your relationship to those two warring factions is going to be a very complicated one. Christianity, the Biblical universe, inculcates a bigger worldview. There's something skewed about the way we've configured the conversation, and that's why it's often hard for people elsewhere to get the liberal-conservative thing and our mania for situating everybody within it somehow. You have to say, "I want to change the subject; it's a different game we're talking about."

As a final introductory point, Barron is convinced that Catholics in the early twenty-first century have to understand and be able to discuss the Bible intelligently, because for many people in his target audience as an evangelist—meaning fallen-away Catholics and secular nones, people of no religious faith—the Bible remains a problem.

"The Bible is this huge, huge stumbling block for some people," he says. "They think it's simply a holdover from the Bronze Age, to use the language of [Christopher] Hitchens and [Richard] Dawkins."

A special challenge, he says, is helping people understand that Catholicism isn't committed to a literalistic reading of Scripture, which tends to be the only Christian approach to the Bible with which many nones are familiar.

> *People often think that the Bible's a book. I always say, begin with the etymology of the word* Bible—*it's* Ta Biblia, *"the books." It's not a book; it's a library. Then my next move is typically to ask, "Do you take the whole library literally? Well, it depends on what section you're in." You're wandering around the library, and some of the books are relatively straightforward. Then you wander into the poetry section, the mythology section, the fiction section, and things are different. We're dealing with books here with widely different authors, genres, audiences, purposes, and so on. To make sense of it all, you have to read it within an interpretive tradition. You don't just pick it up and start reading it. It's like saying, "Here's* Hamlet, *knock yourself out." No, you'd say, "Read* Hamlet *within this long tradition of interpretation, and then you begin to understand it." In the same way, with the books of the Bible you need so much contextualization.*

For all those reasons, therefore, understanding how Barron thinks about, talks about, and makes use of the Bible is key to penetrating not only his own thought but also how he sees the missionary enterprise within a secular culture.

KEYS TO INTERPRETATION

As an evangelist, Barron says, he frequently encounters secular seekers and nones for whom the Bible is a major stumbling block. For one thing, he says, they're often unaware that a literal reading is not the only approach to Biblical interpretation among Christians, and in particular, that it's not the sole method of the Catholic Church. Further, he says, they've often imbibed a truckload of prejudices about the Bible that are hard to get past—that the Bible condones violence, for instance, or that it approves slavery, or that it comes out of a patriarchal world in which women are seen as second-class citizens.

On the back of that experience, Barron has developed a couple of rules of thumb for proper Biblical interpretation. The first, he says, pivots on a distinction between "what the Bible teaches" and "what's in the Bible." He laid that point out in a 2012 YouTube video, prompted by an episode of the *Real Time* show hosted by the comedian, and inveterate critic of religion, Bill Maher.

I agree with the theologian William Placher [an American Presbyterian who shares Barron's postliberal outlook], who said we have to distinguish between what's in the Bible and what the Bible teaches. The authors were in the cultural milieu of the time; they drew on the intellectual furniture of a given time. What the Bible teaches is not always reducible to what's in the Bible. What the Bible teaches is what God intends us to know, what's inspired by God through the Bible for the sake of our salvation. To get that, we have to be attentive to the patterns, themes, and trajectories within the whole of the Bible. A good example is slavery. Was slavery part of the scene during the whole period in which the Bible was written? Yes, sure it was, as it was in almost every ancient culture. It was along for the ride; it was part of the mental furniture of the time. We shouldn't be surprised that Bible authors mention slavery, even sometimes offering indirect words of approbation. But is slavery something taught by the Bible, encouraged by the Bible? Is it what God wants? I would say no, and to get that we look at the totality of the Bible, its great themes. Mind you, the people who opposed slavery in the eighteenth and nineteenth centuries and brought it to an end, in both Europe and America, were precisely Biblical people. They were listening to what the Bible teaches, and not simply reading, dumbly, what's in the Bible. I think that distinction is very important for Biblical interpretation.

At the same time, Barron cautions against allowing that distinction between the Bible's teaching and its content to become an excuse for simply disregarding or playing down anything that's uncongenial, essentially refashioning the Biblical message in one's own image, or suppressing the idea that the voice of God still comes through. That, he believes, was the Achilles' heel of much early Biblical interpretation, among both Protestants and liberals.

"I don't want to make this sound pious, but Aquinas said that it's the divine author that you're really interested in and after," he says. "Yes, the divine author speaks through human authors and their intentionality, and to some extent you have to distinguish the two. But the danger my generation got into was that there was such a focus on the human author, and his intention, that the Word of God got lost."

Second, although Barron is hardly trying to refight the theological battles of the Protestant Reformation, one fixed point for him is that there's just no way to understand the Bible properly apart from the community of the Church. As he puts it, "Who gave you the Bible in the first place? It's a product of the mystical body of the Church." In that sense, though he didn't himself use the term, Barron could be said to be an exponent of what's called canonical criticism, which means pushing beyond the study of individual texts in isolation and instead focusing on the meaning they possess within the finished canon of the Bible, and for the community that regards that entire collection of texts as normative.

To take a practical example, Barron says that one canard he frequently runs into when trying to reach out to secular culture is the charge that the Bible encourages violence, often based on certain Old Testament passages, such as this line from Psalm 68: "God will crush the heads of his enemies, the hairy scalp of the one who walks in sin." Barron says the right way to respond is to put such passages in the broader context of the entire Bible, Old Testament and New.

This is a very ancient problem, and some of the earliest Christian apologists addressed it. You've got these texts in the Bible that seem really out of step with the Cross, with Jesus. In the third century, Origen insisted on reading the whole Bible from the standpoint of the last book of the Bible. He was talking about the Book of Revelation, with its imagery of the Lamb, standing as though slain, who opens the seven seals of the great scroll. That scroll represented the meaning of history and the Scriptures themselves. Who interprets it? Who alone can open that scroll legitimately? It's the Lamb, so the weakest littlest animal—and just to press the point, a lamb that's slain. Of course, that's the crucified Jesus, he's the interpretive key. Origen says once you get that, then whenever you say the Bible must be sanctioning horrific violence, you've obviously got to be wrong. That has to be the wrong interpretation.

"Church Fathers say that all the time, in different ways," Barron says. "If you come away from the Bible with the view that

God is a terrible tyrant, you are ipso facto misreading it. That's an ancient, ancient bit of hermeneutics.

"Reading the Bible as whole is not about pulling something out at random, but asking, What are the great themes and patterns?" Barron says. "They all lead toward the Cross and resurrection of Jesus. It's the resurrection that pulls the whole Bible together. It's like the final cause that draws all the themes and trajectories together, and that's the only way you can really read it properly. You've got to read the whole Bible from the standpoint of the end."

The next step, according to Barron, is to assimilate another traditional way of reading the Bible within the Church, which is what's sometimes called the allegorical method, and which stretches all the way back to St. Paul in the New Testament and comes down through fathers such as Origen and Augustine. In essence, it means understanding when Biblical passages are meant to be taken literally, and when they're being deployed for their symbolic or figurative value.

Consider the "ban." [The reference is to an Old Testament passage in which God orders King Saul to slaughter evil neighboring peoples as well as their cattle.] It can be understood as illustrating the way we have to battle certain forms of evil, which is that they have to be put all the way down. In fact, that's Saul's problem—he plays around with evil. He says, "Well, yeah, I killed almost everybody, but I left a few people and animals alive." He kept the king and the animals for himself, which is a metaphor for how most of us deal with evil most of the time. We sort of address it, but then we leave a little bit on the side for ourselves. Or, take the scene of Samuel hacking Agag to pieces. It's horrific, and the atheists cite that to me a lot. Here's your prophet, here's Samuel, and he's hacking this man to death. But if you follow Origen, it's a figurative

*illustration of battling evil, in this case an evil king, all the
way down.*

Further, Barron insists, the Catholic Church over the centuries has developed an approach to Scripture that navigates between the twin temptations of skepticism on the one hand and blind credulity on the other.

I go back to the great statement of Vatican II, Dei Verbum, *"The Word of God." There's a line there that's enormously clarifying. It says, "The Bible is the words of God, expressed in the words of men." That little iconic statement really packs a punch. In the Bible God speaks to us, and the whole Bible is inspired by God. But God did not dictate to automatons who took down the words literally. Rather, he worked much more subtly, and respectfully, with real human subjects, writers. He expressed himself through these altogether culturally conditioned figures, whose writings were conditioned by the audiences they were addressing and by the genre they were employing. That's why one of the great questions we have to attend to when we're reading the Bible is that of genre—what's the genre of the text we're dealing with? Is it a saga? Is it a legend? Is it a letter? Is it an apocalypse? Is it a history? There are all kinds of genres on display in the Bible. That's why "Do you take the Bible literally?" is just a stupid question. You take some books literally; others you don't. Sensitivity to genre is absolutely key to correct Biblical interpretation. And the ultimate question remains What is God trying to communicate through these texts?*

Reading the Bible just in terms of one's own perspective and experience, Barron says, is "a banalization of the Bible. It's a flattening out. Let the Bible be the Bible. You've got to get comfortable in that world, and it's not our world. There are analogues to it, and that's fine. You learn from it and all that, but you've got to get into it first and move around. It's like a jungle, the Bible, and you need a good guide."

Keep those two rules in mind, Barron argues—focus on what the Bible teaches, not just what it contains, and read it within the context of the Church—then virtually all of the standard barriers to embracing it will fall away.

BARRON'S APPROACH IN ACTION

To appreciate the contextualized, canonical, and nonliteral approach to Biblical interpretation Barron advocates, it's helpful to touch upon two enduring debates in late-twentieth- and early-twenty-first-century Catholic theology, both of which depend, in part, on which way one chooses to read the evidence of Scripture.

The first, strikingly, concerns Hell. Although Barron's great intellectual role model Hans Urs von Balthasar was generally seen as fairly conservative, some of his theological ruminations have run afoul of the Church's more traditionalist wing. Nowhere has that been more the case than in Balthasar's celebrated claim that it's legitimate for Christians to hope that Hell is empty.

That proposition has run into resistance for a variety of reasons, including claims that it clashes with official magisterial teaching in the Catholic Church ranging from the Fourth Lateran Council to St. John Paul II. However, most critiques begin with the Bible, and what appear to be some fairly unequivocal statements from Jesus himself. One oft-cited verse is Matthew 25:46, where Jesus says, "And they [the wicked] will go away into eternal punishment, but the righteous into eternal life."

Barron, however, is basically in the Balthasar camp. He insists, as did Balthasar, that in light of free will the human person can "definitively" refuse God, and thus Hell is always a "real possibility." Whether anyone has actually exercised that option, however, is another matter.

I take the Balthasar view, which is not that we know if all people will be saved, or even that we expect all people to be saved. It's merely that it's legitimate to hope for universal salvation. Further, it's a reasonable hope. It's not just a hope against hope, a wild, unwarranted move. Rather, it's grounded in what Christ accomplished on the Cross and in the resurrection. In that sense, there are reasonable grounds for the hope that all people might be saved. I've gotten in trouble with people for that because there are many who do want Hell to be really emphasized, but I don't see that in John Paul II, in Benedict XVI, and certainly not in Pope Francis.

Note the key interpretive move—Barron is arguing that what the Bible teaches about salvation has to be understood in terms of its great trajectories, all of which, of course, culminate in the Cross and the resurrection. Read in terms of how it ends, in other words, he believes the Bible does not resolve the question of whether Hell is empty, but it at least provides a reasonable basis for hoping the answer just may be yes.

Another concern that I have is evangelical. For the overwhelming majority of unchurched people today, the very idea of Hell is just an appalling absurdity. Beginning the evangelical process by emphasizing it and stirring up fear of it just strikes me, therefore, as a complete nonstarter from a practical standpoint. Look through the writings and speeches of John Paul II, one of the greatest Catholic evangelists of modern times, and you will find precious little on Hell. And you won't find one mention of it in Evangelii Gaudium, *Pope Francis's magisterial summation of the synod on evangelization. Mind you, this doesn't mean for a moment that we should never talk about Hell. Indeed, I have done so frequently, I daresay more than the vast majority of Catholic preachers. I just don't think we should lead with it evangelically.*

Another focus of controversy in which the Bible was keenly relevant was a decades-long tug-of-war among liturgists and theologians over how a phrase of Christ used in the Mass, when Catholics believe the bread and wine become his body and blood, should be translated. Some argued passionately that Christ's reference to the pouring out of his blood should be rendered as "for you and for all for the forgiveness of sins," while others insisted it should be "for many." In English, it was "for all" in the translations approved following Vatican II, but in 2006, Benedict decreed that from then on it would be "for many." (Similar changes were ordered in other languages; in Spanish, for instance, it went from *por todos* to *por muchos*.)

In general it's fair to say that the advocates of "for all" came from the liberal wing of liturgical and theological thought, seeing it as the best way of expressing the doctrinal truth that Christ came to save the entire world, not just a limited portion of it. More conservative voices insisted that not only is "for many" the better translation of the Latin original *pro multis* in the Mass, but that "for all" risked promoting a universality vision of salvation that didn't take adequate account of sin and the need for conversion.

Once again, Barron takes a balanced view, in which the accent isn't on slavish attention to one Biblical phrase seen in isolation but rather is on how it ought to be understood and rendered in light of the whole.

I think pro multis *was a Latin rendering of a Hebrew term that can be construed to mean "for everybody." It was an idiomatic way of saying "for everybody, for the many." I wouldn't put a lot of weight on the transition to "for many," as if it clearly means that there are some who will not be saved. It's a rendering of a term that idiomatically includes both ideas. Depending on what your perspective is, I think it's fine to say Christ shed his blood for everybody. Now, will everybody benefit from that shedding of his blood? That's a different theological question.*

THE BIBLE AND BARRON'S PRIORITIES

One reliable way to gauge how important a subject is to someone is by looking at the role it plays in the things that individual truly cares about, his passions, the apples of his eye. If that's the measure, there's no doubt at all that the Bible is a defining preoccupation for Bishop Robert Barron, because it looms large in the two undertakings to which he might be said to be most personally committed: preaching, and his Word on Fire ministry.

Preaching

As we've seen, Barron identifies himself primarily as an "evangelist," but his evangelical activity takes multiple forms—TV series, YouTube videos, podcasts, columns, books, media interviews, and on and on. Yet in that array of activity, Barron would acknowledge a special pride of place to preaching, which is the way most Catholics become evangelized. As a professor at Mundelein Seminary, and later as rector, he devoted special attention to preparing future priests to be good preachers and homilists, a reflection of how crucial he believes the art of good preaching to be.

Today, Barron says, he regards his range of ministries as "almost entirely" forms of preaching, in one way or another.

Asked to tick off what he regards as the signature qualities of effective preaching, Barron doesn't hesitate about what he puts at the top of the list: Above all else, he says, inspiring preaching has to be Biblical.

"I remember years ago, I listened to a tape of Fulton Sheen, and that's the first thing he said about preaching—good preaching is Biblical," Barron says. "I say that because my formation was in the opposite direction. I think you begin with the Bible. You open up with this weird, strange, beguiling, beautiful, puzzling, mysterious world of the Bible," he says.

"The formation of a Biblical consciousness, a Biblical worldview, is the indispensable thing in preaching," he says. "You're a man of the Bible, and you see the world with Biblical eyes. That's the way to do it. A good sermon allows you to see the world with Biblical eyes."

Asked what makes for a good homily at a Catholic Mass, Barron sounds like something of a broken record, once again insisting that its defining quality ought to be that it's Biblical.

It has to be clearly, unapologetically, and compellingly Biblical. My biggest complaint, and again this goes back to the liberal-postliberal debate, is if your basic orientation is to begin with experience and you try to draw the religious symbols into it, then they get positioned by it. And if you're preaching out of that perspective, you're going to offer a lot of experience and just a little bit of the Bible: "So, here's our Bible story, and that reminds me of my vacation, so let me give you fifteen minutes about my vacation." I think that was a move a lot of us were trained to make, and the idea, obviously, was to engage the people. I've come to see it as a paradox, because it actually works the other way. People are less engaged by that approach, one which so positions the Bible according to our experience that it robs the Bible of its power. I would say instead that what works is densely textured Biblical preaching that takes you on a tour of the Biblical world, opens you to the Biblical spaces and characters, and the Bible's strange way of speaking and its oddity. A preacher is a guide to that world, and I think it's good for a sermon to show how odd the Bible is. My experience is that it's very positive, that people like it, when the Bible opens up. They'll say, "I never thought about that. I never knew that." Or, "That's weird, that's interesting." I find that they like it. It may be a paradox, but my experience is when you lead with experience, it gets tedious fast. So, in terms of homilies, I'd say being Biblical is the number one thing.

Barron says that over the years he's become a student of good preaching. Two figures, admittedly very different, whom he admires in terms of their mastery of the craft are Martin Luther King Jr. and the American Pentecostal televangelist Jimmy Swaggart.

"I'm a big fan of African American preaching, because I think it's very Augustinian," Barron says. "It's lyrical and it's rhythmic and it rhymes; it's like music. I'm a great admirer of Martin Luther King on many levels, but in regard to his preaching, what I particularly admire is how he sings his sermons. Listen to a recording of one of his homilies, and you'll hear these long notes coming out of his mouth, and he's seizing on rhythms. I used to teach the seminarians that way of preaching at Mundelein. It's not just communicating ideas, but you're doing it in this songlike, rhythmic way. Attentiveness to poetic rhythms, I think, is a key to good preaching. All the great ones certainly had that."

Barron is convinced, though, that what made King so effective in the pulpit wasn't just his style or tonality but also his content, which was thoroughly drenched in the language and the spiritual worldview of the Bible.

My favorite sermon by Martin Luther King, Jr., is the "Drum Major Instinct" sermon, from near the end of his life, which is a wonderful example of good preaching. It's also theologically interesting. King studied Tillich too, so we have that in common. But what King really had was the Bible, the Bible, the Bible, all through him. King had cultivated this deeply Biblical view of life. When you listen, he sang the Bible, so he was Barthian in that way. So that's not a bad characterization of a preacher, someone who knows how to sing the Bible.

As for Swaggart, Barron acknowledges that "the poor man had his problems, personally"—a reference to the fact that in 1988 and again in 1991, Swaggart was caught up in prostitution scandals that led to his being defrocked by his denomination, the Assemblies of God, and becoming independent—but despite that, Barron says, he could be a rock-'em, sock-'em preacher when he was at the top of his game. What made Swaggart's preaching so effective, Barron says, is how deep it was in the world of the Bible.

As a kid, I watched Jimmy Swaggart, and I admired him as a preacher; he's darn good. I heard him one time, this was in recent years, well after his fall from grace. He was speaking on King David, and I'd just done all this research on Second Samuel [an Old Testament book in which David figures prominently]. The sermon was on David and David's fall, and it was really impressive. Swaggart was just sitting down, which is unusual, but I think his knee was bothering him. Even though he was sitting, he just had the audience in the palm of his hand. What he was doing was talking about David as the sweet singer of the house of Israel, so basically, he was singing the Bible. That's what great preachers do.

Word on Fire

The other towering concern for Barron, and where the Bible also enjoys pride of place in his thought, is his Word on Fire ministry, which is the umbrella under which his various media projects fall. Over the years, Barron's attracted a network of people who share his basic vision, some of whom are full-time staff and others contributors, collaborators, and supporters. As we'll see in Chapter 10, Barron hopes to see Word on Fire develop into a full-fledged movement in the Catholic Church, whose mission is the New Evangelization.

Though Barron concedes that aim lies down the line, he's already elaborated a set of core principles to flesh out what a Word on Fire movement would be. High on the list, he says, is the Bible, and seeing Word on Fire as a way of fostering a deeper familiarity with and appreciation for Scripture in the Church. Even before the transition to a movement, Barron says, he and his team are hard at work on a project called Word on Fire Bible.

"The idea is to produce an edition of the Bible that would include all kinds of commentary," he says. "Some of it would be from me, things I've written and sermons, and so on, and some of it would come from people such as the theologians and spiritual writers who have profoundly marked me. This Bible would be sort of a focus for formation of Word on Fire groups, with the idea of using that Bible to evangelize young people. That's one of the tools we're developing right now.

"The next step I would see," he says, "is forming our friends more carefully, especially in the use of the Bible. An immersion in this Word on Fire Bible has the potential to form our core group in this common vision and common lifestyle. I'd like to get to that place."

FAVORITE BIBLICAL SCHOLARS

Ever the intellectual, Barron over the years has developed a short list of Biblical scholars he particularly enjoys or finds valuable. One is a figure we've already met, N. T. Wright.

Wright had a big impact on me when I first read him, because he was someone who combined the best of the historical-critical method and all that stuff, while still defending classical Christianity. I thought, Here's a Biblical theologian from whose work I can preach. When I was coming of age it was all Raymond Brown, and I admire him immensely. I saw him several times, and he was a master. He was at Mundelein several times for our Biblical events and he would show up with a tiny New Testament in Greek and that's it. No notes, just that, and he would give a compelling lecture for an hour. Despite my sincere admiration of Brown, though, I think he's hard to preach. I don't think you preach him as readily as you preach N. T. Wright.

Another role model is closer to home for Barron, a Biblical scholar under whom he studied named Father James Doyle.

Jim was a fascinating man. In the early 1960s he decided to become a Trappist monk; he went to Gethsemani and Thomas Merton was his novice master. He was there for two or three years and then decided it wasn't for him, so he went to Rome and got a degree. He was a Bible man. When we had him, we were taking a Gospel of John class, and we were reading Raymond Brown's great commentary on John. Jim said on the first day, "I'd like you to read the first one hundred pages of that for the next class, take it in, and then we'll really get to work" with the Gospel of John itself. It was absolutely the right approach, and it was an eye opener for me. The idea was, yes, know that stuff, the historical-critical method, but what Jim wanted us to do was to get into the real soul of it and to be able to preach it. Also, as I mentioned earlier, I have great respect for Dr. Scott Hahn, who has emerged as the father of a whole generation of Catholic Biblical scholars, including Brant Pitre, Michael Barber, Timothy Gray, and others. And I'd really be remiss not to mention Joseph Ratzinger/Pope Benedict XVI, who splendidly exemplifies a renewal in Catholic Biblical studies.

Chapter Eight

OBSTACLES TO THE FAITH

Plenty of leading Catholic intellectuals, pastors, and pundits have invested considerable energy during the last several decades in diagnosing the discontents of secularism. Perhaps the leading example is emeritus Pope Benedict XVI, who treated his papacy almost like a global graduate seminar in the role of faith in a postmodern, democratic, and secular world. Any future study on the subject will almost certainly have to take into account four cornerstone speeches Benedict delivered over his eight years in office, all of which, in one way or another, pivoted on the topic: Regensburg, Germany, in 2006 (assuming one can get past the opening lines about Islam, the speech is really directed at the West); the Collège des Bernardins in Paris in 2008; Westminster Hall in London in 2010; and the Bundestag in Berlin in 2011.

Although many Catholic figures, albeit generally at lower levels, similarly have thought a good deal about secularism, it's a safe bet that few have spent more time actually talking to secularists than Bishop Robert Barron. In some cases, those exchanges come in person or during media segments, but most often Barron's dialogues have come online, especially in the comments section of YouTube, where he's been willing to log countless hours patiently replying to criticisms, answering questions, issuing intellectual challenges, recommending further reading, and generally trying to keep lines of communication open.

As a result of that experience, as we've already seen, Barron has identified three distinct groups he's trying to engage within the vast secular cauldron.

Lapsed Catholics

Barron is well aware of the depressing statistics from the Pew Research Center's most recent study of the religious landscape in America, which found that nearly one-third of American adults (31.7 percent) say they were raised Catholic, and among that group, fully 41 percent no longer identify with Catholicism. The implication is that a startling 12.9 percent of American adults are former Catholics, and if ex-Catholics formed their own denomination, it would be the second largest in the country. Meanwhile, just 2 percent of U.S. adults have converted to Catholicism from another religious tradition. No other religious group in the country had such a lopsided ratio of losses to gains.

Drilling down into the Pew data, it's clear that not every ex-Catholic walked away for the same reasons. Some joined another, often more progressive mainline Christian church; others embraced a generally more conservative Evangelical or Pentecostal denomination. A few joined other religions entirely. Likely the largest chunk, however, was absorbed into secularism, joining the ranks of the religiously unaffiliated. It's that group which Barron sees as the first target of his evangelizing work, and that of his Word on Fire ministry.

"I've always said that lapsed Catholics are my first target," Barron told me. "But a lot of them are lapsed because they've been drawn, knowingly or not, into the secularist ideology."

During a press conference in Los Angeles in 2015 to introduce him as a new auxiliary bishop, Barron gave a similar answer when asked to name the biggest problem the Church faces.

"It's the massive attrition of our own people," he said. "I don't know how more people don't see that, as problems go on in the Catholic Church. Let's face it, the vast majority of people that we baptize, confirm, educate, and catechize do not stay in the Church. It's an illusion to say, 'They're all coming back.' To be quite frank, people don't realize that. Our number one focus should be on how to reengage Catholics who have fallen away."

"Nones"

Until very recently, in casual conversation Catholics never really found themselves spelling out the word in order to make clear whether they were talking about "nuns" or "nones," but such are the shifting plates of American religion in the early twenty-first century. That same Pew study found there are now approximately 56 million religiously unaffiliated adults in the United States, and this group—colloquially called the nones—is more numerous than either Catholics or mainline Protestants. Only the number of Evangelical Protestants remains larger.

Moreover, if present trends continue, time would seem to be on the side of the nones. Millennials, for instance, show much lower levels of religious affiliation than older generations. Fully 36 percent of young millennials (between the ages of eighteen and twenty-four) are religiously unaffiliated, as are 34 percent of older millennials (ages twenty-five to thirty-three). Those nones, by the way, are increasingly likely to describe themselves in secular terms. The last time Pew did such a study, in 2007, 26 percent of nones said they were atheists or agnostics, but that share had gone up to 31 percent by 2015.

For Barron, that booming cohort of the religiously unaffiliated is his second target audience, with the initial aim to persuade them at least to set aside some of their prejudices and give the argument for faith a more sympathetic consideration.

"Hard-Core" Atheists

Although in a sense this group is a subset of the nones, Barron has come to think of what he calls the "hard-core" atheists, meaning disciples of figures such as Christopher Hitchens, Richard Dawkins, Samuel Harris, and Daniel Dennett, who collectively have been called the "Four Horsemen of the New Atheism," as a different group. In part, he treats them as a separate category because he believes their hostility to faith is much greater, and therefore evangelical strategies directed to them have to be adjusted accordingly.

To be honest, Barron has few illusions that anything he or any other evangelist does is likely to win many of these hard-core atheists over, at least in the short term, always, of course, leaving room for the grace of God. His aim instead is to force some to rethink their arguments, and perhaps to be slightly less aggressive and denigratory when addressing religion and religious believers—which might, he believes, make it slightly easier to reach lapsed Catholics and nones, many of whom are influenced by the thought-world of the New Atheism.

THE "BUFFERED SELF"

Charles Taylor, a Canadian philosopher who's now an emeritus professor at Montreal's McGill University, is a particular favorite thinker for Barron. From Taylor's seminal book *A Secular Age*, which appeared in 2007, Barron picked up the concept of the "buffered self" to describe the central cultural malady associated with widespread secularism.

Basically, the idea is that when culture was dominated by religious belief, it fostered a "porous self." The world was full of other people, angels, demons, and cosmic forces, all of which imbued it with meaning, and people were disposed to absorb those other sources of meaning, which weren't created entirely by the self. In a secular milieu, however, the "buffered self" perceives a strong boundary between the internal and external worlds, people create meaning for themselves, and so they're basically isolated from anything deeper or bigger. To put the point in a nutshell, the "buffered self" has been disconnected from the transcendent, and therefore from God.

To begin, let's consider how Barron defines *secularism*—not as a simple historical and cultural process but as an ideology.

"As I use the term *ideological secularism* is a philosophical view that effectively excludes God from the equation, although it might acknowledge God as a side reality," Barron says. "*Secularism* as I'm using it here is becoming increasingly the dominant philosophy in our culture. It's an exclusive naturalism, often exclusive materialism, which on principle excludes God from the worldview. It sees the very idea of God as a threat to human flourishing. This, of course, is born of a very bad understanding of God."

Ultimately, Barron says, the drive to separate people from any sense of reality or purpose higher than themselves produces disenchantment and disorientation, which opens a door through which evangelists today can walk.

"What I see happening all the time is the hunger for God and dissatisfaction with the buffered self, and dissatisfaction with the purely secularized view of the world," he says.

> *I see a lot of people, especially younger people, who have bought that philosophy, that's what they've been given by the elite culture, and now they're chafing against it, they're reacting against it. That's an opening.*
>
> *My problem with atheists is that they shut down wonder. They say, "Our world is self-contained, all explained, and*

nothing further is needed." But this is far too limiting. I'm with Leonard Cohen, who got the image from Chesterton, that what we have to do is to crack some holes in our heads in order to let in the light, to punch holes in the buffered self.

When you suppress the desire for God, which secularism does necessarily, it's very dangerous psychologically. I see it all the time in the form of addictions and deep depressions. So, I'm doing this out of a deep concern for people. It's dangerous stuff, to shut down the aspiration toward God.

The question then becomes, if that aspiration toward God is natural and, in the end, irrepressible, what's getting in the way for people raised in a secular culture—meaning, the lapsed Catholics, nones, and even the hard-core atheists Barron is trying to reach?

THE PENTARCHY OF PROTESTS

In Eastern Christianity in the early centuries, a theory of Church governance known as the *pentarchy,* from the Greek word for *five,* developed. It held that power in the Church was to be shared among the five major episcopal sees, which corresponded to the major administrative divisions of the old Roman Empire: Rome, Constantinople, Alexandria, Antioch, and Jerusalem.

In essence, the pentarchy was an early way of answering the questions Who's in charge? Who's setting the tone here? Over the years, some ecumenical experts in contemporary Christianity have proposed dusting off some form of the pentarchy as a way to conceive what power sharing in a reunified church might look like.

Based on his experience of interacting with lapsed Catholics, nones, and secularists, Barron believes they've got a pentarchy too, not about power but about protest—five classic, visceral objections to religion in general, and to the Catholic Church in particular, which form the primary obstacles to the faith in the early twenty-first century. Any Catholic evangelist worth his or her salt, Barron says, has to be prepared to confront these objections, because they come up over and over again.

That secularist pentarchy of protest is composed of the following:

- The idea of God
- Religion and science
- Religion and sex
- Religion and violence
- The Bible

In the previous chapter, we covered how Barron views the role and interpretation of the Bible, so here we'll explore how he talks about the other four classic obstacles when he runs into them in conversation, online, and in other venues.

The Idea of God

German theologians often talk about *die Gottesfrage*, meaning "the question of God." Often, they mean it in a basically positive sense. Pope Benedict XVI, for instance, has urged Catholic theologians to spend less time wrestling with second-order matters, such as power in the Church or the fine points of sexual ethics, and more on the *Gottesfrage*, by which he means the stuff that's really most important—who God is, what God wants for humanity, and so on.

Yet Barron says that for many contemporary secularists, the *Gottesfrage* generally is not a positive but a stumbling block. Lots of people in our time, he says, are convinced that there's simply no rational warrant for believing in a Supreme Being, and many are actually convinced that modern science has "disproved" the existence of God. The very first thing a Catholic evangelist must be prepared to do, therefore, is to make a persuasive case that believing in God doesn't mean suspending one's rational faculties or operating solely on the basis of blind faith.

Here's how Barron describes the basic problem: "They think God's a being," he says. "They think God is one big being among many. It's what I call the yeti theory of God. [The yeti is a legendary creature in the folklore of Nepal, basically their version of Bigfoot.] There's supposed to be this thing out there. Some say he's there, some say he's not; so let's go see if we can find him out there. The question then becomes, 'Is there evidence for a yeti? Is there evidence for God?'"

It's precisely the wrong way to think about God. God's not an item in the universe, but you see that assumption in all of the contemporary atheists, from Bertrand Russell to Dawkins and Hitchens. They all operate out of the understanding that God is some big item among many others, and so we have to find evidence. I always go back to Thomas Aquinas, who said that God isn't a being, he's ipsum esse subsistens, *"subsistent being itself." God's not in the genus of being, God is the ground of all being. I use that line from Aquinas, which is really puzzling and confounding, that God is not even in the highest possible genus, namely, the genus of being. Thomas says that God is not an individual, which I think is actually rather mind-blowing, but it means that God is not a thing in the world but rather the reason why there's something rather than nothing. Very few of the contemporary atheists get that, and when you don't get that, you conceive of God as a rival, a competitor with us in the same space. If God gets all the glory, I get no glory. If God is there, my freedom's limited. Sartre came in at that point, and all of his existentialist disciples. If you really press it, I think a lot of it goes back to nominalism, a philosophical view which influenced the reformers in a big way. I think that's the pivot on which a lot of this business turns, and now every high school kid in America thinks God is a threat to their freedom, which is precisely what the true God is not. It's high philosophical stuff, but it has very strong concrete implications.*

When he has laid out what Christianity actually means by "God," Barron's next move is to show that people who believe in that concept of God didn't just check their brains at the door. To do so, once again he falls back on Aquinas, who famously laid out five philosophical arguments for the existence of God—arguments that, Barron is convinced, still retain a persuasive power.

Those arguments are

- *Unmoved mover:* For Thomas Aquinas, "moving" included any kind of change—not just spatial motion. Things change all the time in the world, and those changes are always caused by something else. A plant grows because someone waters it, I change jobs because someone hired me, and so on. However, that chain can't go back indefinitely, because at some point there had to be a force that initiated change without an external cause, and that's what God is.
- *First cause:* In the world, everything that happens has a cause. Once again, however, that chain can't be infinite, because something has to exist without being caused, and that's God.
- *Contingency:* When we look around, it's clear that everything in the world depends on something else, meaning everything is "contingent." I wouldn't be here

without my parents, my wife's Prius wouldn't exist without Toyota, et cetera. However, there has to be something that's not contingent that got the ball rolling, and that is God.

- *Degree:* As we think about the world, instinctively we think about things as more or less "good," more or less "beautiful," et cetera. Yet that evaluation implies some absolute standard of perfect goodness, perfect beauty, and so on, against which everything else is being judged, and that's another way of saying "God."

- *Natural end:* In the world, even nonintelligent beings appear to behave with purpose—acorns, for instance, grow into oak trees without anyone engineering it. Yet since these things can't think for themselves, they must have acquired that orientation toward a goal from some intelligent force, and again, that's a way of talking about God.

Although Barron finds all five of Aquinas's arguments powerful, he says that for most secularists, the one that cuts through the noise best is the argument from contingency. Here's how he presented it in a 2012 column.

You and I are contingent (dependent) in our being in the measure that we eat and drink, breathe, and had parents; a tree is contingent inasmuch as its being is derived from seed, sun, soil, water, et cetera; the solar system is contingent because it depends upon gravity and events in the wider galaxy. To account for a contingent reality, by definition we have to appeal to an extrinsic cause. But if that cause is itself contingent, we have to proceed further. This process of appealing to

contingent causes in order to explain a contingent effect can-
not go on indefinitely, for then the effect is never adequately
explained. Hence, we must finally come to some reality that is
not contingent on anything else, some ground of being whose
very nature is to-be. This is precisely what Catholic theology
means by "God." Therefore, God is not one fussy cause within
or alongside the universe; instead, he is the reason why there
is a universe at all, why there is, as the famous formula has it,
"something rather than nothing." To ask the sophomoric ques-
tion, "Well, what caused God?" is simply to show that the poser
of the question has not grasped the nettle of the argument.

Religion and Science

Commonly, Barron says, people respond to that argument by saying "matter," "energy," or "the universe" can explain things. However, he insists that response just shifts the problem rather than
resolving it.

Energy or matter always exists in a particular modality, which
implies that they could just as well be in another modality: here
rather than there, up rather than down, this color rather than
that, this speed rather than that, this temperature rather than
that, et cetera. But this in turn means that their being in one
state rather than another requires an explanation or an appeal
to an extrinsic cause. The proposal of the fluctuating universe
itself is just as much of a nonstarter, for it involves the same
problem simply writ large: How do you explain why the uni-
verse is expanding rather than contracting, at this rate rather
than that, in this configuration rather than another, et cetera?
Finally, a cause of the very to-be of a contingent universe must
be sought, and this cannot be anything in the universe, nor can

it be the universe considered as a totality. It must be a reality whose very essence is to-be, and hence whose perfection of existence is unlimited. As I have tried to demonstrate, philosophy can shed light on the existence of God so construed. The one thing the sciences cannot ever do is disprove it.

In Chapter 4, we saw how Barron diagnoses *scientism,* a worldview that turns the legitimate triumphs of the empirical sciences into an ideology, claiming that's the only way to establish truth—which by definition consigns God to the realm of the irrational and subjective. He says that what frustrates him most about people who have imbibed such a view is that they assert science is rational and religion isn't, yet they're often not willing to pursue the rational quest to its logical conclusion.

"I'll tease them, saying, 'You drop the question right when it gets really interesting,'" Barron says. "You get to a question such as 'Why is there a world at all?' or 'Why is there something rather than nothing?' and you generally just drop it. Or the atheists will say the world just popped out of nothing. And I'm the one doing magical thinking here? I'm the one who is irrational? I say, pursue reason all the way, and don't abandon it when it's getting really interesting."

In truth, Barron believes, scientism in this sense is a threat not merely to religion but to every nonempirical way of perceiving truth. It imperils poetry and art, for instance, as much as religion, as well as the venerable discipline of philosophy. In fact, about as close as you'll ever hear Barron come to going ballistic, at least in public, came in response to a 2016 YouTube video from Bill Nye, the Science Guy, in which Nye said some disparaging things about philosophy vis-à-vis science, suggesting that philosophy "doesn't always lead you to someplace surprising, inconsistent with common sense."

Barron virtually fumed in a podcast in which he was asked to comment on what Nye had said, calling Nye's answer "a remarkably dumb video . . . it was rambling, incoherent, and it said to me that the man has never read even a page of philosophy.

> *Even by the time of the great figures, Socrates, Plato, and Aristotle, philosophy had clearly distinguished itself from science. Aristotle wrote the* Physics, *and then the* Metaphysics, *meaning "what's beyond physics." What we're hearing now is a tremendous arrogance born of the admittedly massive success of the physical sciences in explaining the world from a particular perspective, and giving rise to technologies that have been of extraordinary help to us. But it's naïve in the extreme to say that all rational forms can be reduced to the scientific form. To say that philosophy is just primitive science . . . Has the man read anything from Aristotle through Wittgenstein? Philosophy is obsolete? Tell Hegel that, tell Heidegger that, tell Wittgenstein that, tell Jacques Derrida that. They knew that philosophy has its own integrity and rational contribution to make.*

The fact that philosophy asks different questions than science, Barron insists, doesn't make it any less rational.

"The sciences can shed light on a whole range of questions that human beings find intensely interesting," he says. "But, what's the beautiful? What makes something morally right or wrong? What's the nature of reality? What does it mean to be 'true'? What's the nature of consciousness? There are all sorts of questions philosophers ask in a rational way, but they're not going to follow the scientific method because it wouldn't apply in those cases. It's just as rational as the sciences, but not reducible to the sciences."

Barron says he also tries to make the point to secularists who regard religion as an implacable foe of science that they've got things exactly the wrong way around. Religion, specifically Christianity, isn't an obstacle to modern science—Christianity actually created the conditions in which scientific thinking could arise.

> *To hold that the world is created is to accept, simultaneously, the two assumptions required for science, namely, that the universe is not divine and that it is marked, through and through, by intelligibility. If the world or nature is considered divine (as it is in many philosophies and mysticisms), then one would never allow oneself to analyze it, dissect it, or perform experiments upon it. But a created world, by definition, is not divine. It is other than God, and in that very otherness, scientists find their freedom to act. At the same time, if the world is unintelligible, no science would get off the ground, since all science is based upon the presumption that nature can be known, that it has a form. But the world, precisely as created by a divine intelligence, is thoroughly intelligible, and hence scientists have the confidence to seek, explore, and experiment.*

Rejecting either of those convictions born of religious faith as simply irrational, or even jettisoning the premises about intelligibility supplied by philosophy because they can't be confirmed through a laboratory experiment, is a self-defeating exercise, Barron argues, that makes even science impossible to justify.

"Sometimes atheists will invoke [Scottish philosopher David] Hume against first cause arguments, because Hume took a radically skeptical position toward the whole idea of causality," Barron says. "Okay, but you're also thereby undermining biology, chemistry, physics, all the natural sciences. They're all based on the principle of causality, in one way or another. In effect, you're cutting off the branch you're sitting on. You're so afraid of the logical power of that argument, you're willing to undermine science itself to avoid it."

For all those reasons, Barron says, Christians of all stripes, but especially the Church's apologists, "must battle the myth of the eternal warfare of science and religion . . . continually preaching, as Pope John Paul II did, that faith and reason are complementary, and compatible, paths toward the knowledge of truth."

Religion and Sex

We've already seen what Barron regards as the critical first move with regard to the Church's teaching on matters such as gay marriage, abortion, contraception, and other aspects of sexual ethics—which is, Don't make that your first move. As he always says, you won't read the Gospels and think Jesus's main concern is that you need to have your sexual life in order, however important that may be. Further, if you don't grasp what Jesus's primary concerns actually are, the sexual teaching won't make sense to you.

That said, Barron is also well aware that the Church doesn't always get to set the agenda. However much he might like to sequence a conversation about the Catholic faith for himself, sometimes the culture asks questions that just won't be made to go away by talking about something else, and they have to be tackled head-on. The first point to be made, he says, is that Church teaching on sex ultimately is about love.

It's about love, not the suppression of sexuality. It's about directing sexuality toward willing the good of the other. We sentimentalize all the time, but I use the more bracing definition. Love is not a feeling, but rather an act of the will, to desire the good of the other as other. Your sexual life, as with everything else in your life, has to be directed that way. That's what the Church's teaching is trying to do, just continually, consistently, move you in the direction of willing the good of the other. And love is the one virtue for which there's no upper limit. You can't love too much. You can have too much faith, which becomes credulity. You can have too much hope, which is presumption. However, you can't have too much love.

Here, we'll look at how Barron typically fields two classic flash points of sex and the Catholic Church: the Church's teaching on gay rights and same-sex marriage, and the clerical sexual abuse scandals.

Homosexuality and Gay Marriage

When it comes to homosexuality, Barron says first he tries to help people not merely to know the bottom line of Church teaching but to appreciate what's behind it and what it's designed to accomplish.

What the teaching is trying to do is to move people into the stance of more radical and complete self-gift, which in the Catholic view, includes not just unity and friendship but procreation and the gift of life. When that sexual ideal is held up uncompromisingly, you're going to get teachings against anything that would undercut procreation and the gift of life. This will strike some people as extreme. Yet the Church is also extreme in its mercy as it reaches out to, accompanies, walks with, and understands gay people. For someone who has a gay orientation, is all that a massively difficult thing to integrate? Yes, absolutely, and we have to be sensitive to that. Do we need shepherds who are willing to walk with and accompany gay people? Yes, as Pope Francis always says. "How far do we go?" All the way, all the way, but without dialing down the moral demand, the moral ideal. I think that's the thing.

While Barron resists "dialing down the ideal," he is hardly what one might consider a cultural warrior on the issue. For one thing, he concedes that some of the language used by the Church over the years to address these issues has been pastorally suspect and, frankly, often counterproductive. The *Catechism of the Catholic Church* declares that a same-sex orientation is "intrinsically disordered." But he says if this is the only thing a gay person ever hears from the Catholic Church, then we've got a "very serious pastoral problem.

"Now, those of us who are trained in the Church's thinking, in its Aristotelian roots, know exactly what that phrase means," he says. "In this aspect of life, there's something ordering you in the wrong way toward what ought to be the proper teleology of this [the sexual] act. That's what it means, but I totally get how that term would have landed with a complete thud in the hearts and minds of gay people."

Barron broadly welcomes the modern emancipation of gays and lesbians, from a past in which they were often mistreated, stigmatized, and driven underground.

Over roughly the past twenty-five years, armies of gay people have come to understand the nature of their sexual attraction, and this is indeed welcome. Repression, deception, and morbid self-reproach are never good things. The result of this greater honesty is that millions have recognized their brothers, sisters, aunts, cousins, uncles, and dear friends as gay. The homosexual person is no longer, accordingly, some strange and shadowy "other," but someone I know to be a decent human being. This development, too, is nothing but positive. The man or woman with a homosexual orientation must always be loved and treated, in all circumstances, with the respect due to a child of God.

As a footnote, however, Barron sees an equal and opposite problem today, and one that's growing, in terms of how people interpret and react to language in the debate over gay marriage, which is that an expression of opposition, however well intentioned or ethically sound, is treated as tantamount to discrimination.

"Any preacher or writer who ventures to make a moral argument against gay marriage is automatically condemned as a purveyor of 'hate speech' or excoriated as a bigot," he says, "and in extreme cases, he can be subject to legal sanction. This visceral, violent reaction is a consequence of the breakdown of a rational framework for moral discourse."

Barron brings sensitivity to other issues in the Church that involve gay persons, such as one he had to face directly during his time as a seminary professor and later the rector of Mundelein Seminary, which is the suitability of men with a same-sex attraction to become priests. The question came to a boil in 2005, when the Vatican's Congregation for Catholic Education issued a controversial document stating that men with "deep-seated" same-sex tendencies should not be admitted to seminaries, and thus should not become Catholic priests. At the time, Pope Benedict XVI, popularly seen as a conservative, had just been elected, and critics charged this was the opening salvo of a wider "witch hunt" designed to drive gays out of the priesthood.

Barron says he adopted the most nuanced perspective, voiced at the time by Cardinal Francis George of Chicago.

The cardinal came out to Mundelein and he said, "I know there's concern about this document and the phrase 'deep-seated homosexual tendencies.'" He said, "Can I address what I think that means?" He said, "I think it means if your sexual orientation is so profoundly central to your identity that the whole of your person focuses around it, we have a problem. Then

your sense of yourself no longer focuses around your relation-
ship with Jesus Christ. But if that relationship with Christ
is central, and your sexual orientation finds its place around
that center, then I don't think we're talking about deep-seated."
That's how he interpreted it. When I became rector, I found
that this issue was clearly on the minds of lots of my students.
So we had a whole formation session on it, and I just repeated
what Cardinal George had said, and I said, "That's my posi-
tion too."

In general, while Barron does not back down from defending the substance of Church teaching on homosexuality and gay
rights, he does question the wisdom of continuing to lead with
such matters in the way the Church engages the culture right now.

I've seen the Church pour all kinds of energy and all kinds of
time into these issues, and you could say culturally right now
it's not working that well. Maybe it's time to shift the empha-
sis. I don't duck it, and if people bring it up, I'll talk about it.
But there are things far more fundamental. If you don't believe
in God, and you don't think there's a supernatural dimension
to life, then we have a lot more elementary work to do. Some
people will just see the Church as oppressive and deeply insen-
sitive to gay people, and I think we can clear that up. I think
we can do so within the framework of our moral teaching, be-
cause we're not saying you're a terrible person . . . We can come
across not as scolding and condescending, as if I've got every
answer, but rather in an inviting way.

Abuse Scandals

Barron says his first inkling that a storm might be brewing with
regard to reports of child sexual abuse by Catholic clergy came in

1992, when he visited his mother in her condo in Chicago after returning from finishing his studies in Paris. He recalled that she had a WELCOME HOME BOB! sign and some champagne on ice. After catching up for a while, he says, his mother mentioned that she had collected some news clippings for him on a table in his room.

"I go to my room, and there was this whole pile of sex abuse clippings," he says. "It was already happening in Chicago. I was unaware of that in Paris, I must say. I said, 'Wow, I know that guy,' and so on. Then my mom told me that, because of all that, when people asked about me she'd tell them I was an author, not, in the first place, a priest. I remember thinking something has really shifted.

"My whole priesthood has been under the cloud of the sex abuse scandal," Barron says. "I can say that for priests it's been horrific, because our work is just compromised in every way, it's undermined. I realize when anyone sees me wearing a Roman collar, they're probably to this day, at some level, making a judgment about me."

To begin with, Barron makes no bones about just how devastating the clerical sexual abuse scandals have been in terms of the Catholic Church's moral authority and its credibility in the public arena.

"It will be mentioned in a thousand years when they say 'Crusades and witch hunts,'" he says. "They'll add, 'and the sex abuse scandal.' I'm convinced of that. I've said it's the worst crisis certainly in American Catholic Church history, and one of the worst in the whole history of the Church."

It is also, Barron says, one of the most frequent objections he encounters to Catholicism when he's talking to lapsed Catholics, nones, and atheists. Typically, he says his first move is to put the question in a different context, to see if he can get people to think about it from a fresh perspective.

First, I'll say, human beings are a bad lot. I mean, we just tend to go bad. Wherever human beings are involved, there will be conflict and stupidity and corruption and all that, and the Church is no exception. Sometimes with people on the Web, I'll ask, "Are there bad Americans?" The question answers itself. Then I'll ask, "Does that mean American ideals are bad? The Constitution, the American ethos?" Of course there are bad Americans; there are terrible Americans. But what about the American ideal, this quasi-mystical reality? It's still wonderful, and rich, and beautiful in its documents, its heroes, and so on. So, in the Church are there bad church people? Obviously. Are there institutional corruptions of tremendous depth? Again, of course. The Church is full of human beings, who go bad. Does that mean the Church in its essential structure is bad, or in its essential ethos is wicked? Then I'll talk about the Church as the Mystical Body of Christ, so we're not just a human institution, we're not just a coming together of like-minded people. We're a Mystical Body, and we're grounded in Jesus. We are cells and molecules in that body, and therefore in sacraments, in the liturgy, in the Eucharist, in the saints, in our great art, in our ethos and all that, we remain the Spotless Bride of Christ. Both those things are true, and we certainly can't deny the first, that there are people in the Church capable of great evil. I fully acknowledge it, that at times the Church has included all kinds of wicked people doing terrible things.

The good news, according to Barron, is that things have changed dramatically in the Catholic Church in terms of child protection.

"I think generally the last fifteen years have brought massive improvement," he says. "I saw it on the front lines as a seminary professor and later as a seminary rector. The process of screening students for the seminary is extremely careful and rigorous, a bit like an FBI investigation. When [Cardinal Blase] Cupich came in, in fact, he brought in a team of former FBI people to comb through the records and raise every possible question, so I know what we've done to address it. I think it's true what they say, that there's hardly any place safer for kids now than the Catholic Church."

Religion and Violence

Barron believes that the Twin Towers attacks on September 11, 2001, produced one of those cultural tipping points that has conditioned secular attitudes about religion ever since. What it did, he says, is cement the widespread impression that there's something inherent in religion that breeds intolerance, radicalism, and hate, which eventually expresses itself in violence. To resist violence, therefore, for many secularists, means to break the grip that religion holds on people's minds.

"That's a giant problem, maybe the biggest if you think about it," Barron says. "We're all in the post–September 11 universe, where the modern myth that religion by its very nature is violent has become reconfirmed. And because it's irrational, the only recourse we have is violence if we disagree, and of course we're going to disagree, so religion is always breeding violence."

Barron says that view of religion has deep cultural roots.

"It's as old as Spinoza, Kant, and Jefferson in our country," he says. "Related to that is the Bible issue, the fact that the Bible seems to be sanctioning so much violence."

Reaching back into the twentieth century, Barron would also say that Christianity's inability to resist the massive bloodshed that rolled through Europe—even, shockingly often, the willing participation of countless Christians in that bloodshed—caused a crisis that still hasn't been resolved.

"In the heartland of Christianity, you had this orgy of violence, the piling up of corpses, a whole continent drenched in blood," he says. "Secularism is like the crater left behind by the bomb. Christianity was obviously incapable of stopping this violence. Nationalistic ties and ethnic ties were far more important than Christian ties. You have French Christians, Russian Christians, German Christians, all Christians, killing each other on a massive scale, and then Christians standing by while six million Jews are killed. I don't think we've begun to recover from that."

By the end of the twentieth century, as Barron sees it, things hadn't become notably more pacific.

"Look at Rwanda in 1994, which is a 90 percent Christian country," he says. "Christians were hacking each other to death. It's another lesson in human beings tending to go bad," he says, adding that the doctrine of original sin makes such failures explicable and even inevitable.

To respond to all that, Barron begins by making the point that while religion may sometimes be a force that drives people to violence, it's hardly the only one.

"Let's be honest. Far more people have been killed in the name of the secular nation-state than have ever been killed in the name of religion," he says. "The most murderous dictatorships of the twentieth century were not religious but were fiercely antireligious. Charles Taylor makes that point over and over again. I mean, give me a break. It is simply a calumny to suggest that religious people are especially responsible for violence in the world."

In his view, however, the only truly effective way to deal with the objection about religion and violence isn't to deny that many religious people, including many Christians, have engaged in violence. It's instead to insist that's not the whole story. Yes, he argues, Christians are as capable of sin and hatred as anyone else, but over the centuries Christianity has also inspired and sustained some of the most heroic models of nonviolence, healing, and reconciliation the world has ever seen—including the supreme act of mercy in history, meaning the sacrificial death of Christ on the Cross.

> *Christianity starts with an act of violence done to the Son of God. It starts with this horrific event, which opens the door [to redemption]. So, we have to keep telling our story of origins. If you think of religion and violence, religious people causing violence, everyone gets that, it's familiar. But religious people enduring horrific violence in imitation of Christ and his Cross, that's our story, which in my mind is far more compelling. Are people violent for religious reasons? Of course, but they're violent for every other kind of reason too. At the drop of a hat, human beings will turn demonic. Original sin is the only empirically verifiable doctrine. We tend to go bad, so we should never be surprised. But there are heroic stories in there too, and I think that's much more compelling.*

Barron goes on, "Within Christianity we have this very long and ancient tradition of nonviolent resistance, and that's the best way for us to engage the violence in the world," he says. "Look at John Paul II in Poland . . . he was not waving the white flag. He was very actively engaging the enemy, but in a nonviolent way, and I love that."

As a final note about religion and violence, Barron defends the Christian just war tradition, which holds that if certain conditions have been met, the use of armed force to stop an unjust aggressor can be morally justified. (He's dubious, however, that any armed conflict in a long time has satisfied those stringent tests, which cover both the cause of the fighting and the means employed in it.)

He's clear that while the Catholic Church always seeks peace, it does not espouse absolute pacifism. At the same time, he says, the Church respects those within its fold who do embrace nonviolence and believes that "we've underplayed the power of that tradition.

Many years ago, when I was at Notre Dame for my sabbatical year, Cardinal George came and gave a talk and Q & A. Michael Baxter [a Catholic theologian who defends "Catholic pacifism"] was there at the time, and he rose to ask, "Tell me about your view on nonviolence." George said, the Church needs the nonviolent the way it needs celibates. He said living as a celibate is a witness to an eschatological way of being [meaning what life will be like in Heaven]. Then he said, "I don't want everyone to be a celibate, and I don't want everyone to be nonviolent. But I do want pacifists to be present in the life of the Church to give an eschatological witness, a glimpse of how things will eventually be in Heaven." I thought that's a good way to balance things. I don't want my president to be nonviolent, because he has an obligation to defend our basic rights. But, as George said to Baxter, I want you operative as an eschatological witness.

Chapter Nine

BARRON THE BISHOP

As Robert Barron tells the story, no one was more surprised than he was in July 2015 when he was named a new auxiliary bishop in the Archdiocese of Los Angeles, serving under Archbishop José Gomez. To set the scene, Barron says he was in his residence at Chicago's Mundelein Seminary one lazy Sunday afternoon, stretched out on his couch watching some golf on TV.

"I love to do that on Sunday. I play golf, and that's the sport I love to watch the most on television. I could spend hours watching golf," he says.

(When I pointed out to Barron that that was a fairly shocking thing for someone who describes himself as an evangelist for baseball to say, he tried valiantly to argue for a both/and perspective. For the record, in all the hours I spent speaking with Barron for this book, it was the one time I found him completely unpersuasive.)

Earlier that Sunday, Barron had celebrated Mass and then had lunch with a Word on Fire benefactor, so he was looking forward to some downtime. Out of the blue, his private line rang, which struck him as odd because during the summer the seminarians are away and calls rarely come in during off-hours. When he answered, he heard the voice of Italian Archbishop Carlo Maria Viganò, at the time still the papal nuncio to the United

States. (Viganò was later replaced by French Archbishop Christoph Pierre.)

For those unfamiliar with the term, the *nuncio* is the pope's ambassador in a given country. (The term comes from the Latin word *nuntius*, which means "messenger.") Although the nuncio is the pope's representative to the government of the country in which he serves, he also plays a lead role in the selection of new bishops in that country, and is therefore the one who calls the man who's been selected to inform him of the appointment.

To this day, Barron says, he doesn't know how Viganò got his private number—though he concedes that if the nuncio asks a fellow cleric for somebody's digits, he'll probably get them. In this case, Barron says the call informing him that he was to relocate to Los Angeles and become an auxiliary bishop lasted only about a minute—and the only reason it took that long, he says, was because Barron, born and bred in Chicago, thought perhaps Viganò was confused, mixing L.A. up with the Windy City, so he interrupted to be sure. (Barron's perplexity was understandable, since about 95 percent of the time when a priest is named an auxiliary bishop, it's in the diocese where he's already serving. That was the case, for instance, with the two new auxiliaries named along with Barron. In fact, Viganò did indeed mean Los Angeles, telling Barron, "We're sending you a long way from home.")

The usual protocol in these situations is that the nuncio asks the candidate if he accepts the appointment, which theoretically leaves open the possibility that someone might refuse—although, given the emphasis on obedience in clerical culture, it's generally understood that the expected reply is yes.

When the moment came that he was asked if he accepted, Barron says he flashed back on conversations he'd had over the years with the late Cardinal Francis George of Chicago, who always told him that he didn't like it when someone turned down a bishop's appointment—rather than finding it humble, he said, George always regarded it as "cowardly and disloyal."

"I said that if it's what the Holy Father wants, I don't know how I can say no," Barron says. "That's how I felt. Unless I'm dying, or there's some dire reason, I couldn't imagine saying no."

One thing that might have entered Barron's mind when he learned of his appointment as a bishop, but that he says never actually occurred to him, might have been the potential parallel with Fulton Sheen. On the heels of Sheen's massive success as a television personality and evangelist, he was named the Bishop of Rochester, New York, in October 1966, his tenure lasting only three years, until he moved on in October 1969.

By most accounts, it was not a happy time. Sheen was an unquestionably gifted orator and teacher, but as an administrator, he didn't seem to fare particularly well. His tenure came in the turbulent period after Vatican II, and perhaps the only area in which Sheen got high marks was irritating everyone almost equally. Liberals saw him as a throwback to the preconciliar Church, calling his decision-making style authoritarian and his positions on faith and morals unenlightened. Conservatives, on the other hand, chafed at his opposition to the war in Vietnam and his support of the Civil Rights movement. Moreover, because he'd had a falling-out with New York's influential Cardinal Francis Spellman, most of Sheen's fellow bishops kept their distance.

Since Barron's résumé is likewise focused more on preaching, teaching, and media work than on governance, he might reasonably have feared that a similar fate could be in store for him. In reality, though, he says the thought never crossed his mind.

"Sheen was at the end of his career," he says. "He was transferred to Rochester as the diocesan bishop in his seventies. Some say it was Spellman's attempt to take one last shot at him. I must say, the idea of any comparison with my situation didn't really occur to me."

Although Barron is palpably sincere when he says he was "flabbergasted," in all honesty, the fact that he became a bishop really shouldn't have been that much of a surprise. For one thing, serving as a seminary rector is one time-honored and reliable path to the episcopacy, not just in the United States but around the world. For another, as we've seen, the "New Evangelization" has been a towering priority for the Catholic Church since the era of Pope John Paul II, and on the contemporary American landscape, Barron is widely regarded as one of its most effective agents and role models. Even the decision to ship him off to Los Angeles makes sense in that light, since L.A. is Hollywood, it's the entertainment and pop culture capital of the world, and if anyone's going to have luck evangelizing that world, it may well be Barron.

In fact, probably the only plausible reason he wouldn't have been made a bishop at some point might have been a feeling that he'd actually be more valuable to the Catholic Church as a full-time evangelist. That, however, is not how things broke, and so Barron set off to Los Angeles in the fall of 2015 and threw himself into his new role.

MARCHING ORDERS

Both by conviction and by instinct, Barron is always extremely respectful of the Church's chain of command. As a result, after he was named to Los Angeles, his first move wasn't to elaborate a personal vision of how he saw his new responsibilities but rather to reach out to his new boss, Archbishop José Gomez, to find out what he wanted from his new auxiliary. Barron says that he called Gomez within a half hour of speaking to the nuncio, but that call was largely devoted to the logistics of announcing his transition rather than discussing a mission statement for his role.

As it happens, Barron says he'd met Gomez only twice before that moment, and the second occasion was a chance encounter in which the only words that passed between the two men involved Barron commenting that it looked as if Gomez had dropped some weight.

"So, I called him and said, 'Archbishop, this is Bob Barron. I guess I'm coming out your way.' He said yes, and I said, 'Well, what's next? What do I do?' He answered, 'We're making the announcement on July 21.' Stupidly, I said, 'I presume that's in L.A.?' He said, 'Well, yes!' He said we'll make the announcement, and that I'd stay at his house. That was it.

"My memory of that day is that I'm in this guest room at the residence in Los Angeles, across from the cathedral," he says. "I'm looking out from the second floor, where you can see the Hollywood sign, and I'm thinking, What happened to me? Where am I? It was just surreal."

The Archdiocese of Los Angeles, with a Catholic population north of 4 million, is the largest ecclesiastical jurisdiction in the country, and one of the biggest in the world. It's so sprawling that for administrative purposes it's divided into five pastoral regions. Gomez tapped Barron to head the region centered on Santa Barbara.

"To be honest I didn't know where Santa Barbara was," Barron says. "I knew it was a city in Southern California, but I had to go to Google to find out exactly where it was. Then everyone said, 'Oh, gosh, Santa Barbara, that's great.'" (A popular tourist destination, Santa Barbara is known as among the most beautiful, and affluent, settings in Southern California.)

Shortly after Barron arrived, Gomez told him he'd drive him out to Ventura to meet the priests who acted as deans of his new pastoral region. In the car on the way back, Barron recalls, he finally had the chance to ask his superior, "What do you want me to do?" Barron says the archbishop pondered the question for a while, and then gave a response that, for those who know Gomez, is vintage in its directness and clarity.

Gomez told him, "Be present to the people, give them hope, and teach them doctrine."

"I remember saying to him, 'Good. I got that,'" Barron says. "'I can do that.'"

In trying to act on that job description—providing presence, hope, and doctrine to his people—Barron says he's found the experience of serving as a bishop deeply rewarding.

Presence

Barron says that meeting his people has been a priority from day one. Characteristically, it wasn't simply a pastoral instinct but also the product of a deep theological conviction born of decades of reading and study about what it means to be a bishop.

I want to be physically present, so I made sure I got out of this house every day during the school year, when things are really busy. From September until early June I was somewhere basically every day, whether it was a hospital, a parish, a deanery meeting, or whatever. In terms of confirmations, there were thirty-eight of them that first year. I felt very strongly about that. I wanted to get to know my region, and I wanted to be personally present so people can see me. I'm big on the bishop as symbol. I go back to Johann Adam Möhler [a nineteenth-century German Catholic theologian], who said that you need to have a single person who symbolizes the unity and the faith in a given area. That's why the parish needs a pastor, because without a pastor, they don't know who they are. The region needs a bishop to know who they are. I represent the apostolic faith, the archbishop, and the Church. I take that really seriously, and I try to express it in the first place with my physical presence.

One discovery produced by that ministry of presence, Barron says, was that despite stereotypes of Santa Barbara as posh and privileged, that's not the whole story in his region.

"I discovered a lot of economic inequity, a lot of poverty," he says. "The gang violence really surprised me. You knew about South-Central and East L.A., but out here I didn't realize it. There's also homelessness. You walk down State Street, and further down the water and towards the real trendy parts of town, and you find a lot of homelessness in Santa Barbara.

"I remember this letter I got, a really articulate letter, from a parishioner in Santa Maria, a town in the far northern section of my region. He said, 'Bishop, I'm really concerned about the gang violence up here,'" Barron recounts. "I thought that area was bucolic, but there were hospitals filled with gunshot victims. So we invited the parishioner to come to a deanery meeting and talk to the priests about it."

In general, Barron says, his drive to be present has reawakened a love for the pastor's role he hadn't had much chance to indulge for a while.

"One thing I've loved about being auxiliary bishop is, it's a rediscovery of the pastoral side," he says. "I did full-time pastoral work years ago, but not for a long time. But I do it a lot now, going out to see people, talking about prayer, talking to schoolkids and teen groups, trying to solve some practical problems. It's all stuff I did years ago, but during my time as an academic, I didn't do it that much.

"What I like best about being a bishop now is the liturgical side of it," he says. "I like being in a parish, saying Mass, preaching, and greeting the people. I like confirmations. I like being out . . . for instance, at a school Mass. I'll say Mass and preach and reach out to the kids. I like that part of being a bishop. You're like the pastor of a big parish. So the Santa Barbara region is my parish, and I love greeting people and reaching out."

Hope

In terms of offering hope, Barron is well aware that his ministry in Los Angeles unfolds against the backdrop of the clerical sexual abuse scandals. Los Angeles was especially hard-hit by the crisis, with cases that reached all the way back to the 1930s and continued through the 1990s coming to light in the 2000s. The archdiocese reached a settlement in 2007 with 508 victims for $600 million, which was the largest single payout ever made by the Catholic Church to resolve sex abuse litigation. To help fund it, a twelve-story Archdiocesan Catholic Center had to be sold off. Former Cardinal Roger Mahony's handling of the scandals came under fire, and when he resigned, in March 2011, many Los Angeles–area Catholics believed he was doing so in disgrace.

Though Gomez didn't say so explicitly, Barron is certain that the marching orders he was given were a product of that experience.

"I'm sure what he told me—give them hope, be present, and teach doctrine—was born of the struggles out here over the last fifteen years," he says. "I think people got demoralized about the Church, and about everything that had happened."

In that context, Barron says, he realizes that offering a hopeful, passionate vision of Catholic life is especially important.

I try to do it by being joyful, and reminding people that there's more to the Church than the sex abuse scandal. I tell them the Church is an ancient community, going back to Jesus himself, and bearing the hope of the Cross and resurrection. I try to project a joyful, confident presence. To be honest, I think the smile goes a long way. I hope they see in me a joyfulness in being Catholic, that there's more to it than the scandal we've been through—without for a second denying those scandals, and how terrible they were, but there's more to it than that. I like to believe that gives people hope.

Doctrine

In many ways, when Archbishop Gomez pressed Barron to make sure he delivers doctrine to his people, he was preaching to the choir. As we've seen repeatedly through this book, a dumbed-down, "beige Catholicism" has been the defining bête noire of Barron's career, by far the aspect of the post–Vatican II period that irritated him the most. He takes as an article of faith that people, including youth, are capable of handling a far more sophisticated version of what faith means than they often get, and failure to provide them with it often has left them ill equipped to handle the onslaughts of secular modernity.

I've taken that charge to present doctrine very seriously. I'm a teacher by nature, and I've taught doctrine for years, but now I'm not going to do it in the context of a classroom. I probably won't mention Möhler and Schleiermacher too often from the pulpit. Nevertheless, I remember doing a homily on Holy Thursday down at the Ventura mission. It was great. We had a Eucharistic procession down the streets, and it's such a beautiful place. I gave a rip-snorting homily on transubstantiation, without using the word, but I talked about the real presence and I did it in a doctrinal way. I've stressed the doctrinal side as a bishop, because I do think there's been drift on that score. I've tried to preach and teach here in a more doctrinally conscious way: "Who's God?" "Who are we?" "What's sin?"

*"What's redemption?" "What's eternal life?" "What's the Eu-
charist?" "What's the Mass?" I've done that partly because the
archbishop asked me to, and partly because I was already convinced it's important. Whenever I get somewhere, I'm going
to teach. I'll do other things too, but I want to teach while I'm
here.*

THE BISHOP OF HOLLYWOOD?

One thing about the Catholic Church that's constantly surprising to people, including most Catholics, is that new bishops are
almost never given any explanation of why they were chosen, who
put them forward, or what the logic was for assigning them to this
particular job. Talk to most bishops even years after their appoint-
ments, and they'll tell you they still have no idea why it happened.

For this reason, trying to explain why so-and-so was sent to a
particular place is a time-honored Catholic parlor game. After the
news broke that Barron was going to Los Angeles, two popular
theories quickly made the rounds.

One was essentially political. By that stage, Cardinal Francis
George had given way in Chicago to Archbishop Blase Cupich,
today also a cardinal, who's widely perceived as more liberal than
his predecessor. Though Barron chafes at the liberal-conservative
dichotomy, he does clearly identify himself as "postliberal," so the
thinking was that he might be more congenial to Gomez, who's
a protégé of Archbishop Charles Chaput in Philadelphia, a hero
to the Church's conservative wing, and seen as fairly by-the-book
when it comes to matters of doctrine.

Barron, however, says Cupich had been nothing but encour-
aging to him since he arrived.

"I worked very well with Cupich," Barron says. "When he
arrived in Chicago, I was rector of the seminary. He never said

a word to me about anything he thought was out of line. Once, there was a very difficult situation, where I had to make a tough call, and Cupich was right with me all the way. There was even a lot of flak afterwards, and he was right in my camp."

Further, Barron says, given that he and Gomez hardly knew each other before July 2015, he finds any political reading of his appointment a stretch.

"If there was some ideological confluence, nobody ever told me about it," he says. "I exchanged a handful of words with him. I can't imagine there was some grand scheme, at least not that I know of."

The more popular way of adding two plus two to get four was to posit that because Barron is America's most visible and effective media priest, he was being shipped off to the West Coast to evangelize the highly secular entertainment and communications businesses.

Barron sees the logic of that hypothesis, yet he insists it was never part of the plan as it was presented to him.

"When I came out here, the reports were 'Barron Goes to Hollywood,' and 'Media Star Goes to L.A.' Well, maybe, but nobody ever said that to me. Later, I thought maybe that did have something to do with it, not in terms of the appointment itself, but maybe in the wake of it. However, nobody ever said that to me, either at first or down the line."

Notably, of course, evangelizing Hollywood also was not part of the marching orders that Gomez delivered to his new auxiliary bishop.

"I honestly don't feel like, boy, I'm here to reach out to Hollywood. Nobody ever told me that, and I've never received it as a mission," Barron says.

He does acknowledge that his media experience and contacts in the industry do, in a sense, present a natural advantage in the Los Angeles area but says he wouldn't overstress it.

I suppose it's helpful, to a degree. I have been reaching out to the entertainment community here, and people involved in media. In terms of my own media work, I don't know. We had it pretty well established and were able to continue it in Chicago, and now it's here. I wouldn't say that being here necessarily makes my Word on Fire work more efficacious. The contacts I've made, and the people in the entertainment world I know, are valuable, but in terms of the actual operation of what I do as an evangelist, it's not really that significant. I think we had that in place before, we had so many projects already under way that we've continued, and it doesn't have much to do with being in Los Angeles.

Granted, no one has ever charged him with trying to plant the flag of the faith in Hollywood or the entertainment industry. Still, given his background, aptitudes, and interests, it does seem a fairly natural challenge for Barron to take on. He says he does want to move in that direction, but his is a deliberately patient, quiet, and largely behind-the-scenes approach.

I'd like to be involved with that, and I've made some inroads with it. I'd like to try to evangelize people who are heavily involved in the entertainment world, and to give them a more substantial sense of the Church and Christianity. I prefer a quieter approach, one that reaches out directly to people. I don't feel it as some pressing obligation that I have, but I would like to pursue it. It's just been very preliminary at this point, but we're trying to look at things like retreats and days of reflection for Hollywood people such as screenwriters, actors, producers, et cetera. I've got a couple contacts in L.A. who know that world pretty well, and they've been in dialogue with me. Through them, I've reached out to other people. We're working on it, and I'd say the quieter, more direct evangelization of those involved in that world is a better path.

Once the ball gets rolling, Barron says, one role model he may propose to entertainment professionals is the great American Catholic novelist Flannery O'Connor, whose best-known collections of short stories include *A Good Man Is Hard to Find* (1955) and *Everything That Rises Must Converge* (1965).

"Flannery O'Connor gives you all the drama you want, all the weirdness, but you're communicating the real essential stuff of Christianity," he says.

THE BISHOP AND THE UNIVERSAL CHURCH

Theologically speaking, when Robert Barron became a bishop, he took on responsibilities not simply to the Archdiocese of Los Angeles or his own pastoral region but to the entire universal Catholic Church. Every one of the more than five thousand Catholic bishops around the world is understood to be part of what's called the College of Bishops, which is seen as the successor to the group of apostles who followed Jesus, and who led the early Church after his ascension into Heaven. Just as the apostles formed a college around Jesus, meaning a body of people united in a single purpose, Catholic theology holds that today the bishops form a college around the pope. As a result, they're all considered to have obligations to the whole Church throughout the world.

Barron obviously knew all that well before his appointment, but he says that one experience in particular since he became a bishop brought the point home to him in a new way. That experience was attending an annual course in Rome sponsored by the Vatican for newly appointed bishops around the world, which is known colloquially as "baby bishops' school." Because the courses are typically held in September and Barron wasn't ordained as a bishop until September 8, 2015, he missed that year's edition, and so he ended up going in September 2016.

"It was a great experience," he says. "It's a bit like a summer camp for bishops, because you stay at a place called the Regina Apostolorum, about five miles west of St. Peter's and the Vatican. It's a seminary, and so my room was a seminary room. It reminded me of my college seminary days. The bed was about two and a half feet wide, and we were all commenting on how the first couple of nights we were in great danger of rolling out and falling on the floor! The meals were good, I must say, in the typical Italian style."

The most impressive thing about the program, he says, was how it brought home the universality of the Church.

The great thing about it was that I was with 157 other bishops, from all over the world. You'd come down for meals and you'd be at table with someone from Ecuador, someone from India, someone from Syria, someone from Boston . . . it made for a very lively exchange. Sometimes I was with English speakers. I can handle French fine, and there were a number of Canadians, a number of French, and then Francophone Africans, so I was able to handle that pretty well. My Spanish is okay, so I spoke some Spanish. My Italian is basically restaurant Italian, so I would try to make my way occasionally in Italian. It was a very illuminating process, and that was the best part of it, actually. There was a whole series of talks, from some pretty high curial officials in Rome. But the best part of it, frankly, was just getting to know these bishops from around the world.

At the end of the day, Barron says the experience of baby bishops' school left a deep impression.

I would say I have a broader sense of the Church's life. Yes, I'm the regional bishop of Santa Barbara, but I'm also a bishop of the Catholic Church. I knew that, of course, but that sensibility is stronger in me now. Yes, you're assigned to this place, and there's something very local about my responsibility. But I'm also a successor of the apostles and a bishop of the Catholic Church. I'm ordained a bishop not just for L.A., but for the whole Church. That can sound grandiose, and I don't mean it in that way, but you've got this truly international responsibility. More important than my status as an American is my status as a Catholic, and as a Catholic bishop somehow connected to all the bishops of the world. That has impacted me, I think, and changed my consciousness.

As it happened, baby bishops' school also gave Barron the chance to meet Pope Francis for the first time when he addressed and then greeted the new bishops. It turned out to be quite the memorable exchange.

It was a great moment. We were there with 157 bishops, and to the pope's great credit, he gave a thirty-minute talk to us, it was not a short talk, and then he greeted every single bishop. I thought maybe he'd greet some, but it was every single one of us. It took a good hour to get through that process. That's an eighty-year-old guy showing a lot of stamina! The three of us who were newly appointed for Los Angeles, Bishop Joe Brennan, Bishop Dave O'Connell, and myself, were together in line. In the past, Pope Francis had referred to us, when talking to Gomez, as "your triplets," as in "How are your triplets doing?" So, when Bishop Brennan went up, he said, "I'm one of the triplets from Los Angeles." I was two people behind him, and I saw the pope's face light up. He said, "Oh, where are the

other two?" We were right there, so we gathered around him.
He spoke to Joe for a little bit, and then to Bishop O'Connell.
Finally he turned to me, and I said, "Hello, Holy Father, I'm
Bishop Barron." He said, "Ah, el Gran Predicador!" meaning
"the Great Preacher," and then something like "who makes the
airwaves tremble." I'm choosing to take that in a positive way!
I was very touched, because, honestly, I didn't know if he knew
me from Adam, or anything about the work I was doing. It
was very moving . . . I'm still kind of going on the fumes of
that. It was very moving to be with him, he's super gracious,
and it was wonderful.

BARRON AND *AMORIS LAETITIA*

Though Catholic bishops are constantly pressed to give their views on virtually every issue confronting the Church, they're facing special pressure today to address the question of whether divorced and civilly remarried Catholics should, after a process of discernment with a priest or bishop, be able to receive Communion. Under traditional Church rules the answer has been no, but in a document on the family and married life titled *Amoris Laetitia*, released in April 2016, Pope Francis appeared to open the door to a cautious yes.

On the other hand, Pope Francis insisted that he did not intend to change Church teaching or Church law on marriage, and he clearly instructed priests that they were not to act on their own but rather to await guidance from their bishop. As a result, bishops around the world have been called upon to clarify how *Amoris Laetitia* will be implemented in their dioceses. Some have determined that the document does not reverse the traditional position, others have found that it creates new possibilities for allowing people to approach the sacraments, and many have not (yet) said anything at all. To date, Pope Francis has resisted attempts to compel him to say something more definitive, which means that, for now, the ball is often in the court of the local bishop.

In Los Angeles, determining the pastoral consequences of *Amoris Laetitia* or anything else does not fall primarily on Barron; rather it's the responsibility of Archbishop Gomez. Still, Barron understands how important the issue has become in the life of the Church, and as he generally does, offers a balanced and nuanced perspective.

> *I read [what Pope Francis said about the divorced and remarried receiving Communion] in terms of what I learned in the seminary years ago, which is that there's a difference between the objective assessment of a situation and the subjective assessment of guilt and responsibility. Those are two different moves, epistemologically. One is relatively easy, in that you can look [at a situation] and say, "Yes, that state of affairs is objectively wrong." The other move is much more complicated. It's the sort of thing a confessor has to do. The question is, To what degree are you responsible for this situation? The pope says, quite rightly it seems to me, you can't simply look out and say any such situation is necessarily a mortal sin. I can say it's less than the moral ideal the Church calls for, but I can't say ipso facto that the person involved is in a state of mortal sin. I've got to do a much more thorough assessment of knowledge, engagement of both mind and will, and mitigating factors. I think that's what he's saying, and to me that's classical Catholic moral theology.*

Barron insists that none of that assessment of subjective responsibility involves any reversal of Church teaching.

"Someone in a state of mortal sin ought not to approach Communion, true. It's been true, and it remains true," he says. "But are you in a state of mortal sin? That's a different question than whether you're doing something objectively wrong. That second question is subtler. It seems to me he's putting stress on that, and emphasizing the importance of the distinction."

Barron also is not in agreement with some Catholics who find the teaching in *Amoris* part of a pattern under Pope Francis of downplaying the Church's moral expectations.

"As I read Chapter 8 [the section of *Amoris* touching on the Communion question], I go back to the first part of the letter," he says. "Francis is really strong on the moral standards. He says a gay relationship is not even analogous to what we mean by marriage; he says very strong things about gender ideology, about ideological colonization. I don't see him dialing down the ideals. I see him dialing up the shepherd's role, and I think that's the right combination."

As for the specter of different bishops appearing to offer different guidance, Barron says that if people understand what's actually going on, there's no problem with it.

> *It would be a problem if, and only if, different answers were being affirmed at the objective level. If one set of bishops were to say, "No, it's no longer objectively wrong to be divorced and remarried,'" then we'd have a serious problem. But I think what's happening is that* Amoris *is bringing more explicitly to expression what's always been assumed at the pastoral level, and that's not a contradiction. I think that's acknowledging the complexity of these different subjective discernments. It's not at all that one thing is objectively wrong in Bavaria, but it's okay in Buenos Aires. I would argue that we're not making that claim, and Francis is not making that claim.*

"You still have to say there's something objectively wrong, but the subjective apprehension of sin is a separate issue," he says. "In that sense, the subtlety or indirection of the pope's approach in *Amoris* is right. It's appropriate, because you're talking about a different epistemological level. The very ambiguity of it is appropriate to that level of discernment."

BARRON AND TRUMP

Speaking in a strictly theological key once more, there is no such thing as "the American Catholic Church," or "the German Church," or anything else. The Catholic Church is universal, not nationalistic, and historically it's fought titanic battles to prevent national loyalties from swamping that universal instinct— efforts to suppress Gallicanism in France in the seventeenth century, Josephinism in the Austrian Empire, and Febronianism in Germany in the eighteenth century, and even "Americanism" in the United States in the nineteenth century, are all cases in point. In Catholicism, neither teaching nor authority is decided on the basis of national boundaries. Moreover, bishops do not answer to a national superior but are directly accountable only to the pope.

Despite all that, national conferences of bishops today are among the most important and influential institutions in the Church. Bishops have long seen value in organizing themselves at the national level, because doing so allows them to pool resources, act in a coordinated fashion, achieve economies of scale, and engage national affairs more effectively. The United States Conference of Catholic Bishops (USCCB), which brings together all the bishops in the country, is a leading case in point.

As a result, when a new bishop is appointed in the United States, he becomes a member of the conference and is expected to take on responsibilities at the national level.

"Ipso facto you've got this national level, so you're drawn into the conference of bishops and so there's that dimension to it as well," Barron says.

We've already seen one example of that aspect of the job, with Barron's election in November 2016 as chair of the bishops' Committee on Evangelization and Catechesis. (The outcome was seen as a tribute to Barron and his reputation, since it's rare for a newly appointed auxiliary bishop to be elected to a chairmanship that quickly.)

"Afterwards, Cardinal Wuerl [of Washington] talked to me. Then Cardinal O'Malley of Boston came up to say, 'I want to congratulate you.' I said, with all sincerity, 'I need a crash course in the USCCB,' and he looked at me kind of puzzled, but it's true. I don't really know the inner workings of the USCCB."

At least Barron is clear on what his priorities—or to put it more accurately, priority—should be.

"What I want to do, and I'll see if this flies, is focus on the nones. Getting after the nones should be a major priority—find them, bring them back, engage them, answer their questions. We're losing young people in droves, and so we need to get them back. I think that should be a priority when it comes to evangelization."

Part of what it means to be a bishop, therefore, is to be engaged at the national level, including in the social and political life of the country. An especially acute form that engagement often takes is reacting to the policies and priorities of whoever happens to be the U.S. president, never more so than in the era of the ever-controversial President Donald Trump.

As we've seen, Barron is not by nature a political animal (even if Aristotle defined all human beings as such). He doesn't really care for the dynamics of partisan politics, and in any event, his real passion is the life of the mind, as well as the evangelizing efforts to which his intellectual and pastoral pursuits lend themselves. Nevertheless, he understands that especially now as a bishop, he can't stay completely out of the fray, because there are important Gospel principles at stake and people rightly expect him to express them.

To begin with, Barron confessed he was as "flummoxed" by Trump's victory as many other people were, assuming that in the end, Hillary Clinton would prevail.

"We had a meeting here at the house on election night with the deans of my region, and when it was over, I said, 'Well, let's go and watch the results.' We all thought we knew what was going to happen, so it was a complete surprise."

The first lesson Barron draws from the rise of Donald Trump is one that's not terribly contested, which is that it reflects the various ways in which America has become a fractured society.

"It does say we're pretty divided, and I get that," Barron says. You see the election results, and then you see the Women's March and all that, and the conclusion is that we're a pretty divided country. It's certainly witness to the polarization."

In addition, Barron believes the Trump phenomenon illustrates the way in which a significant portion of the country felt neglected.

"I agree with those analysts who say there had been a certain ignoring of a large swath of the country, which reacted rather negatively to that," he says. "There's an anger within the body politic that's reflected in the election of Trump, including people who have felt ignored and excluded from the process."

In terms of Trump's early moves, Barron resists being enrolled in the ranks of either enthusiasts or inveterate critics. We spoke in January 2017, so Barron was not reacting to anything Trump has done since that point or to the various statements the U.S. Conference of Catholic Bishops has issued regarding aspects of Trump's policies.

"I think Trump does address some things that probably needed addressing, that weren't being talked about adequately," he says. "I approved of the early moves about abortion, for instance. I like the language he's used with the press about the March for Life, so I think that's good. I think those things probably were overlooked."

As for Trump's executive orders to restrict immigration and the flow of refugees, Barron says, "I wrestle with it.

The Church has the stance of inclusivity. The Church doesn't want to divide families, the Church doesn't want to build walls, but fundamentally the Church wants to build bridges. At the same time, I think that we as a Church, and we as bishops, have been inadequate in articulating more completely what we mean when we say a country has a right to defend its borders. Almost everyone agrees that the way Trump is doing it is excessive, that building walls and so on is not advisable. That said, we pay lip service to the principle that borders can and should be defended, but in my judgment, we don't articulate sufficiently what that would look like. Do we have a program of five steps that says, "Here's a legitimate way to enforce immigration laws"? No, we don't. Looking to the future, that's something that concerns me. Yes, our message has to be building bridges rather than walls, but that doesn't mean we want to encourage completely unrestricted movement. Governments need to strike the right balance, and we could probably be of more help in that regard.

Chapter Ten

FROM MINISTRY TO MOVEMENT

Robert Barron was born on November 19, 1959. Among other things, that apparently means he's a Scorpio. My astrologically literate neighbor believes his star sign helps account for both his deep spirituality and his love of study, and when I suggested that given his faith and worldview there are probably better explanations, she simply scoffed. In any event, his birth date also means that at the time of this writing, he was fifty-seven. By that stage, one has usually mastered the lesson that life is what happens while you're making other plans, an especially applicable insight given Barron's recent experience of unexpectedly being named a bishop.

Dreaming, however, is different than planning, even if the two can be related—dreams sometimes turn into goals, then into plans, and if luck and providence are on your side, plans can become reality. To the extent he has plans right now, Barron says, they're to be the best bishop he can for the people of the Santa Barbara pastoral region, to continue his evangelizing work in various venues, and to remain engaged as a theologian and scholar.

Barron also, however, has a dream. He readily concedes that the extent to which that dream may become real depends on a variety of circumstances, many of which are not under his control, but it's his dream nevertheless: to see his Word on Fire ministry become a full-fledged movement within the Catholic Church, dedicated to the work of the New Evangelization.

"In many ways, I think the Word on Fire ministry is already developing into a kind of movement, and it was Cardinal Francis George who identified that," he says. "Several years ago, he came to our little chapel in Chicago, where we had our offices, and he gave a homily along those lines, suggesting Word on Fire was becoming a movement. That stayed in my mind."

By *movement,* Barron is referring to a vast galaxy of new groups in Catholicism that have sprung up mostly in the twentieth century, many in the period after the Second Vatican Council, which generally have the goal of bringing laypeople together—sometimes together with clergy, sometimes not—and forming them in a particular spirituality, then turning them loose to pursue some sort of mission in the world. Well-known examples include Communion and Liberation, the Neocatechumenate, the Community of Sant'Egidio, the Schoenstatt movement, L'Arche, the Focolare, and the Emmanuel Community.

One complicating factor is that while each of the new movements has had a charismatic founder with a clear vision of what he or she wanted the group to achieve, which Barron certainly supplies, those founders weren't simultaneously bishops who carried administrative and leadership responsibilities for the wider Church. Another is that while the new movements have had great success in other parts of the world, including Europe and Latin America, they haven't been especially successful in the United States, where the typical Catholic still sees the parish as the point of contact with the Church and the primary setting for spiritual development.

Despite those obstacles, Barron is unwilling to let go. He's determined that Word on Fire shouldn't be exclusively about him, that it responds to a legitimate need of the age, and he wants it to continue. Further, he's convinced that what Word on Fire is about isn't just a set of projects or a commitment to "best practices" in the media realm but is an authentic spiritual path that lends itself in a particularly effective way to bringing the postmodern world to the faith, or at least to a more sympathetic consideration of the faith.

To understand Barron's dream, we first have to understand exactly what movements are within Catholicism, and the role they've come to play in the contemporary Church.

THE NEW MOVEMENTS

The "new movements" arose during the twentieth century primarily as a way to form and mobilize laity, so they would see themselves as the front-line carriers of the Church's mission. To date, the Vatican has granted canonical status to more than 120 of these new lay movements, virtually all of them founded within the last one hundred years. During that time, the movements have spawned a bewildering variety of projects, missions, and institutions, to say nothing of controversy. Some accuse the movements of representing a "parallel Church," essentially separate from the regular pastoral life of parishes and dioceses. At their best, however, they encourage laity to see themselves as missionaries in their own walks of life, transforming the secular world from the inside out.

Barron sees the movements as one way of living out the vision of the lay role in the Church propounded by the Second Vatican Council.

> They're a postconciliar phenomenon, and in some ways they're exactly what the council was hoping for. I think they've had an impact on the life of the Church. Their impact will increase, I think, as time goes on. The combination between laity and clergy is a real Vatican II sort of thing, and Word on Fire has been that in spades. We've had laypeople from the beginning

who've been supremely active, even though it's had a clear cler-
ical direction, so I like that model.

Beyond Vatican II, St. John Paul II, who was a great cham-
pion of the new movements, saw them as an authentic eruption
of the Holy Spirit in our time, and as a way of reviving the charismatic dimension of the Church alongside its institutional and
bureaucratic structures. As an expression of that point, John Paul
adopted the custom of holding a major gathering of the movements in St. Peter's Square in Rome on Pentecost Sunday. Asked
if he can see himself one day in the square for that festival alongside other founders, Barron says it's a "really attractive" vision.

"We're moving in our discernment of it," he says. "I'd really
like it to happen."

It's easier to document the number of movements than it is to
establish exactly how many Catholics belong to them, or are influenced by them. Some movements don't have "members" in the
classic sense, and others have small cores of formal members but
wider networks of supporters and collaborators. By most estimates,
the total number of Catholics connected to a movement is relatively small, but their visibility and official favor mean the movements play a disproportionate role in setting the Church's tone.

Brief sketches of three movements—L'Arche, Focolare, and
the Community of Sant'Egidio—will offer a sample of the range
of their activities and outlooks.

L'Arche

Jean Vanier, a Canadian layman and founder of the L'Arche
movement, carries the rare burden of being a public figure widely
flagged as a saint in his own lifetime. Born in Geneva, Swit-
zerland, on September 10, 1928, Vanier is the son of the nineteenth governor-general of Canada, Georges-Philéas Vanier, and

his wife, Pauline Archer Vanier. Sainthood causes for both have been launched in Canada. His father was the Canadian ambassador to France at the end of the Second World War, where the young Vanier saw ex-inmates arriving from Buchenwald, Bergen-Belsen, and Dachau. He later described "their white and blue uniforms . . . They were skeletons. That vision has remained with me—what human beings can do to other human beings, how we can hurt and kill each other."

Studying in France, Vanier befriended a chaplain for mentally handicapped men living at Le Val Fleuri, a large institution about an hour by train from Paris. Vanier later moved to the area, where he bought a small, dilapidated house that he called L'Arche, "the Ark"—a reference to Noah's Ark. Vanier welcomed two mentally handicapped men, Raphael and Philippe, into his home on August 4, 1964, marking the birth of L'Arche.

Vanier's movement came to international attention in the mid-1980s, when Father Henri Nouwen, a Catholic priest whose spiritual books have sold in the millions, settled in a L'Arche community in Ontario, Canada. Nouwen had suffered a nervous collapse from the pressures of worldly success, and his friend Vanier suggested L'Arche as a place he might find relief. L'Arche has since grown to some 149 communities in more than thirty-seven countries on five continents. Vanier is no longer its director, but he still lives in a L'Arche community in France.

"L'Arche is an experience born from suffering," Vanier has said. "The terrible suffering of parents, of people with handicaps . . . the aim of being Christian is to reveal the compassionate face of Christ."

Focolare

Founded in Italy in 1943 by laywoman Chiara Lubich, Focolare claims to reach 182 countries, touching 2 million people. Its core idea is universal brotherhood, which prompts the *focolarini,* as members are known, to be especially involved in ecumenism and interreligious dialogue.

As Focolare is structured today, it has three levels of affiliation. Consecrated members take vows of celibacy, live in Focolare communities, and turn over their earnings to the community. Married members turn over what they can afford. Affiliates have a looser connection. All told, there are eighteen Focolare-related groups and associations. While Focolare is unambiguously rooted in Catholic tradition, it also welcomes members from other backgrounds, including Protestants, Anglicans, Orthodox, Jews, Muslims, Hindus, Buddhists, and Sikhs, as well as people with no particular religion. The Focolare constitution requires that the president be a woman, one of the few mixed bodies of women and men to have such a stipulation.

In the United States, one example of the Focolare commitment to unity is its standing dialogue with the American Muslim Society led by Imam W. D. Mohammed, widely considered the moderate alternative to the Nation of Islam. Launched in the mid-1990s, the dialogue has become a model for Christian-Muslim relations in other parts of the world.

The Community of Sant'Egidio

Launched in 1968 by Italian Church historian Andrea Riccardi, then a high school student in Rome, Sant'Egidio ("St. Giles" in English) takes its name from an old Carmelite convent in the Trastevere district of Rome, where early members gathered for worship. Inspired by Vatican II and the leftist student energies of the time, members began living and working among the poor along the city's periphery. They founded "popular schools" for disadvantaged children.

Today, there's a perception that Sant'Egidio is Pope Francis's favorite among the new movements. For instance, when Francis brought several Syrian refugees back to Rome with him aboard the papal plane after a day visit to the Greek island of Lesbos in April 2016, he entrusted their care to Sant'Egidio.

For its work on international conflict resolution, Sant'Egidio is nicknamed "the U.N. of Trastevere." A breakthrough success came on October 4, 1992, when they brokered a peace accord in Mozambique, ending a civil war that had left more than 1 million people dead. The community proudly says the Mozambique deal was "the first intergovernmental agreement ever negotiated by a nongovernmental body."

Sant'Egidio is also active on human rights issues, especially its campaign to abolish the death penalty worldwide. In 2001 the community delivered a petition with 2.7 million signatures to the United Nations supporting abolition of capital punishment. The community also enjoys a reputation for liturgical and spiritual depth. Vespers at the Church of Santa Maria in Trastevere attract overflow crowds, usually composed of a wide cross section of visitors and locals, including a striking number of young adults.

In 1986, when John Paul II called leaders of the world's religions to Assisi to pray for peace, Sant'Egidio welcomed the initiative despite criticism from some quarters that it risked relativism. Every year since, they have sponsored an interreligious gathering to keep "the spirit of Assisi" alive. Members of Sant'Egidio have been leaders in ecumenical and interreligious dialogue, sometimes operating a sort of "back-channel" ecumenism alongside the Church's official dialogues and relationships. Pope Francis traveled to Assisi in 2016 to take part in one of those Sant'Egidio gatherings.

WORD ON FIRE AS A MOVEMENT

We've already heard Barron say that the idea of Word on Fire becoming a movement was first planted in his mind by Cardinal George of Chicago, who in many ways, acted as a mentor for Barron personally as well as a sponsor of his ministry.

"I think he saw Word on Fire as the beginning of something that might grow and have an impact on the wider Church," Barron says. "I think he believed in that, and he wanted it to be part of his legacy. We're very happy to claim him as the grandfather of Word on Fire, and he really was. Very early he got behind it, he gave me the freedom to do the *CATHOLICISM* series, and in all kinds of ways he was the grandfather of the whole movement."

Barron says part of George's enthusiasm for the idea of a movement came from his background as a member of the Oblates of Mary Immaculate religious order, and the story of St. Eugène de Mazenod, who founded the order in Provence, France, in 1816 (it received papal approval in 1826). Mazenod became the Bishop of Marseille in 1837 but continued to be active in leading and inspiring the order.

"De Mazenod was involved in seminary work and he drew a lot of his former students around him," Barron says. "Eventually he became a bishop, yet was the director of this community. I asked George a lot about that, how'd it happen, how'd it start."

Beyond Cardinal George's support and encouragement, Barron says, in some ways the ministry has already been moving in the direction of becoming a movement organically: "It's grown up like a plant," he says. "We didn't really plan it." The basic idea is drawing people, especially young people, not only to a project but to a way of life.

"That's been a great part of the Word on Fire thing," he says. "There's the institutional side, but there's also the movement side, and it's all these young people who have expressed an interest in it. I'm still trying to think it through.

"The idea though came from below," he says. "It came from these kids who approached me about, in their language, an 'order.' They didn't know the right canonical terminology. But, they said, We want to give our lives to this, not just make this our profession."

That desire, Barron says, has gradually given rise to an authentic Word on Fire community.

"There's a community now," he says. "They first came together as people who are dedicated to the work of the ministry, but then a lot of them now pray together, and they are exploring what it means to live a life dedicated to evangelization. They're prayerfully dedicated to a lot of the themes I have been developing in my writing and media work, and they want to make it central. It's both lay and clergy together, although it's in a very seminal form."

To illustrate the way that's worked, Barron tells the story of a chance encounter in Los Angeles.

> *I met a fellow out here in L.A. the day I was announced as a bishop. I walked out of the cathedral, and up comes this young man—a big guy, with tattoos, and he says, "I just want to meet you. You've made such a difference in my life. I came back to the Church because of Word on Fire." Later Father Steve [Grunow] says to me, "Do you know who that was? That was Joe Gloor, who's on MTV." [Gloor hosted a show on MTV called* I Used to Be Fat.*] He's a trainer and a bit of a celebrity. Well, now Joe is the assistant content director for Word on Fire and part of our Word on Fire family.*

Barron says that traveling to Krakow, Poland, in July 2016 for World Youth Day, the massive global gathering of Catholic youth pioneered by Pope John Paul II, helped cement the idea of Word on Fire as a movement, especially the experience of taking part in a high-octane liturgy for English-speaking pilgrims at a center sponsored by the Knights of Columbus.

It just sang to my heart, and one of the great moments of my priesthood was that night. It was dazzling, seeing the banners hanging above those 25,000 kids of St. John Paul II, St. Faustina, and Jerzy Popiełuszko, and St. Maximilian Kolbe, who died within a forty-five-minute drive of that arena. It was overwhelming to me, and I thought of the young people who have been part of our ministry. For example, our first Word on Fire couple, Sean and Rozann Lee, met at Word on Fire, married, and now have two children. And what are their children's names? Kolbe, for St. Maximilian, and Mary Flannery for Flannery O'Connor! That generation is totally on board with everything we've been talking about. When you talk to the younger generation about Church and political machinations, and jockeying for office, they're bored, but what turns them on is "Yes, tell me the story of Maximilian Kolbe again!"

Barron says that while there's a much wider network of millions who follow Word on Fire and perhaps even contribute to it in some way, the core group right now is composed of about ten people, including Brandon Vogt, the content director of the ministry, and Father Steve Grunow, who followed Barron from Chicago. That core group, Barron says, predominantly made up of young people, "is beginning to think self-consciously about this as a movement.

"I feel increasingly strong about it as I get older," Barron says.

You feel your own mortality, and you want something to go on. It's not going to go on if I just keep making videos, and writing books, and all that. It goes on if there's a community around it. Forming that community, that strikes me as more and more important the older I get. It's funny, I'm in my late fifties, and I'm thinking that all the great people were dead before they got to my age! They had short lives. When I was in Krakow for World Youth Day, we visited the Dominican Church of the Holy Trinity, where St. Hyacinth's relics are located. Dominic founds his order, they just get under way, and he says to his friend Hyacinth, "Okay, you go to Krakow," and to other of his followers, "You go to Bologna, you go to Paris," and he just starts sending them. It's the same with St. Francis, who's sending people right and left within months of their coming together. I get that there's a certain urgency about it. We're already kind of a national and global thing, so let's take advantage of it, let's do it.

Given that sense of urgency, Barron says he's anxious to move forward.

"What I want to do now the most is to get the movement off the ground, something that involves both laypeople and priests, and take the vision wider," he says. "I'm very much aware of that, and canonically, institutionally, personally, I want it to happen."

One point that's important for Barron is that the Word on Fire movement needs to bring both clergy and laity together.

"I realize it's got to be more than me, more than just the work, and I want to inspire these younger people that do it," he says. "I was involved in priestly formation for so long, so maybe it'll also be the priests focused vocationally around evangelization."

For that reason, Barron says, the models in the Church to which he's most attracted are groups that bring clergy and laity together around a common spirituality. One example he cited is Opus Dei, which was founded in Spain in 1928 by St. Josemaría Escrivá, with a spirituality premised on the sanctification of ordinary work and seeing one's work as a pathway to holiness. (As a technical matter, Opus Dei is not a movement but a "personal prelature" in canon law, meaning a nongeographical group organized around a particular spiritual path and led by a prelate.)

Though his core group now may be small, Barron says, that's largely because there has been no conscious effort to foster the sort of movement he's describing. Given the wide reach of Word on Fire's platforms, he believes, growth could be rapid.

"I have a feeling once we open the floodgates of all our social media, saying we have this movement and we're inviting people to join at different levels, it could happen very quickly," he says.

A WORD ON FIRE SPIRITUALITY

For a new movement to sustain itself in the Catholic Church, recent history suggests that it needs three things. First is a charismatic founder, whose vision, energy, and personality draw people into the enterprise. Second is a clear mission, not simply a vague desire to "do good" or "love God," which the whole Church shares and for which there's no special need for any new outfit. Third, the movement requires a spirituality that undergirds its mission, a particular kind of formation that no other group in the Church provides in quite the same way.

In effect, without even trying, the nascent Word on Fire movement already has two of those things. Barron could have been selected by Hollywood central casting for the role of charismatic founder—just watching the way young Catholics from around the world reacted to him in the streets of Krakow during the July 2016 World Youth Day, you would have thought you were taking a stroll with Justin Bieber. Moreover, Word on Fire already has a clear sense of purpose, which is the New Evangelization, including bringing the faith to the social media world.

Word on Fire also has the building blocks of a distinctive

spirituality in Barron's writings and talks, and in several of the decisions they've had to make along the way about what makes for effective evangelization and what doesn't. Barron and his core team have elaborated eight core principles.

Here are those pillars of Word on Fire spirituality, none of which will be surprising given the arc of Barron's thought and career.

Unwavering Christocentrism

For a movement inspired by a man whose "big book" as an academic was titled *The Priority of Christ*, and whose major complaint with the post–Vatican II Church was that personal experience took center stage over the encounter with Christ, this principle of Christocentrism seems the obvious place to begin.

"The idea is that everything revolves around and returns to Christ, so relationships, theology, politics, art, philosophy—all find their center in Christ," Barron says.

In a variety of venues over the years, Barron has made the point that Christianity is a stubbornly historical religion, centered on Christ.

"It's not a philosophy (though it can employ philosophical language), nor is it a spirituality (though a spirituality can be distilled from it)," Barron said in an April 2017 review of the movie *The Case for Christ*.

"Rather, it is a relationship to a historical figure about whom an extraordinary historical claim has been made, namely, that he rose bodily from the dead," he says.

The Evangelization of Culture

"We have an *ad extra* focus," Barron says of Word on Fire, using a Latin phrase that means "to the outside." In Catholic parlance, it's usually set in contrast with an *ad intra* orientation, meaning focused on the Church's internal life.

"We want to move into the culture," Barron says. "Despite its secularism, our culture is Christ-haunted, and so evangelizing it from within has been the strategy. Members understand that secularism is the greatest challenge to the faith today, and that evangelizing that culture is the key to evangelizing its adherents."

Special Commitment to the New Media

"Word on Fire is committed to new and emerging technologies," Barron says, "seeing them as powerful vehicles to connect with people far from Christ and his Church.

"If the Church did not get involved in that world, and didn't use it evangelically, it would be missing an enormous opportunity," he adds. "I don't think it's an exaggeration to say the Internet is the greatest invention in the field of communication since the printing press, and I'm taking into consideration TV. I think the new media represent a means of communication that's explosive in its implication, and if the Church does not get into that world, it would be a giant mistake."

Rootedness in the Mystical Body

Word on Fire members forge strong friendships with the Church's saints. According to Barron, they lean especially on the intercession of Thérèse of Lisieux, Thomas Aquinas, John Paul II, Fulton Sheen, and John Henry Newman as heroes of the New Evangelization and patrons of Word on Fire.

We've seen how foundational the saints are both to Barron's personal spirituality and to his approach to evangelization. He sees the saints as exemplars of both the beauty and the goodness of the Catholic tradition, and their magnetic power to capture hearts and minds remains undimmed.

After the council, our concept of the Church became the "People of God," which carried both positives and negatives. And we largely forgot the idea of the "Mystical Body," a union that spans across space and time, and even transcends death. When you forget that, then the Church just turns into an institution of like-minded people, and who needs it? But if you know that the Church is a Mystical Body, and you realize that, you can't know Jesus apart from it.

Affirmative Orthodoxy

The formula *affirmative orthodoxy* first arose during the Benedict XVI years to capture what seemed to be his style as pope, and both elements of the term are important. Benedict is thoroughly "orthodox," in the sense of defending classic Catholic belief and practice, but he seemed equally determined to be "affirmative" in presenting it, emphasizing that to which the Church says yes rather than no.

Here's how Benedict put it in a 2006 interview with German radio: "Christianity, Catholicism, isn't a collection of prohibitions: it's a positive option," he said. "It's very important that we look at it again, because this idea has almost completely disappeared today."

As applied to Word on Fire, Barron says, "Instead of condemning the unevangelized, Word on Fire members relate with joyous verve, and extend an invitation to receive all of Christ's gifts through his Church."

(As a footnote, Barron is kind enough to say that Word on Fire got this principle from me. What he means is that I coined the term *affirmative orthodoxy,* obviously not that I invented its content.)

Via Pulchritudinis

As we've seen, the way of beauty is a core Barron conviction. In a culture that's allergic to claims about truth, and resistant to moral dictates about the good, beauty still resonates, and so it's the right place to begin an evangelical appeal.

Barron believes that Pope Francis illustrates the point in an especially compelling way.

"He exudes a joyfulness about the Christian life, like *Gaudium et spes* says," Barron says. "He puts the beatitudes at the heart of Christian life, and I'm totally with Francis on that."

Collaborative Apostolate

Vatican II wanted clergy and laity to collaborate more thoroughly and effectively, and Barron says that from the beginning, such collaboration has been one of the defining features of Word on Fire.

"I'm in charge of it, Father Steve [Grunow] has been a key player, but then it's all laypeople," he says. "It's a very lay sort of movement, so the collaborative model absolutely is the only path."

Grounded in the Eucharist

As Barron puts it, "Christ offers himself to us in the Blessed Sacrament, which serves as food for evangelization and the source of our collective ardor. We at Word on Fire especially prioritize Eucharistic prayer and adoration, among other devotions."

In a speech to a Eucharistic congress in the Philippines in

2016, Barron developed why the Eucharist is so central to any Catholic spirituality.

"It's the Bread of Life, it's what keeps us alive spiritually," he said. "We should all stretch out our hands as though we were starving for the Bread of Life.

"It's indispensable to our Eucharistic faith that we acknowledge that we're sinners, that we are lost, walking in the wrong way," Barron said. "If we're off-kilter, which we are, if we are worshipping the wrong way, we need to be brought back, and that process is painful. We need to go through a painful realignment," he explained, insisting that's precisely what the Eucharist prompts believers to do.

"MAKE NO LITTLE PLANS"

Barron's fellow Chicagoan, famed urban planner and designer Daniel Burnham, once counseled, "Make no little plans. They have no magic to stir men's blood, and probably themselves will not be realized." In that spirit, even though Barron realizes that for now he may have to be content with baby steps toward the realization of his dream of a Word on Fire movement, that doesn't mean he lacks big plans for what he'd like to see it become.

I would say our mission is to engage the culture, through the new media, for the purpose of evangelization. We envision it along the lines of Opus Dei or Communion and Liberation, that your whole spirituality, your lifestyle, is focused on evangelical mission. I've got the idea of Word on Fire centers. We've talked about developing these centers eventually in the major cities. We have a lot of Word on Fire people both in this country and in Europe, so why not Word on Fire centers in

Rome, London, Paris, New York, L.A., Chicago? There will also be a priestly dimension. I would like this to grow into a priestly order as well, never exclusively so, but according to a collaborative model. If I'm dreaming big, we'll have both priests and laity, and maybe houses all around the place where people could live and be formed. That's a little bit like the Opus Dei model.

Barron goes on, "I know that can sound kind of grandiose, maybe, but I want this to be more than just this media ministry I had for a while, which did some good things but then faded away. I want this to go on beyond me. In addition, as I've said, people have come from below, from the grass roots, and approached me about making this more than just a ministry."

Barron is strongly convinced that Word on Fire fills a new niche, rather than simply replicating what others either have done or are doing.

"When the Church is kind of at a low ebb, or it's challenged in its work of evangelization, the idea is that this would be a cutting-edge response," he says. "We'd have smart, dedicated, focused people establishing these centers. I also think a presence at universities would be a great thing. I'm happy to work with others who are already doing that work, but it's kind of a more urban phenomenon, with media and communications, combined with the intellectual side."

Barron concedes that for now, all this is "down the line," but that doesn't make him any less determined to do more than talk about a movement, saying he's in complete earnest about taking concrete steps to make it real.

"I think the preliminary stage is to take our core group, which we'll expand, and then really form them," he says. Once they open the doors, Barron says, he's convinced "a lot" of people will respond.

We have such a platform through our social media, which is in the millions, and many people have expressed passion and interest for this sort of thing. I'm actually a little afraid of that. I'm afraid I'll say, "Hey, we have this thing and you can join up at these varying levels, even priests interested in becoming Word on Fire priests." Then they'll flood in and I'll need the money and wherewithal to train them. I'm a little afraid that we would get a strong response, and I wouldn't be able to manage it. I'd be like St. Francis: What do I do with all these people?

Of course, as Barron acknowledges, "There are worse problems to have!"

Barron understands that in trying to found a new movement in the United States, he may be swimming against the tide. Aside from the Knights of Columbus, which is a fraternal organization rather than a movement, although it performs some of a movement's functions, to date there has never been a successful new movement with a global following that originated in the United States.

So far the movements have come from Europe and elsewhere. But I'm intrigued by the practicalities of it. In many ways, we have a much bigger platform and institutional capacity than most of these movements had at the beginning. That's also true of religious orders. The Jesuits, for instance, started with these six people at Montmartre [a hill in Paris were St. Ignatius Loyola founded the order] and off it goes. Maybe I just need the evangelical confidence to say, "Let's just Duc in altum [a Latin phrase meaning "set out into the deep," used often by Pope John Paul II] and get this going."

"It's a bit like the *CATHOLICISM* series," he says, "where I'm launching out without fully knowing where we'll go, but with a certain insouciance born of faith, I suppose. We'll see, but that's where we are." Extending the *CATHOLICISM* comparison, Barron says he feels the same way today that he did about the series as he and his team were originally discussing the idea—that it's important, and that one way or another, it's going to happen.

"It's like an egg that's getting ready to hatch," he says. "I do feel that."

No matter what happens in his life going forward, Barron says, he envisions himself remaining keenly involved with his Word on Fire community, playing the role of "father."

> *I'd be the father of the community. I would visit, be present to them, teach, preach, inspire . . . I'd be the spiritual father. "Spiritual father" is an image that I've always been very at home with. When I was rector of the seminary, I told the students that they will be called "Father" one day and that means they'll be spiritual fathers to their people. To me that's a very rich image, and it's very inclusive of all that a priest does. For this movement, I'd be the father. I'd try to inspire it, lift it up, preach to it, and shape it.*

Barron is an avid student of Catholic theology, which means he's well aware that the track record of Catholic theologians and intellectuals trying to found new movements is mixed. His hero Hans Urs von Balthasar, for instance, tried to inspire a group called the Community of St. John, which he cofounded with the Protestant mystic Adrienne von Speyr, but it never really took off.

"I think it was too much tied to him, his publishing house, and his presence," Barron says, adding that he doesn't intend to make the same mistake.

On the other hand, there's also the example of Father Luigi Giussani, an Italian priest and theologian who wrote pioneering works resisting what he saw as various "reductions" of Christian faith in the modern era, especially the attempt to boil it down to either a set of ecstatic experiences or a moral code. Instead, Giussani insisted, Christianity is a relationship with Christ that orders, and gives meaning to, all of life.

Along the way, Giussani founded a movement, originally for young students and eventually for everyone, that came to be called Communion and Liberation. Though it has been controversial over the years, with some Italians seeing it as a right-wing alternative to more liberal currents in the Church, today it's among the largest and most influential new movements in the world. It sponsors an annual event in Rimini, Italy, with an average attendance of 700,000.

A famous story, quite possibly apocryphal, is told in Catholic circles of a conversation between Balthasar and Giussani, in which Giussani told the Swiss theologian how much he admired his books and wished he could develop such elegant theological ideas.

"Yes," Balthasar is said to have replied, "but you founded a people."

When I suggested to Barron that if the Word on Fire movement develops in line with his dreams, he could end up being remembered as the American Giussani, he paused for a moment, smiled, and then replied.

"That wouldn't be bad," he said. "You could do a lot worse. I'd be okay with that."

Conclusion

Bishop Robert Barron and I share passions for both baseball and Catholicism. Speaking for myself, I believe baseball and the Church are deeply kindred spirits—both feature obscure rules that make sense only to initiates, both have communions of saints, both reward patience, and in both, casual fans can dip in and out, but for serious devotees the liturgy is a daily affair.

Another thing baseball and Catholicism have in common is that fans love to speculate about the future, especially in terms of who the next hot commodity in "the show" will be. There are whole TV programs, blogs, columns, and so on devoted to which pitching coach might land a manager's job, which minor-league prospect might be a game changer, which star player on a struggling team might get traded to a contender, and so on. Similarly in the Church, a time-honored parlor game is to speculate on which priests are being groomed to become bishops, which bishops in small dioceses might get bigger ones, who's going to make the cut the next time the pope creates new cardinals, and who might be in line for a major Vatican gig. Of course, the granddaddy of all such exercises is trying to guess who might be the next pope.

Generally, such guesswork misses more than it hits, but that doesn't stop people from being fascinated by it. It's anybody's guess what Barron's future may hold, but one thing does seem a reasonably safe bet: He's unlikely to finish his career as an auxiliary bishop. Barron simply has too much of the "right stuff"—intelligence, media savvy, a solid commitment to Church teaching yet a capacity for nuance and pastoral sensitivity, and a personality that allows him to engage and win over a wide range of people.

Ironically enough, while the rest of us can't help thinking about what the future may bring, Barron himself doesn't seem terribly preoccupied with it. Right now, he's loving the chance to dive back into direct pastoral contact with people in his Santa Barbara region of L.A. after spending most of his career as a professor and seminary administrator. At the same time, he's still fully engaged with the work of his Word on Fire ministry—churning out YouTube videos and writing columns, rounding out his new *CATHOLICISM: The Pivotal Players* film series, and giving talks. He's also keeping one foot in the academic world, among other things publishing a book on 2 Samuel in 2015 as part of the Brazos Theological Commentary on the Bible series.

As we saw in the last chapter, it's not that Barron doesn't have ambitious plans for Word on Fire, wanting to see it become nothing short of a full-fledged movement in the Catholic Church. However, one has the sense that he is fundamentally a happy man just as things stand, and that if the phone never rings again with a higher gig in the Church, he would be satisfied.

To say Barron is content, of course, is not the same as to say that everyone else is content with Barron. We saw in Chapter 1 that he sometimes draws criticism from both the left and the right—some liberals view him as too uncritical of the Church and triumphalistic about it, and some conservatives worry that his capacity for nuance can mean "going soft" on matters such as same-sex marriage, the need to combat Islamic radicalism, and even the theological debate over whether it's legitimate to hope that Hell is empty.

None of that blowback, however, seems to ruffle Barron's feathers. He's heard the criticism, is aware of it, and may even think there's some merit to it. At the end of the day, however, he appears comfortable in his own skin. As an evangelist, Barron believes in being fast on one's feet, and also in being flexible. As he puts it, "If it works, great. If it doesn't, try something else." He'd apply the same principle to himself—if you find my approach helpful, fantastic. If not, try someone else.

(Although that principle would seem to be no more than common sense, it's utterly characteristic of Barron that he invokes Ludwig Wittgenstein to explain it, arguing that one of the weaknesses of modern philosophical liberalism is that it tended to be overly "univocal" in its approach to method.)

Barron also isn't overly concerned about what his good friend the late Father Andrew Greeley described as the "original sin" of the clerical world, which is envy. Greeley, who experienced a fair bit of clerical envy himself, often said that the minute a Catholic priest gets a touch of fame and success, others will come out of the woodwork to try to tear him down, and Barron concedes he's had a few brushes with that tendency.

"People claim, 'Oh, he's just trying to get attention,' stuff like that," he says. "Whenever you go into the media, that's automatically the problem. People always say, 'He's an attention hog, just trying to make a name for himself, never met a microphone he doesn't like.'"

Once again, however, he doesn't seem overly perturbed.

"I'm a sinner, I'm sure there's some of that in me," he says, "but I also know that's part of the game."

Robert Barron, in other words, is a calm man in an increasingly hysterical time. If he were to offer no other contribution to the Church, and to the world, his gift for being both unwaveringly firm in his convictions and unflappably gentlemanly in the way he goes about articulating them, might alone qualify him for *Time* or Business Insider lists of the world's most intriguing personalities.

None of this is to say that Barron is anything less than forceful in his presentation of what he sees as the beauty, goodness, and truth of the Catholic tradition, or that he's incapable of mounting a strong defense of that tradition when he feels the situation calls for it. Rather uniquely among today's public personalities, however, Barron is able to be forceful without using force, and to deliver a defense without getting defensive.

As a final query about Barron, therefore, it's worth pondering what that basic calm is about.

Part of it is his upbringing and background. Barron was born into a solid Catholic family in Chicago but one, he says, that was never overly "demonstrative" about its faith. His childhood experience involved prayer and regular Mass attendance, but no sense of spiritual and cultural warfare, and gave him the ability to relate to people of different walks of life without instinctively passing judgment or feeling the need to wag a finger.

Part of it too is his intellectual formation. Granted, it's not as if academics are incapable of being demagogues or bombasts, and there are plenty of examples of that. Still, when one's rhetoric is routinely peppered with terms such as *propaedeutic, exegetical,* and *epistemological,* it's frankly a little more difficult to come off as fire-breathing and confrontational.

Then there's Barron's passion for teaching. In one way or another, Robert Barron has always seen himself as a teacher, which involves exercising the fine art of persuading people that something is worth knowing, and then guiding them as they come to know it. Teachers who routinely berate or get into shouting matches with their students, who become defensive at every question or every perceived slight, don't succeed in conveying a love of their subject, which may also explain why for Barron, restraint and patience are often the better parts of virtue.

Part of it as well is a conscious decision, born of Barron's sense of what works evangelically in a postmodern, secular culture.

You're not going to get a lot of nones coming back to church if you're ranting and raving. I don't want to be part of the outrage machine. You have to begin with the positive . . . I did a video on this, taking as my point of departure the image of Cardinal [Timothy] Dolan walking up the aisle of St. Patrick's in New York, because that's one of the great evangelical icons of our time. When I first saw him do it, walking up and the smiling and the backslapping and everything, I was just captivated. I'm not Dolan, but I try to offer some version of this more inviting way of doing things, finding positive things in the culture you can identify with. That's a conscious strategy.

I suspect, however, that the real explanation for Barron's calm lies in his faith—not just the content of it, because plenty of Catholics who believe in the same things do become unraveled in trying to explain or defend their positions, but how deeply persuaded Barron is that what he's trying to say to the world is completely, thoroughly true.

In effect, it's the "smartest kid in class" syndrome, though in this case Barron would say the real smarts come not from himself but from the great tradition. In any event, if you're sure you know the answers, then you never have to sweat the test.

In the end, that calm resolve has been key to Barron's success, and it is also why he's such an important role model for Catholicism in the twenty-first century. That's likely nowhere more the case than in the ever more polarized, and ever more secularized United States. What Barron offers is a road map to a Catholic way of engaging the culture that's simultaneously clear about what the Church stands for but also open, and that attracts rather than alienates.

I've spent a fair bit of time trying to invent sound bites to capture the Barron spirit: "Clarity without clamor," "acuteness without acrimony," and "passion without polemics" are all formulas with which I toyed, but in the end, better judgment prevailed, and I opted to let Barron speak for himself.

Perhaps the vintage expression of the Barron spirit came in one of those rare moments when he almost did lose his cool. It happened in 2014, when Bill Maher, the atheist comic who hosts *Real Time* on HBO, interviewed Christian political activist Ralph Reed. Among other things, Maher got Reed to agree that he suspends his critical faculties when it comes to his religious beliefs, which drove Barron to go on YouTube to respond.

> *Faith is not infrarational, meaning "below reason." That's credulity, that's superstition, that's accepting things on no evidence, that's childish. God gave us brains, and he wants us to use them. Authentic faith never involves a* sacrificium intellectus, *as the medievals said, a "sacrifice of the intellect." In fact, that's a sign that your faith is inauthentic. If you feel obligated to leave your mind aside to have faith, it's not real faith. Real faith is not infrarational, it's suprarational, it's beyond reason, but inclusive of it . . . There may be darkness on the far side of reason, but never on the near side. There's never a suspending of one's critical faculties. Authentic faith awakens the mind.*

That, in a nutshell, is how Robert Barron sees the great Catholic tradition, meaning its art, its saints, its literature, its theology, all of it. Nothing in his experience has ever awakened his lively mind in quite the same way—and he wants yours to be awakened too.

To put his basic drive into more spiritual terms, Robert Barron wants your entire life to be set ablaze with the "Word on Fire."

Acknowledgments

I want very specially to thank my intrepid editor, Gary Jansen, who first made the suggestion that a collaboration between John Allen and me might produce an interesting book. I also want to express my gratitude toward my Word on Fire colleagues, Fr. Steve Grunow, Brandon Vogt, and Joseph Gloor, all of whom read the initial drafts of the manuscript and made extremely valuable recommendations and corrections. I'm grateful as well to Fr. Paul Murray, one of the very best spiritual writers on the scene today, who read through the interview and helped especially with the formulation of the title. Finally, I want to acknowledge the hard work, patience, and dedication of the indispensable John Allen.

—*Bishop Robert Barron*

The obvious place to begin in giving thanks on this project is with Bishop Robert Barron, whose graciousness, availability, intelligence, and good humor were unfailing. I also want to thank Gary Jansen, our editor at Penguin Random House, whose smarts about publishing and dedication to a project are unmatched. Beyond those two, I'd like to thank my colleagues at Crux, especially Inés San Martín, Shannon Levitt, Terri Lynn, Clair Giangravé, and Christopher White for their friendship and support. Finally, as always, endless gratitude goes to Shannon and Ellis for the love.

—*John L. Allen Jr.*

About the Authors

BISHOP ROBERT BARRON is the founder of Word on Fire Catholic Ministries and Auxiliary Bishop of the Archdiocese of Los Angeles. He is also the host of *CATHOLICISM,* a groundbreaking, award-winning documentary about the Catholic faith, which aired on PBS.

Bishop Barron is a #1 Amazon bestselling author and has published numerous books, essays, and articles on theology and the spiritual life. He is a religion correspondent for NBC and has also appeared on FOX News, CNN, and EWTN.

Bishop Barron's website, WordOnFire.org, reaches millions of people each year, and he is one of the most-followed Catholics on social media. His regular YouTube videos have been viewed more than 20 million times and he has over 1.4 million followers on Facebook. Bishop Barron's pioneering work in evangelizing through the new media led Francis Cardinal George to describe him as "one of the Church's best messengers." He has keynoted many conferences and events all over the world, including the 2016 World Youth Day in Kraków and the 2015 World Meeting of Families in Philadelphia, which marked Pope Francis's historic visit to the United States.

Bishop Barron's latest film series and study program, *CATHOLICISM: The Pivotal Players,* debuted in September 2016 and has been syndicated for national television.

JOHN L. ALLEN JR. is the editor of Crux, specializing in coverage of the Vatican and the Catholic Church. He has written nine books on the Vatican and Catholic affairs and is also a popular speaker on Catholicism both in the United States and internationally. Veteran religion writer Kenneth Woodward of *Newsweek* described John as "the journalist other reporters—and not a few cardinals—look to for the inside story on how all the pope's men direct the world's largest church." John's articles have appeared in the *Boston Globe,* the *New York Times,* CNN, NPR, *The Tablet, Jesus, Second Opinion, The Nation,* the *Miami Herald, Die Furche,* and the *Irish Examiner.* He is a senior Vatican analyst for CNN, and was a correspondent for the *National Catholic Reporter* for sixteen years.

A native of Kansas, John received a bachelor's degree in philosophy from Fort Hays State University and a master's degree in religious studies from the University of Kansas. He has received honorary doctorates from the University of St. Michael's College in Toronto, Ontario; Lewis University in Romeoville, Illinois; St. Michael's College in Colchester, Vermont; Assumption College in Worcester, Massachusetts; and the University of Dallas in Texas.